NOTABLE LATINO WRITERS

NOTABLE LATINO
WRITERS

Volume 3

Piri Thomas — Jose Yglesias

659 - 1000

Essays

Appendices

Indexes

from

The Editors of Salem Press

SALEM PRESS, INC.
PASADENA, CALIFORNIA   HACKENSACK, NEW JERSEY

∞ The paper used in these volumes conforms to the American National
Standard for Permanence of Paper for Printed Library Materials, Z39.48-1992
(R1997)

Essays originally appeared in *Cyclopedia of World Authors, Fourth Revised Edition* (2004), *Critical Survey of Drama* (2003), *Critical Survey of Poetry* (2002), *Critical Survey of Short Fiction* (2001), *Critical Survey of Long Fiction* (2000), and *Identities and Issues in Literature* (1997). New material has been added.

Library of Congress Cataloging-in-Publication Data
Notable Latino writers / from the editors of Salem Press.
    p. cm. – (Magill's choice)
Includes bibliographical references and indexes.
ISBN-13: 978-1-58765-243-1 (13-digit set : alk. paper)
ISBN-13: 978-1-58765-246-2 (13-digit vol. 3 : alk. paper)
ISBN-10: 1-58765-243-9 (set)
ISBN-10: 1-58765-246-3 (vol. 3)
    1. American literature–Hispanic American authors–History and criticism.
2. Hispanic Americans–Intellectual life. 3. Hispanic Americans in literature.
I. Salem Press. II. Series.
    PS153.H56N68 2005
    810.9'868–dc22
                                                                        2005017567

First Printing

PRINTED IN THE UNITED STATES OF AMERICA

Table of Contents

Key to Pronunciation

Vowel Sounds

Symbol	Spelled (Pronounced)
a	answer (AN-suhr), laugh (laf), sample (SAM-puhl), that (that)
ah	father (FAH-thur), hospital (HAHS-pih-tuhl)
aw	awful (AW-fuhl), caught (kawt)
ay	blaze (blayz), fade (fayd), waiter (WAYT-ur), weigh (way)
eh	bed (behd), head (hehd), said (sehd)
ee	believe (bee-LEEV), cedar (SEE-dur), leader (LEED-ur), liter (LEE-tur)
ew	boot (bewt), lose (lewz)
i	buy (bi), height (hit), lie (li), surprise (sur-PRIZ)
ih	bitter (BIH-tur), pill (pihl)
o	cotton (KO-tuhn), hot (hot)
oh	below (bee-LOH), coat (koht), note (noht), wholesome (HOHL-suhm)
oo	good (good), look (look)
ow	couch (kowch), how (how)
oy	boy (boy), coin (koyn)
uh	about (uh-BOWT), butter (BUH-tuhr), enough (ee-NUHF), other (UH-thur)

Consonant Sounds

Symbol	Spelled (Pronounced)
ch	beach (beech), chimp (chihmp)
g	beg (behg), disguise (dihs-GIZ), get (geht)
j	digit (DIH-juht), edge (ehj), jet (jeht)
k	cat (kat), kitten (KIH-tuhn), hex (hehks)
s	cellar (SEHL-ur), save (sayv), scent (sehnt)
sh	champagne (sham-PAYN), issue (IH-shew), shop (shop)
ur	birth (burth), disturb (dihs-TURB), earth (urth), letter (LEH-tur)
y	useful (YEWS-fuhl), young (yuhng)
z	business (BIHZ-nehs), zest (zehst)
zh	vision (VIH-zhuhn)

Complete List of Articles

Volume 1

Volume 2

NOTABLE LATINO WRITERS

Piri Thomas

Puerto Rican novelist

Born: New York, New York; September 30, 1928
Also known as: Juan Pedro Tomás

NONFICTION: *Down These Mean Streets,* 1967; *Savior, Savior, Hold My Hand,* 1972; *Seven Long Times,* 1974.
SHORT FICTION: *Stories from El Barrio,* 1978 (juvenile).

Piri Thomas (PIH-ree TAW-muhs) was born in 1928, just before the Great Depression struck, the first child of a Puerto Rican couple, Juan (also known as Johnny) and Dolores Montañez Tomás. In 1941, when Piri was thirteen, his father, whom he called "Poppa," lost his job and went to work with the Works Progress Administration (WPA), a Depression-era government jobs program. The work was hard manual labor, and Poppa became distant and cool toward his son, who desperately wanted paternal affection and approval.

At an early age, Thomas became conscious of the problems of having dark skin. His own mother was light-skinned, and his brothers and sisters were light in color, with straight hair. Only the narrator and his father had the hair with tight curls and the dark brown skin that marked them as members of a disadvantaged race. The young narrator's awareness of race increased when his family moved out of Harlem to an Italian neighborhood, where he was subjected to racial slurs and had to fight the Italian boys. Standing up to the Italians gradually won him acceptance, though, and he learned to make his way in the world by fighting.

Thomas's family returned to Harlem, where the boy became a member of a Puerto Rican youth gang. In 1944, the family moved to Long Island, enjoying the prosperity of Poppa's wartime job. Thomas's own stay in the suburbs did not last, though. The snubs of his schoolmates made him even more conscious of

his color than he had been in the Italian neighborhood, and he dropped out of school and returned to Harlem. He became friends with Brew, a black man from the South, and Thomas's puzzlement about his own racial identity led him to ask Brew to take him south. The two men went to Virginia, where they took work on a merchant ship.

After his travels, Thomas returned to Harlem, where he fell in love with a young woman from Puerto Rico and who was waiting for him. He also, however, began to use heroin and developed a serious habit. After kicking his heroin habit with the help of a friend from his boyhood gang days and his friend's mother, he took up another dangerous pursuit: armed robbery. Another Puerto Rican introduced him to two white men who had been in prison, and the four began robbing small businesses. A daring attempt to rob a nightclub full of patrons ended with Thomas shooting a policeman and being shot himself. Barely escaping death, he was sentenced to five to fifteen years at Sing Sing Prison.

Soon transferred from Sing Sing to Comstock State Prison, Thomas remained behind bars from 1950 to 1956. His youth on the mean streets of New York served him well in prison, where only the strong and aggressive could avoid being raped and ex-

---

Zorro unleashed his imaginary whip, making the cracking sound he usually did when pleased. Zorro Jones had Zorro of the movies as his hero. Zorro, protector of the downtrodden poor, always left his mark Z with his sword on his enemy's property or on his behind. Zorro Jones planned to do the same in El Barrio as he grew up. His brown-colored skin covered a lithe, muscular body that promised the world a giant.

—from *The Blue Wings and the Puerto Rican Knights*

ploited. In prison, he also began to think seriously about his life and to read widely. For a time, he explored the religious beliefs of the Black Muslims. Thomas finally won parole and found himself back in New York, ready to turn his life around.

Down These Mean Streets is Thomas's own story, and questions of identity and race lie at its core. Psychologically, it is the coming-of-age story of a young man who must struggle with the conflicts in his family and in his own mind in order to make sense of his life. Through gang involvement, drug addiction, a criminal career, and a prison sentence, the protagonist wrestles with his own versions of the problems that confront all people: problems of self-definition, of tension with parents, of sexual relationships, and of religious meaning.

As a Puerto Rican, Thomas is a member of a group that has an ambiguous status. Puerto Rico is not a state or a part of any state, yet it is still part of the United States. Puerto Ricans are culturally different from the people of the mainland United States, but they are U.S. citizens. As a blend of national and racial ancestries, Puerto Ricans often do not fit neatly into the racial categories used by North Americans. Both of Thomas's parents are from Puerto Rico, but Thomas grew up in New York; thus, there is a gap between him and his parents. To make matters even more complicated, Thomas and his father are dark-skinned, while Thomas's mother and his brothers and sisters are light-skinned. This would not be a problem in Puerto Rico, where racial consciousness is less pronounced than in the mainland United States, but it proved to be a big problem for the young Piri. He continually felt "hung up between two sticks," in his phrase. In his novel, there are continual hints that his father's own discomfort about having dark skin is a source of the coldness the son feels from his father.

Down These Mean Streets was both controversial and influential. It was criticized for its violence, explicit sexuality, and expression of strong racial feelings. During the 1970's, the book was banned from the shelves of school libraries in a number of communities, including Queens in New York; Levittown, Long Island; Darien, Connecticut; and Salinas, California. Responding to these attempts at book banning, Thomas became an out-

W H A T   T O   R E A D

Down These Mean Streets

Down These Mean Streets (1967) is an autobiographical novel that tells of the author's experiences growing up as a dark-skinned Puerto Rican in New York, becoming involved in drugs and crime, and going to prison.

The book's thirty-five chapters are divided into eight sections, with each of the sections devoted to an important place and time in the author's life. The first section, entitled "Harlem," deals with Thomas's childhood in and around New York's Spanish Harlem. The second section, "Suburbia," deal with life in the suburbs of Long Island, where the family moves after Thomas's father gets a wartime job at an airplane factory. The third, fifth, and final chapters all concern Harlem, the site of the "mean streets" of the book's title.

Thomas is the narrator of the book, and the style draws heavily on the speech of New York's Puerto Rican and black populations. Racism and prejudice, both as sociological forces and as sources of psychological pain, are central themes in the work. Some of Thomas's difficulties in fitting in with American society are the result of poverty, but he also experiences real discrimination, and opportunities are closed to him because of his skin color. His anger and resentment at being continually rejected, though, are his true reasons for becoming a drug addict and a criminal. His story is ultimately the story of his ability to rise above his anger.

Down These Mean Streets was the first work by a Puerto Rican author writing in English to attract a large readership. A best-seller when it appeared in 1967, it became an inspiration for the "Nuyorican" literary movement. The book was criticized for its violence, explicit sexuality, and expression of strong racial feelings, and was banned from the shelves of many school libraries in the 1970's. In response, Thomas has become an outspoken opponent of all forms of censorship.

— *Carl L. Bankston III*

spoken opponent of all forms of censorship and an advocate for the poor and disenfranchised. As he says in the afterword to the thirtieth anniversary edition of *Down These Mean Streets:*

> In writing *Down These Mean Streets*, it was my hope that exposure of such conditions in the ghetto would have led to their improvement. But, thirty years later, the sad truth is that people caught in the ghettoes have not made much progress, have moved backwards in many respects—the social safety net is much weaker now. Unfortunately, it's the same old Mean Streets, only worse. I was taught that justice wears a blindfold, so as not to be able to distinguish between the colors, and thus make everyone equal in the eyes of the law. I propose we remove the blindfold from the eyes of Lady Justice, so for the first time she can really see what's happening and check out where the truth lies and the lies hide. That would be a start. *Viva* the children of all the colors! *Punto!*

— Carl L. Bankston III

Learn More

Fox, Geoffrey. *Hispanic Nation: Culture, Politics, and the Constructing of Identity.* Tucson: University of Arizona Press, 1997. A general work on the growth of Hispanic ethnic groups in America. Contains a discussion of Puerto Rican literature that gives special attention to the influence of Piri Thomas.

Hernandez, Carmen Dolores. *Puerto Rican Voices in English: Interviews with Writers.* New York: Praeger, 1997. Interviews with fourteen Puerto Rican authors, including Piri Thomas, who write in English. The book will help readers understand the dilemma of the Puerto Rican writer, who must work in two cultural traditions, and it presents readers with the views of Thomas and his fellow authors on their work.

Holte, James Craig. *The Conversion Experience in America: A Sourcebook on Religious Conversion Autobiography.* New York: Greenwood Press, 1992. Thomas, who described his religious experience in *Savior, Savior, Hold My Hand,* is included in this collection of essays about authors of religious conversion autobiographies. The essay about Thomas includes a short biography, a discussion of his book and the critical response it received, and a bibliography.

Luis, William. *Dance Between Two Cultures: Latino Caribbean Literature Written in the United States.* 1997. Reprint. Nashville, Tenn.: Vanderbilt University Press, 2001. Thomas is included in this analysis of prose and poetry written by Puerto Rican Americans, Cuban Americans, and Dominican Americans. Luis places these authors' works in a broader social, political, historical, and racial context.

Sandín, Lyn Di Ioria. *Killing Spanish: Literary Essays on Ambivalent U.S. Latino/a Identity.* New York: Palgrave Macmillan, 2004. Examines characters in Latino literature who are ambivalent about their American identities and their Caribbean and/or Latin American origins. Sandín looks at *Down These Mean Streets* by Thomas and novels by other authors in which poverty, race, and class force protagonists to embrace the street as their new home.

Santiago, Roberto, ed. *Boricuas: Influential Puerto Rican Writings— An Anthology.* New York: Ballantine Books, 1995. An anthology of the most influential Puerto Rican writings of the twentieth century, both on the island and in the mainland United States. Intended to serve as a handbook on the Puerto Rican experience, this can help readers place the writings of Piri Thomas in literary and historical context.

Turner, Faythe, ed. *Puerto Rican Writers at Home in the USA: An Anthology.* Seattle: Open Hand, 1991. A collection of stories, poems, and essays about the Puerto Rican experience in America, including writing by Piri Thomas.

Thomas, Piri. "The World of Piri Thomas." http://www.cheverote.com/. Accessed March 22, 2005. The author's Web site contains considerable information about his life and works: a multi-page biography that includes links to the letters he wrote while in prison, links to his poems and excerpts from his prose pieces, and more.

Rodolfo Usigli
Mexican playwright

Born: Mexico City, Mexico; November 17, 1905
Died: Mexico City, Mexico; June 18, 1979

DRAMA: *El niño y la niebla*, wr. 1936, pr., pb. 1951; *Medio tono*, pr. 1937, pb. 1938 (*The Great Middle Class*, 1968); *Estado de secreto*, pr. 1938, pb. 1963; *La mujer no hace milagros*, pr. 1939, pb. 1949; *La familia cena en casa*, pr., pb. 1942; *El gesticulador*, pb. 1944, pr. 1947; *Otra primavera*, pr. 1945, pb. 1947 (*Another Springtime*, 1961); *Corona de sombra*, pr., pb. 1947 (*Crown of Shadows*, 1946); *Jano es una muchacha*, pr., pb. 1952; *Un día de éstos*, pr. 1954, pb. 1957 (*One of These Days*, 1971); *Corona de fuego*, pr., pb. 1960; *Corona de luz: La virgen*, pr. 1963, pb. 1965 (*Crown of Light*, 1971).

LONG FICTION: *Ensayo de un crimen*, 1944.

POETRY: *Conversación desesperada*, 1938.

NONFICTION: *México en el teatro*, 1932 (*Mexico in the Theater*, 1976); *Caminos del teatro en México*, 1933; *Itinerario del autor dramático*, 1940; *Anatomía del teatro*, 1966.

Rodolfo Usigli (rew-DOH-foh ew-SEE-lee) has been hailed as the father of Mexican theater. He introduced authentic dramatic representations of Mexico through works that addressed its history, its politics, and the psychological makeup of its people. The psychological factor is the core of his theater.

Usigli was born in Mexico City, Mexico, on November 17, 1905, the product of Italian, Austrian, and Polish ancestry. Usigli demonstrated his interest in the theater at an early age. When he was eleven years old, he worked as an extra in the Castillo-Taboada troupe at Mexico's Teatro Colón. He wished to study drama, but there were no established schools of drama in Mexico at that time. Therefore, he designed his own curriculum whereby he read and analyzed on a daily basis six plays by well-known dramatists. He then attended local performances, at which he compared the dramas he studied with the actual stage productions. His commentaries were published in Mexican newspapers. By the time he reached the age of twenty, he had become a respected theater critic.

Usigli met with little success in finding producers for his first dramatic attempts. His difficulties with managers, producers, and critics may perhaps be traced to unhappy childhood experiences. Usigli was born with slightly crossed eyes, a person Spanish-speakers call *bizco.* His classmates punned on the word and nicknamed him *Visconde* (Viscount), which also alluded to his conviction of being superior to them. He later underwent corrective surgery for his eyes but never lost his conviction about his superiority, which often expressed itself in an arrogance and defensiveness that theater authorities found unappealing.

From 1932 to 1934, Usigli offered courses in the history of the Mexican theater at the University of Mexico and served as director of the Teatro Radiofónico, which broadcast plays in conjunction with the Ministry of Education. During this period, he was also associated with the Teatro Orientación, which was created to introduce Mexico to the masterpieces of world theater, performing plays translated from French, Italian, English, German, and Russian. Usigli prepared the Spanish versions for the stage. In 1935, Usigli was awarded a scholarship to study dra-

---

He was courteous, but it is not known whether he was because he was Mexican or merely intelligent. Courtesy is the strength of the weak and the perfection of the strong. Or at least it was formerly. . . . He pretends not to attract attention and, naturally, attracts it. Accursed attention.

—from *Mexico in the Theater*
(trans. Wilder P. Scott)

matic composition at Yale University. During this period, he wrote *El gesticulador* (the pretender), one of his greatest works. On his return to Mexico, he was appointed director of the school of drama and theater and director of the department of fine arts at the University of Mexico. In 1940, he founded his own theater, the Teatro Media Noche, to produce his Mexican plays, but ongoing problems with producers soon ended this venture.

During the period from 1943 to 1946, Usigli served Mexico in a diplomatic capacity, becoming the cultural attaché at the Mexican embassy in Paris. During his tenure in Europe, he had the opportunity to meet his idol, playwright George Bernard Shaw. Also during this period, he completed another of his great works, *Crown of Shadows*, part of a trilogy about the three Mexican myths of sovereignty. (The other works in the trilogy are *Corona de fuego*—crown of fire—and *Crown of Light*.) After completing his tour of duty, Usigli returned to Mexico and of-

fered courses at the University of Mexico in the history of the theater and playwriting. He completed The Corona Trilogy and several other plays.

Usigli resumed his diplomatic career from 1956 until 1962, serving as Mexico's ambassador to Lebanon and Norway. During this period and after his return to Mexico, he continued to produce dramatic works.

In his plays, Usigli does not merely criticize the Mexican people and their society. Rather, he seeks to ennoble them by offering them models of their own potential greatness. Usigli accomplishes this by introducing the concept of myth formation. The concept of myth formation has its roots in Georg Wilhelm Friedrich Hegel's conception of the historical process as a series of syntheses that revolve around transcendental historical figures such as Maximilian and Montezuma, who represent superior cultural symbols. From a cultural and theatrical perspective, a myth is a transcendental synthesis embodied in one of these figures that offers a new perspective, a positive direction for the country's future growth. Its direct appeal to the faith of the Mexican audience causes them to reevaluate their mythical past and to experience a catharsis of nationality with those national sentiments and values that most ennoble it. In recognition of his efforts to create a Mexican national theater, Usigli was awarded the Premio Nacional de Letras in 1972.

There are four elements that constantly recur in Usigli's plays: fantasy, myth, family types, and humor. Fantasy is present in all of his works. Through examples that illustrate his philosophy, he sets the course that propels the action and motivates the characters: madness, absurdity, dreams, superstition, double identity, and illusions. The element of the fantastic is reinforced by dramatic techniques such as the play of lights, visions, flashbacks, and anonymous voices. Myth is of utmost importance in Usigli's works. He sees Mexico as an outstanding example of a fusion of two cultures, the indigenous and the Hispanic, both of which are myth-oriented. Within the framework of Usigli's Hegelian view of history, the central characters become transcendental myth figures. He uses myth to reinterpret historical

W H A T   T O   R E A D

The Great Middle Class

In the sociological drama *The Great Middle Class* (1938) the Sierra family is transformed into a symbol of middle-class life. Each family member has a particular problem. The father has lost his job with the government because of his political affiliation and has taken refuge in pursuing other women, but the mother's overwhelming religious character prevents her from seeing that anything is wrong. David, the eldest son and moderator of the family, suffers from tuberculosis. His brothers and sisters each have their own difficulties, but only David realizes that the only salvation is unity. An atmosphere of dissension, pessimism, confusion, and egotism prevails. However, the family members share a sense of unity that will surface during a grave crisis.

At the end of the drama, the circumstances are much more serious than at the beginning. The father moves the family to another province, and he must sell much of the family furniture in order to pay the rent. The mother is able to acknowledge her family's difficulties and suffers when she learns what her children have been through. The difference, however, lies in the sense of consolidation and unity among the members of the family and their attempts to rescue one another. They feel a new freedom in thought and action, born of the now-prevailing atmosphere of mutual love and respect.

The Sierra family is a typical example of the trials and tribulations of any middle-class family anywhere in the world. Usigli, by presenting the life of the Sierra family in a universal light, successfully transcended national boundaries and won the empathy of other frontiers. Psychologically, Usigli appealed to a fundamental element of Mexican society: the clan instinct, the overpowering desire of family members to overcome their personal differences, no matter what the sacrifice or price, in order to ensure the continuation of their line.

— *Anne Laura Mattrella*

events, clarifying their significance and offering a new and positive direction for Mexico's future. Another recurring element found in Usigli's dramatic productions is the character types based on members of the family. He treats all social levels—lower, middle, upper, and aristocratic—to portray segments of Mexican society. Usigli's acute awareness of the inconsistencies in Mexican life and culture are often expressed in witty dialogue and amusing episodes.

The Great Middle Class, El gesticulador, and *Crown of Shadows* are considered to be Usigli's finest works. Each portrays a conflict that tests the spirit. Human emotions are presented so as to diminish the distance between the public and the stage. Ridicule is not provoked from pathetic situations; rather, the audience feels a sense of spiritual elevation at the conclusion of each of these dramas.

Usigli dedicated his life to the creation of a Mexican national theater. He combined practical experience, a keen sense of the Mexican spirit, a thorough knowledge of the theater, stylistic creativity, and a new ideology to establish the basis for a new Mexican theater. His dramas are neither didactic nor doctrinal, but objective in their thematic treatment. Usigli's desire was to bring the past and the present into harmony, to see them in a positive light, and to appeal to the faith of the Mexican people to overcome their weaknesses and gain a new and optimistic perspective on their country's future. Through his acting, translating, teaching, and writing, he played a decisive part in the creation of a Mexican national theater.

— *Anne Laura Mattrella*

Learn More

Beardsell, Peter R. *A Theatre for Cannibals: Rodolfo Usigli and the Mexican Stage.* Rutherford, N.J.: Fairleigh Dickinson University Press, 1992. A study of the dramatic works of Usigli and the Mexican theater of his times. Bibliography and index.

Jones, Willis Knapp. Introduction to *Two Plays: "Crown of Light," "One of These Days,"* by Rodolfo Usigli. Translated by Thomas Bledsoe. Carbondale: Southern Illinois University Press, 1971.

In his introduction to the translation of two of Usigli's plays, Jones provides information on Usigli's life and dramatic works.

Savage, Ronald Vance. "Rodolfo Usigli's Idea of Mexican Theatre." *Latin American Theatre Review* 4, no. 2 (1971): 13-20. This essay examines the Mexican theater according to the viewpoint of Usigli.

Tilles, Solomon H. "Rodolfo Usigli's Concept of Dramatic Art." *Latin American Theatre Review* 3, no. 2 (1970): 31-38. A discussion of drama as conceived by Usigli.

Luis Miguel Valdez

Mexican American
playwright and political activist

Born: Delano, California; June 26, 1940

DRAMA: *The Theft*, pr. 1961; *The Shrunken Head of Pancho Villa*, pr. 1965, pb. 1967; *Las dos caras del patroncito*, pr. 1965, pb. 1971; *La quinta temporada*, pr. 1966, pb. 1971; *Los vendidos*, pr. 1967, pb. 1971; *Dark Root of a Scream*, pr. 1967, pb. 1973; *La conquista de México*, pr. 1968, pb. 1971 (puppet play); *No saco nada de la escuela*, pr. 1969, pb. 1971; *The Militants*, pr. 1969, pb. 1971; *Vietnam campesino*, pr. 1970, pb. 1971; *Huelguistas*, pr. 1970, pb. 1971; *Bernabé*, pr. 1970, pb. 1976; *Soldado razo*, pr., pb. 1971; *Actos*, pb. 1971 (includes *Las dos caras del patroncito*, *La quinta temporada*, *Los vendidos*, *La conquista de México*, *No saco nada de la escuela*, *The Militants*, *Vietnam campesino*, *Huelguistas*, and *Soldado razo*); *Las pastorelas*, pr. 1971 (adaptation of a sixteenth century Mexican shepherd's play); *La Vírgen del Tepeyac*, pr. 1971 (adaptation of *Las cuatro apariciones de la Vírgen de Guadalupe*); *Los endrogados*, pr. 1972; *Los olivos pits*, pr. 1972; *La gran carpa de los rasquachis*, pr. 1973; *Mundo*, pr. 1973; *El baille de los gigantes*, pr. 1973; *El fin del mundo*, pr. 1975; *Zoot Suit*, pr. 1978, pb. 1992; *Bandido!*, pr. 1981, pb. 1992, revised pr. 1994; *Corridos*, pr. 1983; *"I Don't Have to Show You No Stinking Badges!,"* pr., pb. 1986; *Luis Valdez—Early Works: Actos, Bernabé, and Pensamiento Serpentino*, pb. 1990; *Zoot Suit, and Other Plays*, pb. 1992; *Mummified Deer*, pr. 2000.

SCREENPLAYS: *Zoot Suit*, 1982 (adaptation of his play); *La Bamba*, 1987.

TELEPLAYS: *Fort Figueroa*, 1988; *La Pastorela*, 1991; *The Cisco Kid*, 1994.

EDITED TEXT: *Aztlán: An Anthology of Mexican American Literature*, 1972 (with Stan Steiner).

MISCELLANEOUS: *Pensamiento Serpentino: A Chicano Approach to the Theatre of Reality*, 1973.

L uis Miguel Valdez (lwees mih-GEHL VAL-dehz), political activist, playwright, director, essayist, and founder of El Teatro Campesino, is the most prominent figure in modern Chicano theater. Born on June 26, 1940, to migrant farmworker parents, he was second in a family of ten brothers and sisters. In spite of working in the fields from the age of six, Valdez completed high school and received a scholarship to San Jose State College, where he developed his early interest in theater. *The Shrunken Head of Pancho Villa* was written while Valdez was a student there. After receiving a bachelor's degree in English and drama in 1964, he joined the San Francisco Mime Troupe, whose work was based on *commedia dell'arte* and the theater of Bertolt Brecht. These experiences heavily influenced Valdez's work, especially in terms of style and production.

A 1965 meeting with César Chávez, who was organizing migrant farmworkers in Delano, California, led to the formation of El Teatro Campesino, the cultural and propagandistic arm of the United Farm Workers (UFW) union. Valdez created short improvisational pieces, called *actos*, for the troupe. All the *actos* are characterized by the use of masks, stereotyped characters, farcical exaggeration, and improvisation. *Las dos caras del patroncito* (the two faces of the boss) and *La quinta temporada* (the fifth season) are *actos* from this early period that highlight the plight of the farmworkers and the benefits of unionization.

"*This ain't your country. Look what's happening all around you. The Japs have sewed up the Pacific. Rommel is kicking ass in Egypt but the Mayor of L.A. has declared all-out war on Chicanos. On you!*"

—from *Zoot Suit*

Arte Público Press

Valdez left the union in 1967, bringing El Teatro Campesino with him to establish El Centro Campesino Cultural. He wanted to broaden the concerns of the troupe by fostering Chicanos' pride in their cultural heritage and by depicting their problems in the Anglo culture. *Los vendidos* (the sellouts), for example, satirizes Chicanos who attempt to assimilate into a white, racist society, and *La conquista de México* (the conquest of Mexico) links the fall of the Aztecs with the internal dissension of Chicano activists. In 1968 El Teatro Campesino moved toward producing full-length plays, starting with Valdez's *The Shrunken Head of Pancho Villa.* Expressionistic in style, the play explores the conflict between two brothers—an assimilationist and a *pachuco,* a swaggering street kid—and the impact this extremism has on the tenuous fabric of a Chicano family. Recognition followed, with an Obie Award in New York in 1969 for "creating a workers' theater to demonstrate the politics of survival" and an invitation to perform at the Theatre des Nations festival in Nancy, France. Later in 1969, Valdez and the troupe moved to Fresno, California, where they founded an annual Chicano theater festival, and Valdez began teaching at Fresno State College.

In 1971 Valdez moved his company permanently to the small town of San Juan Bautista in California. There, El Teatro Campesino underwent a fundamental transformation, as the group began increasingly to emphasize the spiritual side of their work, as derived from prevalent Christian as well as newfound Aztec and Mayan roots. This shift from an agitational focus to a search for spiritual solutions was met with anger by formerly admiring

W H A T   T O   R E A D

Zoot Suit

The first Chicano play on Broadway, *Zoot Suit* (1992) grew out of California Chicano guerrilla theater, incorporating bilingual dialogue and ultimately alienating Mexican Americans. In it, Valdez questions the Los Angeles newspaper accounts of the Columbus Day "Zoot Suit" riots and the related Sleepy Lagoon murder trial (1942). The drama uses song, dance, and a unifying narrative based on the traditions of the Mexican *corrido* (a ballad form that often reflects on social issues).

A zoot-suiter "master of ceremonies" called Pachuco narrates the action, dispelling illusion, showing reality, and providing flashbacks that characterize the protagonist, Henry Reyna, who is vilified in the white media, as heroic. This defiant, existential street actor wears the colors of Testatipoka, the Aztec god of education.

Reyna, a loyal American about to ship out for the war in the Pacific, becomes a scapegoat for the Los Angeles police. When a minor scuffle with a rival gang interrupts his farewell celebration, he bravely steps in to break up a one-sided attack. Newsboys shouting inflammatory head-

audiences in Mexico City at the Quinto Festival de los Teatros Chicanos in 1974. The company continued to flourish, however, touring campuses and communities yearly and giving financial support and advice to other theater troupes.

Fame came with *Zoot Suit,* the first Chicano play to reach Broadway. Although its run was relatively brief, owing to negative criticism, the play was very popular on the West Coast and was made into a film in 1981, with Valdez both the director and the writer of the screenplay. During the 1980's, Valdez and El Teatro Campesino continued to tour at home and abroad, presenting works by Valdez and collectively scripted pieces that interpret the Chicano experience. The 1986 comedy *"I Don't Have*

lines and a lawyer predicting mass trials prepare viewers for legal farce. The prosecution twists testimony proving police misunderstandings and Henry's heroism to win an unjust conviction. White liberals distort the conviction of the zoot-suiter "gang" for personal ends, and even Pachuco is ultimately overpowered and stripped by servicemen. The play ends as it began: with the war over, the incarcerated scapegoats released, and police persecution renewed.

Leaving viewers with the choice of multiple possible endings, Valdez not only reflects the Mayan philosophy of multiple levels of existence but also offers alternate realities dependent on American willingness to accept or deny reality: a calm Henry and supportive family group united against false charges, Henry as victim of racist stereotypes reincarcerated and killed in a prison fight, Henry the born leader dying heroically in Korea and thereby winning a posthumous Congressional Medal of Honor, Henry a father with several children, Henry merged with El Pachuco, a living myth and symbol of Chicano heritage and Chicano oppression. Thus, Reyna the individual portrays Chicanos in crisis in general. The plays shows Chicanos undermined by a prejudiced press, racist police, and an unjust legal system that distorts facts and denies Chicanos their rights.

— *Gina Macdonald*

to Show You No Stinking Badges!" is about the political and existential implications of acting, both in theater and in society. In 1987 Valdez wrote the screenplay for the successful film *La Bamba*, the story of Ritchie Valens, a young Chicano pop singer who died in an airplane crash in the late 1950's. This work reached a large audience.

After a gap in playwriting of almost fifteen years, Valdez wrote *Mummified Deer*. This play reaffirms his status as the "father of Chicano drama" and continues his exploration of his heritage through the juxtaposition of ritual and realism. The play takes its inspiration from a newspaper article concerning the discovery of a sixty-year-old fetus in the body of an eighty-four-year old woman. According to scholar Jorge Huerta, the mummified fetus serves as a metaphor for "the Chicanos' Indio heritage, seen through the lens of his own Yaqui blood." The play's major dramatic action operates in the historical/fictional past.

Valdez's contributions to contemporary Chicano theater are extensive. Writing individually and with others, he has redefined the cultural forms of the barrio: the *acto*, a short comic piece intended to move the audience to political action; the *mito* (myth), which characteristically takes the form of an allegory based on Indian ritual, in an attempt to integrate political activism and religious ritual; and the *corrido*, a reinvention of the musical based on Mexican American folk ballads. He has placed the Chicano experience onstage in all of its political and cultural complexity, creating what no other American playwright has, a genuine workers' theater that has made serious drama popular, political drama entertaining, and ethnic drama universal.

— Lori Hall Burghardt

Learn More

Broyles-Gonzales, Yolanda. *El Teatro Campesino: Theater in the Chicano Movement*. Austin: University of Texas Press, 1994. Study drawing on previously unexamined materials, such as production notes and interviews with former ensemble members, to demystify the roles Valdez and El Teatro Campesino played in the development of a Chicano theater aesthetic.

Conlogue, William. *Working the Garden: American Writers and the Industrialization of Agriculture.* Chapel Hill: University of North Carolina Press, 2001. Refutes the stereotype that farm-centered works are pastoral. Examines work by Valdez and other writers to show how these works address migrant labor, gender roles, and other significant issues.

Elam, Harry J., Jr. *Taking It to the Streets: The Social Protest Theater of Luis Valdez and Amiri Baraka.* Ann Arbor: University of Michigan Press, 2001. Explores the political, cultural, and performative similarities between El Teatro Campesino and Baraka's Black Revolutionary Theater. An intriguing examination of the political theater of these two marginalized groups, Chicanos and African Americans, and their shared aesthetic.

Huerta, Jorge A. *Chicano Theatre: Themes and Forms.* Ypsilanti, Mich.: Bilingual Press, 1982. Well-written and well-illustrated study that begins with Valdez's experiences in Delano in 1965. It contains an excellent immediate description with dialogue of these first energies and is written in the present tense for immediacy and energy. Provides some discussion of the beginnings of the San Francisco mime troupe and strong description of the *actos* and their literary history in Europe.

_____. "Labor Theatre, Street Theatre, and Community Theatre in the Barrio, 1965-1983." In *Hispanic Theatre in the United States,* edited by Nicolás Kanellos. Houston, Tex.: Arte Público Press, 1984. Placed at the end of a longer study of Hispanic theater, this essay takes on more importance by indicating Valdez's contribution in a continuum of history. Good on contemporaries of El Teatro Campesino; strong bibliography.

Kanellos, Nicolás. *Mexican American Theater: Legacy and Reality.* Pittsburgh: Latin American Literary Review Press, 1987. Begins with an examination of Valdez's transformation from director of El Teatro Campesino to the urban commercial playwright of *Zoot Suit* in 1978. Cites Valdez's contribution to the "discernible period of proliferation and flourishing in Chicano theatres" from 1965 to 1976, then moves on to examine other offshoots of the impulse.

Martinez, Manuel Luis. *Countering the Counterculture: Rereading Postwar American Dissent from Jack Kerouac to Tomás Rivera.* Madison: University of Wisconsin Press, 2003. Martinez analyzes writings by Valdez and other Chicano nationalists whose works convey their opinions of participatory democracy and progressive culture.

Valdez, Luis Miguel. "*Zoot Suit* and the Pachuco Phenomenon: An Interview with Luis Valdez." Interview by Roberta Orona-Cordova. In *Mexican American Theatre: Then and Now,* edited by Nicolás Kanellos. Houston, Tex.: Arte Público Press, 1983. The opening of the film version of *Zoot Suit* prompted this interview, in which Valdez reveals much about his motives for working, his view of Chicano literature and art, and his solutions to "the entrenched attitude" that will not allow Chicano participation in these industries.

Luisa Valenzuela

Argentine novelist and short-story writer

Born: Buenos Aires, Argentina; November 26, 1938

LONG FICTION: *Hay que sonreír,* 1966 (*Clara,* 1976); *El gato eficaz,* 1972; *Como en la guerra,* 1977 (*He Who Searches,* 1979); *Libro que no muerde,* 1980; *Cola de lagartija,* 1983 (*The Lizard's Tail,* 1983); *Novela Negra con Argentinos,* 1990 (*Black Novel with Argentines,* 1992); *Realidad nacional desde la cama,* 1990 (*Bedside Manners,* 1995); *La travesía,* 2001.

SHORT FICTION: *Los heréticos,* 1967 (*The Heretics: Thirteen Short Stories,* 1976); *Aquí pasan cosas raras,* 1975 (*Strange Things Happen Here: Twenty-six Short Stories and a Novel,* 1979); *Cambio de armas,* 1982 (*Other Weapons,* 1985); *Donde viven las águilas,* 1983 (*Up Among the Eagles,* 1988); *Open Door: Stories,* 1988; *Simetrías,* 1993 (*Symmetries,* 1998); *Cuentos completos, y uno más,* 1998.

NONFICTION: *Peligrosas palabras,* 2001 (essays).

Luisa Valenzuela (LWEE-sah vah-lehn-ZWAY-lah), Argentine novelist, short-story writer, journalist, and scriptwriter, is one of Argentina's most significant authors to emerge since the boom in Latin American literature during the 1960's. As the daughter of Luisa Mercedes Levinson, a prominent Argentine writer, Valenzuela was initiated at an early age into the world of the written word. Her father, Pablo Francisco Valenzuela, was a doctor. She was reared in Belgrano and received her early education from a German governess and an English tutor. In 1945, she attended Belgrano Girls' School and then an English high school. She began writing for the magazine *Quince abriles* in 1953 and completed her studies at the National Preparatory School Vicente López in 1955. Subsequently she graduated with a bachelor of arts degree from the University of Buenos Aires. She wrote for the Buenos Aires magazines *Atlántida, El hogar,* and *Esto es* and worked with Jorge Luis Borges in the National Li-

brary of Argentina. She also wrote for the Belgrano Radio and was a tour guide in 1957. It was during this time that her first short stories were published, in the magazine *Ficción.*

In 1958, when she was twenty years old, Valenzuela left Buenos Aires to become the Paris correspondent for the Argentine daily newspaper *El Mundo.* There she wrote programs for Radio Télévision Française and participated in the intellectual life of the then-famous *Tel Quel* group of literary theorists and structuralists. She married French merchant marine Theodore Marjak, resided in Normandy, and gave birth to a daughter, Anna-Lisa, in 1958. Three years later she returned to Buenos Aires and joined Argentina's foremost newspaper, *La Nación,* where she became assistant editor. After she was divorced from her husband in 1965, she went to the University of Iowa's Writers'

Workshop on a Fulbright grant in 1969. In 1972, she received a scholarship to study pop culture and literature in New York. She then became an avid traveler, living in Spain, Mexico, New York, and Buenos Aires; participating in conferences; continuing her journalism; and cultivating her fiction.

Her first novel, *Clara,* presents the story of a naïve country girl turned prostitute in Buenos Aires; the girl's picaresque adventures in a male world alternate between the humorous and the sinister. As the novel progresses, the antiheroine's forthrightness slowly changes into a pathos under the constant attack of the city's anonymity, alienation, and male brutality. Valenzuela won the Instituto Nacional de Cinematografía Award in 1973 for the script "Hay que sonreír," based on her first novel. Her New York-Greenwich Village experience resulted in *El gato eficaz* (the efficient cat), an experimental novel sustained largely by the innovative use of language and an imaginative plot. In 1975, she returned to Buenos Aires and joined the staff of the journal *Crisis.* After participating in more workshops and conferences, she left Buenos Aires and settled in New York in 1978, where she conducted creative writing workshops and taught Latin American literature at Columbia University, as well as at other universities in the United States.

Although she has lived much of her life outside Argentina, Valenzuela, like other Argentine women writers, could not escape her involvement with an Argentine society torn by vio-

---

They are two, I repeat: José María and María José, born of the same womb on the same morning, perhaps a bit mixed up. And the years went by for them, too, till they reached this point where a vast assortment of impossibilities began to weigh on them, over and above the desire to do as they wish. They can't just go on: they're stuck in the mud and out of gas.

—from "Legend of the Self-Sufficient Child"
(trans. Christopher Leland)

lence, class struggle, dictatorship, and dehumanization. Thus, much of her fiction, though written and published outside her native country, where it was banned, treats such themes as violence, political repression, and cultural repression, especially as they relate to women. Yet, as critics point out, her work continually undermines social and political myths while (unlike that of

---

W H A T   T O   R E A D

"Other Weapons"

Called by feminist critics a landmark in Latin American feminist literature, "Other Weapons" is a depiction of woman as wife-whore-slave in the extreme, for the female in the story is reduced to total passivity by torture at the hands of her male master. In an almost autistic state of isolation, her consciousness effaced, the woman feels completely isolated in time and space, cut off from the past, with no hope for a future.

The story falls within a tradition of sadistic Bluebeard stories, stories in which a powerful male figure uses the woman as a sex object, keeping her shut off from the world and imprisoned within herself. The story is told in a fragmentary fashion, in third person but from the woman's perspective, as she haltingly tries to "find herself out." Complete with whips and voyeuristic peep holes where the man's colleagues can watch the man sexually dominate the woman, "Other Weapons" is a paradigm of the sadistic male who uses the phallus as a weapon.

The final revelation of the story comes when he tells her that she was a revolutionary who had been ordered to kill him but was caught just when she was aiming at him. He says everything he did was to save her, for he forced her to love him, to depend on him like a newborn baby. "I've got my weapons, too," he repeats over and over. However, when he starts to leave, she remembers what the gun is for, lifts it and aims.

— *Charles E. May*

---

so many political writers) refusing to replace old mythic structures with new but equally arbitrary and authoritative ones.

— *Genevieve Slomski*

Learn More

Kantaris, Elia Geoffrey. *The Subversive Psyche: Contemporary Women's Narrative from Argentina and Uruguay.* New York: Oxford University Press, 1995. Examines Valenzuela's fiction and literary theories to describe her treatment of sexuality. Kantaris argues that Valenzuela and other writers from Argentina and Uruguay often challenge Western theories of gender and identity.

McNab, Pamela J. "Sexual Silence and Equine Imagery in Valenzuela and Cortázar." *Bulletin of Hispanic Studies* 76 (April, 1999): 263-279. Compares how Valenzuela and Julio Cortázar use horse imagery to fill the gap between language and silence in their short stories.

Medeiros-Lichem, María Teresa. *Reading the Feminine Voice in Latin American Women's Fiction: From Teresa de la Parra to Elena Poniatowska and Luisa Valenzuela.* New York: P. Lang, 2002. A feminist critique of Valenzeula's work.

Niebylski, Dianna C. *Humoring Resistance: Laughter and the Excessive Body in Latin American Women's Fiction.* Albany: State University of New York Press, 2004. Analyzes how Valenzuela and other Latin American women writers use humor and other literary techniques to approach questions of identity and community.

Shaw, Donald L. *The Post-Boom in Spanish American Fiction.* Albany: State University of New York Press, 1998. Shaw includes a chapter about Valenzuela in his examination of Latin American fiction that first appeared in the mid-1970's. This literature differed from the works published in the preceding "Boom" period: it was more reader friendly, situated in the here and now, and not readily assimilated into the postmodern movement.

Tomlinson, Emily. "Rewriting Fictions of Power: The Texts of Luisa Valenzuela and Marta Traba." *Modern Language Review* 93 (July, 1998): 695-709. Discusses the feminist exploration of themes of power in the writings of the two authors.

César Vallejo

Peruvian poet

Born: Santiago de Chuco, Peru; March 16, 1892
Died: Paris, France; April 15, 1938

POETRY: *Los heraldos negros,* 1918 (*The Black Heralds,* 1990); *Trilce,* 1922 (English translation, 1973); *Poemas en prosa,* 1939 (*Prose Poems,* 1978); *Poemas humanos,* 1939 (*Human Poems,* 1968); *España, aparta de mí este cáliz,* 1939 (*Spain, Take This Cup from Me,* 1974); *Obra poética completa,* 1968; *Poesía completa,* 1978; *César Vallejo: The Complete Posthumous Poetry,* 1978; *Selected Poems,* 1981.

LONG FICTION: *Fábula salvaje,* 1923 (novella); *El tungsteno,* 1931 (*Tungsten,* 1988).

SHORT FICTION: *Escalas melografiadas,* 1923; *Hacia el reino de los Sciris,* 1967; *Paco Yunque,* 1969.

DRAMA: *La piedra cansada,* pb. 1979; *Colacho hermanos: O, Presidentes de América,* pb. 1979; *Lock-Out,* pb. 1979; *Entre las dos orillas corre el río,* pb. 1979; *Teatro completo,* pb. 1979.

NONFICTION: *Rusia en 1931: Reflexiones al pie del Kremlin,* 1931, 1965; *El romanticismo en la poesía castellana,* 1954; *Rusia ante el segundo plan quinquenal,* 1965; *El arte y la revolución,* 1973; *Contra el secreto profesional,* 1973.

César Vallejo (SAY-zahr vah-YAY-hoh) vies with the Chilean poet Pablo Neruda for recognition as the best Spanish American poet of the twentieth century, yet the semantic difficulty of his poetry has often meant that he is not as well known outside the Spanish-speaking world as he deserves to be. Author of a novel, a novella, four dramas, a collection of short stories, a collection of essays on Marxism and literary theory, two books on Soviet Russia, and more than two hundred newspaper articles, Vallejo is mainly remembered for his poetry.

Born the eleventh child to a family of mixed Spanish and Indian origins, Vallejo as a child witnessed at first hand hunger, poverty, and the injustices done to Indians. His first book of poems, *The Black Heralds,* showed him still to be under the influence of *Modernismo*—which favored allusions to Greco-Roman mythology—but also hinted at the emergence of a radically new personal poetic voice. The major theme of this collection was anguish at the injustice and futility of life, a feeling that was deepened by the death of his older brother, Miguel. Some poems in *The Black Heralds* openly question God's role in the universe, some demonstrate the stirrings of an Amerindian consciousness, and others hint at the growth of social concern for the plight of the Indians.

In 1920, Vallejo's involvement in political matters concerning the Indian population led to his imprisonment for nearly three months. This experience heightened his feeling of loss at the death of his mother and contributed to a state of depression that was to torment him for the rest of his life. *Trilce* was conceived during his imprisonment; in this work, Vallejo used startling and innovative techniques—such as neologisms, colloquialisms, and typographical innovation—to express his anguish at the disparity that he felt existed between human aspirations and the limitations of human existence.

In 1923, Vallejo left Peru for Europe; he was never to return to his homeland. While in Paris, he was unable to find stable employment; he barely made a living from translations, language tutoring, and political writing. His experience of poverty was ac-

---

A cripple walks by arm in arm with a child
After that I'm going to read André Breton?
Another shakes from cold, hacks, spits blood.
Is it possible to even mention the profound I?
Another searches in the mud for bones, rinds.
How write after that about the infinite?

—from "A man walks by with a loaf of bread on his shoulder" (trans. Clayton Eshleman)

companied by a growing interest in Marxism. In the late 1920's, Vallejo became a frequent visitor to the bookstore of *L'Humanité*, the Communist newspaper. He read Marxist and Leninist theory, and as a result, his work reflected this shift toward the political sphere. He also traveled twice to the Soviet Union during these years to see Communism at work firsthand. Vallejo was

W H A T   T O   R E A D

Spain, Take This Cup from Me

Although first published as part of *Human Poems* (1968), Vallejo's *Spain, Take This Cup from Me* actually forms a separate, unified work very different in tone from the majority of the other posthumous poems—a tone of hope, although, especially in the title poem, the poet seems to suspect that the cause he has believed in so passionately may be lost. In this poem, perhaps the last that Vallejo wrote, the orphan—now all human children—has found a mother. This mother is Spain, symbol of a new revolutionary order in which oppression may be ended. The children are urged not to let their mother die; nevertheless, even should this happen, they have a recourse: to continue struggling and to find a new mother.

In *Human Poems*, man is captive of his body and hardly more intelligent than the lower animals, but in *Spain, Take This Cup from Me* he is capable of true transcendence through solidarity and the will to fight injustice. Spain thus becomes a text—a book that sprouts from the body of an anonymous soldier. The poet insists that he himself is nothing, and that his actions rather than his words constitute the real text. This may represent a greatly evolved negation of poetic authority, first seen in "The Black Heralds" with the repeated cry, "I don't know!" Nevertheless, *Spain, Take This Cup from Me* rings with a biblical tone, and the poet sometimes sounds like a prophet.

— Lee Hunt Dowling

expelled from France in 1930 for his political activities (he had to go to Spain), and he joined the Communist Party in 1931.

While he published no new poetic works during the 1930's, he continued to write poetry based on his experience of life in Europe. About half of these poems, which were published post-humously under the title *Human Poems*, focus on the collective experience of humankind. A number of the poems express en-thusiasm for the collective ethos of communism, some express dismay at the exploitation and pain experienced by the prole-tariat, and others express disillusionment with politics and poli-ticians.

In July, 1936, the Spanish Civil War broke out, and Vallejo was irresistibly drawn to this international political struggle. He trav-eled to Spain on two separate occasions and wrote some emo-tional poems about the conflict, subsequently collected in

Spain, Take This Cup from Me. Some of the best poems of this collection focus on a Republican war hero. "Masa" (Mass), for example, perhaps Vallejo's most famous poem, focuses on a moment on the battlefield when a dead Republican militiaman is miraculously brought back to life through the collective love of humankind.

Vallejo died on Good Friday in 1938, muttering that he wanted to go to Spain, on the very day that Francisco Franco's troops split the Republican forces in two by reaching the Mediterranean Sea, thereby sealing the fate of the Republicans. Vallejo thus did not live to see the demise of the Republican forces he supported. A number of poems were discovered among his posthumous papers by his widow, Georgette de Vallejo, who the following year published them under the title *Human Poems.* They had been written from the late 1920's to the mid-1930's and had been typed up over a period of about six months preceding Vallejo's death.

— *Stephen M. Hart*

Learn More

Dove, Patrick. *The Catastrophe of Modernity: Tragedy and the Nation in Latin American Literature.* Lewisburg, Pa.: Bucknell University Press, 2004. Dove analyzes *Trilce* and works by other authors to determine how literature reflects and comes to terms with societal catastrophe in Latin America.

Franco, Jean. *César Vallejo: The Dialectics of Poetry and Silence.* New York: Cambridge University Press, 1976. A good introduction to Vallejo's work.

Hart, Stephen. *César Vallejo: A Critical Bibliography of Research.* London: Tamesis, 2002. Describes and evaluates the manuscripts, books, essays, articles, translations, and theses that have been written about Vallejo since his death.

_____, ed. *César Vallejo: Selected Poems.* London: Bristol Classical Press, 2000. Hart's introduction and notes on Vallejo include excerpts of poetry in Spanish. (The text is in English.) Also includes a bibliography and glossary.

Hedrick, Tace. *Mestizo Modernism: Race, Nation, and Identity in Latin American Culture, 1900-1940.* New Brunswick, N.J.: Rutgers University Press, 2003. Hedrick argues that Modernism had a different meaning for Latin American writers and artists than it did for Americans and Europeans. He examines what being "modern" and "American" meant to Vallejo, Gabriel Mistral, Frida Kahlo, and Diego Rivera.

Higgins, James. *The Poet in Peru: Alienation and the Quest for a Super-Reality.* Liverpool, England: Cairns, 1982. Contains a good overview of the main themes of Vallejo's poetry.

McGuirk, Bernard. *Latin American Literature: Symptons, Risks, and Strategies of Poststructuralist Criticism.* New York: Routledge, 1997. An analysis of Latin American literature from 1890-1990, including the work of Vallejo. McGuirk examines the confrontation between theory, politics, and culture that is present in literature of this period.

Weiss, Jason. *The Lights of Home: A Century of Latin American Writers in Paris.* New York: Routledge, 2003. Weiss explores the lives and work of Vallejo and other twentieth century Latin American writers who lived in Paris. He describes what their experiences in Paris meant to them and how it affected their writing.

Mario Vargas Llosa

Peruvian novelist

Born: Arequipa, Peru; March 28, 1936
Also known as: Jorge Mario Pedro Vargas Llosa

LONG FICTION: *La ciudad y los perros*, 1962 (*The Time of the Hero*, 1966); *La casa verde*, 1965 (*The Green House*, 1968); *Los cachorros*, 1967 (novella; *The Cubs*, 1979); *Conversación en la catedral*, 1969 (*Conversation in the Cathedral*, 1975); *Pantaleón y las visitadoras*, 1973 (*Captain Pantoja and the Special Service*, 1978); *La tía Julia y el escribidor*, 1977 (*Aunt Julia and the Scriptwriter*, 1982); *La guerra del fin del mundo*, 1981 (*The War of the End of the World*, 1984); *La historia de Alejandro Mayta*, 1984 (*The Real Life of Alejandro Mayta*, 1986); *¿Quién mató a Palomino Molero?*, 1987 (*Who Killed Palomino Molero?*, 1987); *El hablador*, 1987 (*The Storyteller*, 1989); *Elogio de la madrastra*, 1988 (*In Praise of the Stepmother*, 1990); *Lituma en los Andes*, 1993 (*Death in the Andes*, 1996); *Los cuadernos de don Rigoberto*, 1997 (*The Notebooks of Don Rigoberto*, 1998); *Fiesta del Chivo*, 2000 (*The Feast of the Goat*, 2001); *El paraíso en la otra esquina*, 2003 (*The Way to Paradise*, 2003).

SHORT FICTION: *Los jefes*, 1959 (*The Cubs, and Other Stories*, 1979).

DRAMA: *La señorita de Tacna*, pb. 1981 (*The Young Lady from Tacna*, 1990); *Kathie y el hipopótamo*, pb. 1983 (*Kathie and the Hippopotamus*, 1990); *La Chunga*, pb. 1987 (English translation, 1990); *Three Plays*, pb. 1990; *El loco de los balcones*, pb. 1993.

NONFICTION: *La novela en América Latina: Dialogo*, 1968; *Literatura en la revolución y revolución en la literatura*, 1970 (with Julio Cortázar and Oscar Collazos); *La historia secreta de una novela*, 1971; *Gabriel García Márquez: Historia de un deicidio*, 1971; *El combate imaginario*, 1972; *García Márquez y la problemática de la novela*, 1973; *La novela y el problema de la expresión literaria en Peru,* 1974; *La orgía perpetua: Flaubert y "Madame Bovary,"* 1975 (*The Perpetual Orgy: Flaubert and "Madame Bovary,"* 1986); *José María Arguedas: Entre sapos y halcones,* 1978; *La utopía arcaica,* 1978; *Entre Sartre y Camus,* 1981; *Contra viento y marea, 1964-1988,* 1983-1990 (3 volumes); *A Writer's Reality,* 1991 (Myron I. Lichtblau, editor); *Fiction: The Power of Lies,* 1993; *Pez en el agua,* 1993 (*A Fish in the Water: A Memoir,* 1994); *Making Waves,* 1996; *Cartas a un joven novelista,* 1997 (*Letters to a Young Novelist,* 2002); *Claudio Bravo: Paintings and Drawings,* 1997 (with Paul Bowles); *El lenguaje de la pasión,* 2001 (*The Language of Passion: Selected Commentary,* 2003); *La verdad de las mentiras,* 2002.

Peru's leading contemporary novelist, Mario Vargas Llosa (MAH-ree-oh VAHR-gahs YOH-sah), is regarded as one of the creators (along with such writers as Julio Cortázar, Gabriel García Márquez, and Carlos Fuentes) of the new Latin American novel. The son of Ernesto Vargas Maldonado and Dora Llosa Ureta, Mario Vargas Llosa was born in the town of Arequipa in southern Peru. His parents were divorced before he was born, and he was taken by his mother to live at Cochabama, Bolivia, with her parents, who spoiled him. When he was nine, he and his mother left for Piura, in northwestern Peru; however, a year later, his parents remarried, and they moved the family to Lima.

Those ingrates wanted women and nighttime fun so much that finally heaven ("the devil, you mean, that cursed trickster," *Father García says) ended up giving them exactly what they wanted. And that was how it came to be, noisy, frivolous, and nocturnal: the Green House.*

—from *The Green House*
(trans. Gregory Rabassa)

Jerry Bauer

694

The pampered and sensitive boy found himself no longer the center of attention. At the Catholic school he attended in Lima, he was younger than most of his classmates and was consequently ridiculed. At home, his artistic activities had to be kept from his father, who (like many Peruvians) regarded writing as no work for a man. For Vargas Llosa, literature became an escape and, as he later described it, a way of justifying his existence. Intending to "make a man of him," Vargas Llosa's father sent his son to a military academy in Lima, the Leoncio Prado. The machismo and brutality he encountered there proved highly traumatic for the young man.

This experience ended in 1952, when Vargas Llosa returned to Piura for his final year of secondary school. In Piura he worked part-time on the newspaper *La Industria* and wrote a play called "La huida" (the escape). Returning to Lima, Vargas Llosa studied for his degree in literature at the University of San Marcos, while being employed as a journalist with Radio Panamericana and the newspaper *La Crónica*. In 1955 he married Julia Urquidi, a Bolivian; the marriage ended in divorce. In 1965 he married his first cousin Patricia Llosa, with whom he had two sons and a daughter.

Vargas Llosa made a brief visit to Paris in 1958 and won a prize in a short-story competition sponsored by *La Revue française*. The winning story, "El desafío" (the challenge), was published in his first book of short stories. The book won for Vargas Llosa the Premio Leopoldo Alas award in Spain, where it was published in 1959. That same year the author traveled to the University of Madrid on a scholarship but decided to move on to Paris without completing his doctoral dissertation. He lived there for seven years, working as a Berlitz teacher, as a journalist, and with URTF, the French radio and television network.

In Paris, Vargas Llosa met other Latin American and French writers and intellectuals but worked and wrote in relative isolation until the publication of his first novel, *The Time of the Hero*, which caused a sensation throughout the Spanish-speaking world. Highly experimental in style, the novel portrays an educational institution that deliberately corrupts innocence and

W H A T   T O   R E A D

The Time of the Hero

The Time of the Hero (1962) is set at a military academy and explores the relationships among a group of cadets as they enter adulthood. The various hierarchies under which the cadets live structure the plot, which works itself out through multiple narrators.

The story concentrates upon what the existential philosopher Jean-Paul Sartre termed the time of election, when one becomes the self one has chosen to be. Vargas Llosa explores this moment, not only for the adolescents but also for their officers and for Peru's power structure. By stressing the limited options available to the cadets and by revealing the hideous strength of the social hierarchies into which they must blend, he creates a narrative web of tragic intensity.

The cadets are from varying social strata, providing the perfect mechanism for portraying the country's social structure. They form a small cell (the "Circle") to ensure their survival. Through a series of mistakes, the cell is implicated in the death of a cadet. The guilt associated with the cadet's murder spreads through the school, and its moral implications are realized most clearly in the reactions of three characters: Gamboa, the perfect officer; Alberto, the author of pornographic novels and the typical bourgeois; and the Jaguar, the invincible strong man who created the Circle. Each of them comes to terms with the reality of death and is indelibly marked: Gamboa's career is ruined because he disputes his superior officers' decisions; Alberto returns to the suburb instead of becoming the writer he should have been; and the Jaguar escapes through his love for another, but his life is constantly threatened by corruption. The fragmented conversations, the disjointed interior monologues, the tension between adolescent and adult realities—all of these aspects create a dramatic field upon which the battles for honor are lost.

— *Mary E. Davis*

perverts idealism in its students (indicting both the Leoncio Prado and the Peruvian military regime that it represents). The Peruvian military authorities burned a thousand copies of the book on the grounds of the Leoncio Prado and dismissed the work as the product of a demented Communist mind. In Spain, however, it received the Premio de la Crítica Española, and it has been translated into more than a dozen languages.

The Green House appeared three years later. The title refers both to a Piura brothel and to the rain forest. The social messages—the complicity between army and church, the horrors of human exploitation—coexist with the intense inner conflicts of the characters. Some critics disparaged the novel's characters as one-dimensional, failing to understand that for Vargas Llosa a novel is primarily a chronicle of action, not an inner revelation of the forces that motivate action. The book was awarded numerous prizes in Spain and Peru.

In 1966 Vargas Llosa left Paris for London, accepting an appointment as visiting lecturer in Latin American literature at the University of London; he also traveled and lectured throughout Great Britain and Europe. He then spent a semester as writer-in-residence at the University of Washington in Seattle.

After the publication of his third novel, *Conversation in the Cathedral,* a monumental two-volume indictment of Peruvian life under the corrupt dictatorship of Manuel Udria (he ruled from 1948 to 1956), Vargas Llosa lectured briefly at the University of Puerto Rico. The doctoral dissertation he had begun in 1959, a study of the fiction of his close friend Gabriel García Márquez, was finally published in 1971. Two years later a fourth novel appeared: *Captain Pantoja and the Special Service.* While it once again attacked the unholy alliance of church, army, and brothel, it was written in a new farcical style. This comic vein continues in the author's next novel, *Aunt Julia and the Scriptwriter,* a satirical account of the discovery of a Bolivian genius in his genre: radio melodramas.

Besides being a writer of fiction, Vargas Llosa has published much literary criticism. For him, writing literary criticism is a creative act, not unlike that of writing a novel or a short story, in which the critic indulges in the same arbitrariness and fantasy as the author.

Finally, Vargas Llosa has taken an active role in Peruvian politics, running for president in 1990. As a spokesman for democratic centrism, he has been harshly criticized by his erstwhile colleagues on the left. Not only in speeches and journalistic pieces but also in novels such as *The Real Life of Alejandro Mayta* and *The Feast of the Goat,* Vargas Llosa has cast a skeptical eye on revolutionary ideology and its real-world outcomes. Political controversy, however, has not diminished his reputation as one of the leading writers in Latin America.

— Genevieve Slomski

Learn More

Booker, M. Keith. *Vargas Llosa Among the Postmodernists.* Gainesville: University Press of Florida, 1994. One of the most comprehensive treatments of Vargas Llosa's work. Includes chapters such as "The Reader as Voyeur" and "Literature and Modification."

Castro-Klaren, Sara. *Understanding Mario Vargas Llosa.* Columbia: University of South Carolina Press, 1990. Offers an insightful analysis of Vargas Llosa's major works of fiction and views the works in their political and cultural context.

Gerdes, Dick. *Mario Vargas Llosa.* Boston: Twayne, 1985. A varied and useful collection of critical essays by Gerdes; includes a chronology of events and a bibliography.

Guillermoprieto, Alma. *Looking for History: Dispatches from Latin America.* New York: Pantheon, 2001. Discusses Vargas Llosa's political career.

Köllmann, Sabine. *Vargas Llosa's Fiction and the Demons of Politics.* New York: Peter Lang, 2002. Evaluates the relationship of Vargas Llosa's fiction to his political writing, focusing on three political novels. Köllmann concludes that politics is a demon for Vargas Llosa, provoking him to creativity.

Kristal, Efraín. *Temptation of the Word: The Novels of Mario Vargas Llosa.* Nashville, Tenn.: Vanderbilt University Press, 1998. Kristal examines the overarching reasons for Vargas Llosa's political passions and divides Vargas Llosa's writing career into sections corresponding to results of his ideas on capitalism and the decline of the Cuban Revolution.

Moses, Michael Valdez. *The Novel and the Globalization of Culture.* New York: Oxford University Press, 1995. Discusses the cultural context of Vargas Llosa's major works of fiction.

Vargas Llosa, Mario. "Mario Vargas Llosa." http://www.mvargasllosa.com/. Accessed March 22, 2005. The author's Web site contains basic information about life, his books, awards he has received, and a detailed chronology.

Maruxa Vilalta

Spanish-born Mexican playwright

Born: Barcelona, Spain; September 23, 1932

DRAMA: *Los desorientados,* pb. 1959, pr. 1960 (adaptation of her novel); *Trio,* pr. 1964, pb. 1965 (includes *Un país feliz, Soliloquio del tiempo,* and *La última letra*); *El 9,* pr. 1965, pb. 1966 (*Number 9,* 1973); *Cuestión de narices,* pr. 1966, pb. 1967; *Esta noche juntos, amándonos tanto,* pr., pb. 1970 (*Together Tonight, Loving Each Other So Much,* 1973); *Nada como el piso 16,* pr. 1975, pb. 1977 (*Nothing Like the Sixteenth Floor,* 1978); *Historia de Él,* pr. 1978, pb. 1979 (*The Story of Him,* 1980); *Una mujer, dos hombres, y un balazo,* pr. 1981, pb. 1984 (*A Woman, Two Men, and a Gunshot,* 1984); *Pequeña historia de horror (y de amor desenfrenado),* pb. 1984, pr. 1985 (*A Little Tale of Horror [and Unbridled Love],* 1986); *Una voz en el desierto: Vida de San Jerónimo,* pb. 1990, pr. 1991 (*A Voice in the Wilderness: The Life of Saint Jerome,* 1990); *Francisco de Asís,* pr. 1992, pb. 1993 (*Francis of Assisi,* 1993); *Jesucristo entre nosotros,* pr. 1994, pb. 1995; *El barco ebrio,* pb. 1995; *En blanco y negro: Ignacio y los jesuitas,* pr., pb. 1997; *1910,* pr. 2000, pb. 2001.

LONG FICTION: *El castigo,* 1957; *Los desorientados,* 1958; *Dos colores para el paisaje,* 1961.

SHORT FICTION: *El otro día, la muerte,* 1974.

M aruxa Vilalta (mah-REW-shah vee-LAHL-tah) was born in Barcelona, Spain, on September 23, 1932. Her family, exiles from the Spanish Civil War, emigrated in 1939 to Mexico, where Vilalta continued to reside. After completing her primary and secondary education at the Liceo Franco Mexicano in Mexico City, Vilalta studied Spanish literature at the college of philosophy and letters of the National Autonomous University of Mexico. She was married in 1951 and has two children.

Vilalta began her writing career as a novelist in 1957, with *El castigo* (the punishment). When, in 1959, she adapted her second published novel, *Los desorientados* (the disoriented ones), for the stage, Vilalta was so impressed by the immediacy of the theatrical medium and the concrete life it gave to her characters that she dedicated herself thereafter almost exclusively to playwriting. While her early plays, especially *Number 9*, won for her considerable critical attention, it was in 1970, with *Together Tonight, Loving Each Other So Much*, that she really established herself as one of Mexico's leading experimental dramatists. This was the first of three plays that would win for her the coveted Alarcón Prize for the best play of the year; in 1978, *The Story of Him* won that prize on a unanimous vote, something rather rare in the award's history.

In 1975, with the prizewinning *Nothing Like the Sixteenth Floor*, Vilalta began directing her own plays, and as a director, she has been closely associated with the National Autonomous University of Mexico, which is considered the major locus for experimental play production in Mexico. Vilalta is also a noted essayist and theater critic for Mexico's leading daily newspaper, *Excelsior.*

Vilalta is known at home and abroad as an experimentalist, a playwright who with every new work further explores the possibilities of the theatrical medium. Her plays have been showcases for significant theatrical innovations since the mid-twentieth

> *"Let's not be pessimists. Let's try to have constructive thoughts. Thoughts that are educative, productive, depurative, communicative, seductive, sensitive, digestive, abortive, cohesive, copulative, operative, ponderative, lucrative and lubricative, imperative, volitive, incentive, and incisive. In any case, thoughts to live with."*
>
> —from *Number 9*
> (trans. W. Keith Leonard and Mario T. Soria)

century, and they have been associated with names such as Eugène Ionesco, Samuel Beckett, Harold Pinter, and Bertolt Brecht. Vilalta has been concerned with the most pressing issues of the twentieth century, such as the loss of direction in a seemingly absurd world, humankind's horrifying capacity for cruelty, and the corrupting allure of power. Given these concerns, it is not surprising that Vilalta's plays are themselves often violent and shocking and that her characters are dehumanized grotesques.

Vilalta's playwriting fits within a universalist trend in Latin American theater, and for this reason, her plays are not peculiarly Mexican, either in their language, their characters, or their setting. This goes hand in hand with Vilalta's rejection of more realistic stage conventions, which she considers too much associated with a local theater of customs or manners, what in Spanish is called *costumbrismo*. Instead, Vilalta usually prefers a nonrepresentational theater, whose characters belong to no specific country. When she does place them geographically, as in *Nothing Like the Sixteenth Floor,* it is in Manhattan, New York, and not in Mexico City.

Vilalta's conscious effort to avoid things typically Mexican clearly places her on one side of a long-standing debate among fellow playwrights about how indigenous their art should be and the degree to which it should be valued based on international appeal. A similar debate has been waged by artists in most Latin American countries, who recognize the necessity to deal with their own reality but also do not want to be potentially isolated from world audiences. Many have chosen the same solution as Vilalta, which is to write plays that can be read as allegories. Thus, while on one level they may not have anything overtly Mexican about them, the issues with which they deal—the dehumanization of the labor force, the cruelty individuals inflict on one another, the institutionalization of violence—most certainly do. It is by indirection, then, that Vilalta makes a powerful commentary on the specific world in which she lives, while not actually having to place her characters there.

Vilalta often expresses her thematic concerns through the theatrical metaphor of game playing. Usually she keeps the

W H A T   T O   R E A D

1910

Vilalta's play *1910* (2001) won critical acclaim. The epic dramatizes the commoners' experience of the Mexican Revolution. As playwright and director, Vilalta intended to demonstrate how theater was the perfect medium for the Mexican Revolution, which played out as the history of passions. Vilalta's 168 characters portray anonymous townspeople and farmers, not famous military or governmental figures. She intended to demythicize the revolution. Rather than political heroics or the official story of history, *1910* portrays child soldiers, women guerrilleras fighting among the men, violence inflicted by the *campesinos* on themselves, and thoughtless yet pure acts of heroism. Vilalta's Mexico reveals the realities of all wars.

Like most of Vilalta's plays, *1910* exposes sociopolitical problems that extend beyond Mexico. She denounces governments that practice dictatorial abuses behind a facade of democracy while they dehumanize their citizens. Power in interpersonal relations is examined in all its facets and degrees, from the abuser to the abused.

— *Kirsten F. Nigro*

number of players at two or three, and the intensity of the games may well explain her preference for one-act plays. The rules for the games her characters play are not always easy to follow, because they do not necessarily adhere to everyday logic. Their logic resides in the games themselves, which should be interpreted as metaphors and not concrete depictions of reality offstage.

Vilalta represents a considerable presence in Mexican experimental drama, and her plays show the clear influence of many major theater innovators of the twentieth century. Vilalta is not merely derivative, however, for she adapts these influences to her own ends. The result is a very personal theater, one that is not particularly Mexican in any obvious way but that still manages to make an indirect commentary on the social and political realities of Mexican culture. Moreover, although the vision of humankind that Vilalta paints is bleak in the extreme, critical and audience enthusiasm for her plays, both in Mexico and abroad, would seem to indicate playgoers' recognition that, by emphasizing the negative, Vilalta ultimately hopes to provoke change for the better.

Vilalta's work, like much experimental theater since the 1960's, means to assault rather than comfort audiences, and has a definite political intent while not being allied with any specific ideology. Instead, it makes a statement with a broad application, regardless of geography or culture. As a result, Vilalta has won audiences throughout Latin America, in the United States, Canada, and numerous European countries. In Mexico itself, Vilalta has three times received that country's most prestigious drama award, the Alarcón Prize of the Mexican Critics Association— for *Together Tonight, Loving Each Other So Much, Nothing Like the Sixteenth Floor,* and *The Story of Him. Number 9* was selected for publication in the United States as one of the best short plays of 1973. Vilalta's major plays have been published in English as well as in French, Italian, Catalan, and Czech.

Vilalta won the Sor Juana Inés de la Cruz award for best play in 1976 for *Nothing Like the Sixteenth Floor.* That same year, she was awarded the El Fígaro award for best play for *The Story of Him.* In 1991, she received the award for best play for *A Voice in the Wilderness: The Life of Saint Jerome* from the Agrupación de Periodistas Teatrales. The drama also won the Claridades award for best play of the year. The Asociación Mexicana de Críticos de Teatro gave the drama *Francis of Assisi* its award for the best creative research.

— *Kirsten F. Nigro*

Learn More

Bearse, Grace, and Lorraine E. Roses. "Maruxa Vilalta: Social Dramatist." *Revista de estudios hispánicos* 43 (October, 1984): 399-406. An analysis of Vilalta's role as a social dramatist.

Cajiao Salas, Teresa, and Margarita Vargas, eds. *Women Writing Women: An Anthology of Spanish American Theater of the 1980's.* Albany: State University of New York Press, 1997. The authors analyze Vilalta's dramaturgy and provide detailed bibliographical information. They include an English translation by Kirsten F. Nigro of *A Woman, Two Men, and a Gunshot.*

Gladhart, Amalia. *The Leper in Blue: Coercive Performance and the Contemporary Latin American Theater.* Chapel Hill: University of North Carolina Press, 2000. This study explores contemporary controversial playwrights with social and political messages. Gladhart examines several of Vilalta's plays.

Magnarelli, Sharon. "Maruxa Vilalta: *Una voz en el desierto.*" In *Latin American Women Dramatists: Theater, Texts, and Theories,* edited by Catherine Larson and Margarita Vargas. Bloomington: Indiana University Press, 1998. Vilalta is one of the fifteen playwrights included in this collection of critical essays examining their lives and work. Magnarelli's essay focuses on *Una voz en el desierto: vida del San Jeronimo,* discussing the relation to performance and art in the two plays.

"Maruxa Vilalta." In *Dictionary of Mexican Literature.* Westport, Conn.: Greenwood Press, 1992. A concise biographical treatment of Vilalta.

José Antonio Villarreal

Mexican American novelist

Born: Los Angeles, California; July 30, 1924

LONG FICTION: *Pocho*, 1959; *The Fifth Horseman*, 1974; *Clemente Chacón*, 1984.
SHORT FICTION: "The Last Minstrel in California" and "The Laughter of My Father" (in *Iguana Dreams*, 1992).

The parents of José Antonio Villarreal (hoh-SAY ahn-TOH-nyoh VEE-yah-ree-AHL) were born in Mexico and moved to the United States in 1921. His father fought for Pancho Villa during the Mexican Revolution. Villarreal's family served as migrant workers in the fields of California before settling in Santa Clara in 1930. As a child he read such works as classical mythology, Mark Twain's *The Adventures of Tom Sawyer* (1876) and *Adventures of Huckleberry Finn* (1884), Jonathan Swift's *Gulliver's Travels* (1726), and Henry Fielding's *Tom Jones* (1749). He has cited James Otis's *Toby Tyler: Or, Ten Weeks with a Circus* (1881) as his favorite childhood book.

Villarreal received a B.A. in English from the University of California at Berkeley. He has taught at various universities, including the University of Colorado, the University of Texas at El Paso, the University of Texas-Pan American, the University of Santa Clara, and the Universidad Nacional Autónoma de México.

Villarreal has the distinction of having written what is considered to be the first Chicano novel, *Pocho*, published in 1959, before the Civil Rights movement began in earnest. Villarreal maintains his individuality within the Chicano movement; he acknowledges his cultural debt not only to the Chicano culture but to the mainstream cultures of the United States and Mexico as well. He considers Chicano literature to be a part of American literature and compares Chicano writers to the regional writers of the southern or western United States. He acknowledges

Mexican literature as an influence on his writing but feels that, except for the difference of language, the literatures of Mexico and the United States are very similar.

Villarreal considers the best Chicano literature to be that which informs the rest of American society about the condition of Hispanics living in the United States. He does not hesitate to criticize radical propagandistic writings by Chicanos which, in his opinion, alienate the general public and are read only by Chicanos, who are already familiar with their predicament. Villarreal has gone as far as to say that Chicano literature has come to be considered a separate and distinct body of literature largely because of the promotional efforts of academics who must justify their jobs and graduate programs.

Villarreal's first novel, *Pocho*, suggests that the Mexican Revolution was the beginning of the proliferation of Hispanic communities in the American Southwest. Subsequently, many other Chicano novelists have also referred to the revolution as the point of departure for Chicano culture. The novel's title is a derogatory term for an Americanized Chicano. The father of the protagonist, Richard Rubio, had participated in the Mexican Revolution and then crossed into the United States. As he matures, Richard rejects his parents' Mexican Catholic values in order to assimilate into American society. As he witnesses a demonstration by farm and cannery workers, Richard's perspective is detached— he seems to have forgotten that his own birth was in a melon

> *At one-thirty in the morning, the General sent another assault wave to the base of the Bufa. "To keep the Federals alert," he said. He lay on a field cot and slept, protected by a sarape from the light rain and early morning chill. He slept but a few minutes, waking when the machine-gun fire ceased. It was as if the silence had disturbed his sleep.*
>
> —from *The Fifth Horseman*

field in California's Imperial Valley. Villarreal modeled *Pocho* after James Joyce's *A Portrait of the Artist as a Young Man* (1916).

In his second novel, *The Fifth Horseman,* Villarreal took his assimilationist philosophy one step further by attempting to write a novel that could be considered part of the Mexican literary tradition, even though the novel is written in English. As in *Pocho,* the Mexican Revolution provides the historical setting. Several scenes appear to be strongly influenced by Mexican novels about the revolution.

The Fifth Horseman also recalls the many American novels about the Mexican Revolution that were written in the 1920's and 1930's, long before the Chicano rights movement; moreover, the novel's title is even reminiscent of *The Four Horsemen of*

W H A T   T O   R E A D

Pocho

Pocho (1959) is generally regarded as the first novel by an American of Mexican descent to represent the experiences of emigration from Mexico and acculturation to the United States. Although this pioneering work went out of print shortly after publication, a second edition appeared in 1970 during the Chicano Renaissance, and it has since been studied in many literature classes.

Set in the years between 1923 and 1942, the years of the Great Depression, the novel recounts the quest for personal and cultural identity of Richard Rubio, son of a soldier exiled after the Mexican Revolution and now a migrant farmworker in Santa Clara, California. As a *pocho,* a member of the first generation born in the United States, Richard grows up deeply attached to the traditions of his family yet very attracted to the values of his American peers.

In addition to trials faced by every young person—the struggle with authority, the search for independence, the thirst for knowledge, and the hunger for sexual experi-

the Apocalypse (1916), the novel about World War I by the Spaniard Vicente Blasco Ibáñez. By thus acknowledging his American, Mexican, and Spanish heritage, Villarreal asserts his belief that the best literature is universal.

In his third novel, *Clemente Chacón*, Villarreal depicts the plight of Chicanos in the 1960's and 1970's. The narrative has certain surreal qualities, which are perhaps the author's way of suggesting that Chicanos had become totally divorced from their history by the second half of the twentieth century. For example, in the novel's epilogue, a senator from Texas named Porfirio Díaz talks to the U.S. president about the problem of illegal Mexican aliens.

— Douglas Edward LaPrade

ence—Richard faces special challenges in self-definition. He confronts poverty, family instability, a blighted education system, racial prejudice, a society torn by economic crises, and world war. His passage from childhood into adulthood is given unique shape by the Depression, by the turmoil of life as an itinerant farmworker and by the powerful tensions between Mexican and American cultures.

Poverty inspires his dreams of success. He identifies intensely with his macho father but cannot abide his violence, coldness, and self-destructiveness. Drawn to the beauties of the Catholic Church, he nonetheless rejects faith. He is deeply attached to his mother but finds her helplessness repugnant. Obliged to become the man of the family as a teenager, he finds that his responsibilities clash with his solitary nature, his love of books, and his emerging personal identity as a writer.

His choice to join the Navy is more personal than patriotic. To resolve his conflicts he chooses exile from his shattered family, escapes from his poverty without prospects, and seeks release from the fragments of the two cultures he has not yet pieced together. He leaves to face what he knows will be a struggle for a new identity as a man, as an artist, and as an American.

— Virginia M. Crane

Learn More

Alarcón, Daniel Cooper. *The Aztec Palimpsest: Mexico in the Modern Imagination.* Tucson: University of Arizona Press, 1997. Discusses images of Mexico in *Pocho.*

Bruce-Novoa, Juan. *Chicano Authors: Inquiry by Interview.* Austin: University of Texas Press, 1980. Includes an interview with Villarreal that is an excellent source of information about the author's childhood and education; the interview also offers valuable insights into Villarreal's attitudes toward Chicano literature and literature in general.

Leal, Luis. *"The Fifth Horseman* and Its Literary Antecedents." Introduction to *The Fifth Horseman.* Garden City, N.Y.: Doubleday, 1974. This essay makes many references to Mexican and American novels about the Mexican Revolution that serve as sources or background for *The Fifth Horseman.*

Saldívar, Ramón. *Chicano Narrative.* Madison: University of Wisconsin Press, 1990. Includes a subchapter entitled *"Pocho* and the Dialectics of History," which explains how the protagonist must ignore history so he can assimilate in the United States.

Victor Villaseñor

Mexican American novelist, short-story writer, biographer, and screenwriter

Born: Carlsbad, California; May 11, 1940
Also known as: Victor Edmundo Villaseñor

LONG FICTION: *Macho!*, 1973.
SHORT FICTION: *Walking Stars: Stories of Magic and Power*, 1994.
SCREENPLAY: *The Ballad of Gregorio Cortez*, 1982.
NONFICTION: *Jury: The People vs. Juan Corona*, 1977; *Rain of Gold*, 1991; *Wild Steps of Heaven*, 1996; *Thirteen Senses: A Memoir*, 2001; *Burro Genius: A Memoir*, 2004.

Victor Edmundo Villaseñor (VEE-tohr ehd-MEWN-doh VEE-yah-sehn-YOHR) is one of the significant chroniclers of the Mexican American experience; his novel *Macho!* was, along with Richard Vásquez's 1970 novel *Chicano*, one of the first Chicano novels issued by a mainstream publisher. Villaseñor was born to Mexican immigrant parents in Carlsbad, California. His parents, Lupe Gómez and Juan Salvador Villaseñor, who had immigrated with their families when young, were middle class, and Victor and his four siblings were brought up on their ranch in Oceanside. Villaseñor struggled with school from his very first day, being dyslexic and having spoken Spanish rather than English at home. He dropped out of high school, feeling that he would "go crazy" if he did not, and went to work on his parents' ranch. He briefly attended college at the University of San Diego, where he discovered that reading books could be something other than drudgery, but left college after flunking most of his courses. He became a boxer for a brief period, then went to Mexico, where he suddenly became aware of Mexican art, literature, and history. He began to be proud of his heritage, rather than confused and ashamed, meeting Mexican doctors and lawyers—"heroes," he says—for the first time. He read extensively.

> *Juan wasn't able to support his family by working*
> *only one shift at the Copper Queen, so he decided to*
> *change his name to Juan Cruz and get a second job*
> *on the night shift. After all, he was going on*
> *thirteen. He figured that he could hold down both*
> *shifts. . . . Hell, the big, thick-necked* gringo *boss*
> *couldn't tell him apart from all the other Mexicans.*
>
> —from *Rain of Gold*

Returning to California at his parents' insistence, Villaseñor worked in construction beginning in 1965 and painstakingly taught himself how to write. James Joyce's *A Portrait of the Artist as a Young Man* (1916) was particularly inspirational. He wrote extensively, producing many novels and short stories. They were steadily rejected until Bantam Books decided to take a chance and publish *Macho!* in 1973. The novel's protagonist is a young man named Roberto García, and the novel covers roughly a year in his life, first in his home village in Mexico, then in California, then in Mexico again. Somewhat unwillingly, Roberto journeys northward with a group of *norteños* from his village to earn money working in the fields of California. Roberto's personification of—and finally, inability to fully accept—the traditional social code of machismo; his conflicts with others, notably fellow *norteño* Pedro; and the larger labor struggle between migrant workers and landowners in California provide the central action of the book. *Macho!* received favorable reviews. The year of its initial publication Villaseñor married Barbara Bloch, the daughter of his editor; they have two sons, David and Joe. Villaseñor built a house on his parents' property, and as his sons grew older he enjoyed horseback riding with them.

Villaseñor's second major published work was nonfiction. *Jury: The People vs. Juan Corona* details the trial of a serial killer. Villaseñor had read about the case after *Macho!* had been accepted for publication, and it captured his interest—Corona had been arrested for murdering twenty-five derelicts. Villaseñor extensively interviewed the members of the jury that convicted Corona and thoroughly examined the complex and controversial trial. (The jury had deliberated for eight grueling days before reaching a verdict.) After the book's publication, he received some criticism for his interpretations of the events.

Villaseñor subsequently wrote the screenplay for *The Ballad of Gregorio Cortez*, based partly on writer Américo Paredes's account of the adventures of Cortez, a real-life figure, eluding the Texas Rangers around 1900. Villaseñor tells the story using multiple points of view, effectively relating the story of a man driven by circumstances into the life of a bandit while showing the prejudices and racism of the times. Written for television, the film won an award from the National Endowment for the Humanities; it was also released to theaters.

Rain of Gold, published in 1991 after more than ten years of research and writing, is the multigenerational story of Villa-

Paul Stachelek

W H A T   T O   R E A D

Macho!

The protagonist of *Macho!* (1973) is Roberto, a young Mexican who immigrates illegally into the United States. Victor Villaseñor suggests that Roberto extracts his identity from the soil of the fields that he works. On the first and last pages of the book, Villaseñor describes how volcanic ash has enriched the soil of a Mexican valley. At the end of the novel, Roberto has returned to this valley to work the land, applying what he has learned in the United States.

These homages to volcanic ash suggest that soil is not just the earth's outer covering but also its soul. Likewise, the soil is the soul of the people who work it. The novel refers to the Mexican Revolution, a popular movement to redistribute the ownership of land, to say that land is fundamental to understanding not only the Mexican people but also the country's politics and history.

According to Villaseñor, Mexico's geography dictates the country's indigenous law. Mexico is mountainous, so villages are isolated. As a result of their isolation, these villages developed their own systems of justice and never ap-

señor's family. It begins in the days before the turbulence of the Mexican Revolution and continues through life after migration to the United States in the early twentieth century, and it is told with some dramatic fictionalization. It was dubbed the "Chicano *Roots*" by those who compared it with Alex Haley's story of his African American family's history. *Rain of Gold* tells readers much about Mexican history and about anti-Hispanic prejudice in the American Southwest. The book was almost published two years earlier by G. P. Putnam's, but Villaseñor became unhappy with the company at the last minute for insisting that the book be called "Rio Grande" ("a John Wayne movie," he scoffed) and wanting to cut its length and call it fiction in order to boost sales.

peal to a higher authority. This law of the land is a violent code of honor, and the novel documents how this code places a premium on a woman's virginity and on a man's ability to fight. The definition of "macho" must necessarily emanate from an understanding of this law of the land.

The novel makes frequent references to César Chávez's movement in the 1960's to unionize agricultural workers in the United States. Villaseñor offers a complex portrait of Chávez, not allowing him to become a cardboard cutout representative of Mexicans who identify themselves with the soil. Chávez's movement distinguishes between the illegal Mexican immigrants, whom Chávez wanted deported, and the Mexican Americans, whose rights he sought to protect through unionization.

Villaseñor concludes that Chávez is a "true-self hero," one who is not labeled readily as macho, but who trusts his own conscience and is not afraid to have enemies. In this respect, Chávez is like Abraham Lincoln, Benito Juárez, John F. Kennedy, and Martin Luther King, Jr. On the novel's final page, Villaseñor qualifies Roberto also as a true-self hero when the protagonist returns to his native valley to work the fields.

— *Douglas Edward LaPrade*

The company agreed to let him buy back his book, for which Villaseñor remortgaged his home. Published in its original form and with the original title (a translation of La Lluvia de Oro, his mother's birthplace in Mexico) by Arte Público, it was well received and was widely considered Villaseñor's masterwork.

Wild Steps of Heaven recounts the history of Villaseñor's father's family in the highlands of Jalisco, Mexico, before the events covered in *Rain of Gold*; Villaseñor considered it part two of a "Rain of Gold" trilogy, and he planned to follow it with the story of his mother's family. He draws on stories told by his father and members of his extended family, relating them in a folkloric style that sometimes verges on Magical Realism. *Walk-*

ing Stars: Stories of Magic and Power, published two years before *Wild Steps of Heaven,* consists of stories for young readers that attempt both to entertain and to inspire; each of the stories, most based on events in the early lives of his parents, concludes with notes in which the author discusses the stories' meanings, emphasizing the spiritual magic that people's lives embody.

— *McCrea Adams*

Learn More

Barbato, Joseph. "Latino Writers in the American Market." *Publishers Weekly,* February 1, 1991, 17-21. Discusses the publishing of *Rain of Gold* and includes an interview with Villaseñor.

Guilbault, Rose Del Castillo. "Americanization Is Tough on 'Macho.'" In *American Voices: Multicultural Literacy and Critical Thinking,* edited by Dolores Laguardia and Hans P. Guth. Mountain View, Calif.: Mayfield, 1992. Focuses on the concept of macho, central to Villaseñor's first book. Also has an interview with Villaseñor.

Kelsey, Verlene. "Mining for a Usable Past: Acts of Recovery, Resistence, and Continuity in Victor Villaseñor's *Rain of Gold.*" *Bilingual Review* 18 (January-April, 1993): 79-85. Extensive review and close reading of Villaseñor's book.

Tatum, Charles M. *Chicano Literature.* Boston: Twayne, 1982. Includes a discussion of Villaseñor.

Helena María Viramontes

Mexican American
novelist and short-story writer

Born: East Los Angeles, California;
February 26, 1954

LONG FICTION: *Under the Feet of Jesus*, 1995; *Their Dogs Came with Them*, 2000.
SHORT FICTION: *The Moths, and Other Stories*, 1985; "Miss Clairol," 1987; "Tears on My Pillow," 1992; "The Jumping Bean," 1993.
NONFICTION: "Nopalitos: The Making of Fiction," 1989; "Why I Write," 1995.
EDITED TEXTS: *Chicana Creativity and Criticism: Charting New Frontiers in American Literature*, 1987, revised 1996 (with María Herrera-Sobek); *Chicana (W)rites: On Word and Film*, 1995 (with Herrera-Sobek).

Helena María Viramontes (heh-LAY-nah mah-REE-ah VEE-rah-MON-tays) made a name for herself as a fiction writer, educator, and active participant in Latino literary and artistic groups. One of the founders of Southern California Latino Writers and Filmmakers, Viramontes also lectured in New Delhi, India, and participated in a women's writing discussion group in the People's Republic of China. Her work was included in several major anthologies, including *The Oxford Book of Women's Writing in the United States* (1995).

The major themes of Viramontes's fiction, the oppression of women and the problems faced by working-class Chicanos, can be traced to her childhood experiences. Viramontes's parents, Mary Louise and Serafin Viramontes, met as migrant workers and settled in East Los Angeles, where Viramontes was raised with six sisters and three brothers. In "Nopalitos," she depicts her mother as a kind, energetic woman who often took in friends and relatives who needed a place to stay. Viramontes de-

> La llorona *only comes at night. When it's day,*
> *Veronica will always stay. That's what I say. I don't*
> *like Veronica. . . . I'm ascared of her cause her*
> *mama died a few months back, when the so hot so*
> *hot you could fry your toes on the tar street. And*
> *every time I seen her, I remember if it's possible for*
> *my mama to die too.*
>
> —from "Tears on My Pillow"

scribes her father, a construction worker, as a man who worked hard but responded to the stresses of his job and family responsibilities with drinking and angry outbursts.

Viramontes started writing while attending Immaculate Heart College, from which she received a B.A. in English in 1975. In 1977 her story "Requiem for the Poor" received first prize in a competition sponsored by the California State University in Los Angeles's *Statement* magazine; in 1978 she received the same prize for "The Broken Web." In 1979 she entered the creative writing program at the University of California at Irvine (UCI), where her story "Birthday" won first prize for fiction in the University's Chicano Literary Contest.

After leaving the UCI creative writing program in 1981 Viramontes continued to write and to take a leading role in local literary and artistic organizations. Two short stories, "Snapshots" and "Growing," were published in *Cuentos: Stories by Latinas* (1983); in 1984 "The Broken Web" appeared in the anthology *Woman of Her Word.* These and other stories first published in magazines such as *XhismeArte* and *Maize* were gathered in Viramontes's first book, *The Moths, and Other Stories.*

The stories in *The Moths, and Other Stories* focus on women, usually Latinas, struggling against traditional social and cultural roles. Oppressive fathers, misguided husbands, and priests who are blind to women's real needs and problems contribute to the pain experienced by Viramontes's female protagonists. However, the rebellious adolescent girls in "Growing" and "The Moths" find that their mothers collaborate in the loss of freedom and in the social limitations placed upon *mujeres,* or women. In "The Long Reconciliation" Amanda, a married Mexican woman, chooses to abort a child rather than allow it to starve, but the price she must pay is her husband's rejection and abandonment. The concerns of older women are also depicted in "Snapshots" and "Neighbors." In "The Cariboo Cafe" Viramontes extends her representation of women to include the plight of Central American mothers whose children have been "disappeared." In addition to sharing common themes, the stories in *The Moths* are linked by Viramontes's skillful handling of multiple narrators and stream of consciousness.

In 1987 Viramontes, along with María Herrera-Sobek, organized a conference at UCI on Mexican American women writers. Viramontes's short story "Miss Clairol" was included in the conference proceedings, *Chicana Creativity and Criticism,* which she also coedited. Viramontes's growing reputation was enhanced in 1989 by a National Endowment for the Arts grant, an invitation to attend a storytelling workshop with Nobel Prize laureate Gabriel García Márquez at the Sundance Institute, and the publication of her autobiographical essay "Nopalitos" in *Breaking Boundaries: Latina Writing and Critical Readings.* In 1991 she was awarded a residency at the Millay Colony for the Arts.

Viramontes returned to the University of California writing program in 1992, the same year in which "Tears on My Pillow" appeared in *New Chicana/Chicano Writing.* In 1993 Viramontes received her M.F.A., completed the manuscript that was published as *Under the Feet of Jesus* in 1995, and published another story, "The Jumping Bean," in the anthology *Pieces of the Heart.* Viramontes began to teach creative writing at Cornell University in the fall of 1993.

Viramontes's novel *Under the Feet of Jesus* combines realism with lyrical passages to depict the harsh circumstances faced by a family of migrant farmworkers. Abandoned by her husband, Petra, the mother, lives with Perfecto, a man thirty-seven years her senior, who is torn between his obligations to Petra and her family and his desire to return to his home in Mexico.

W H A T   T O   R E A D

Under the Feet of Jesus

Under the Feet of Jesus (1995) traces the day-to-day lives of a group of Chicano migrant farmworkers, revealing the struggles they endure. Viramontes is the daughter of migrant workers, and the book is dedicated to her parents and to the memory of César Chávez, who fought for the rights of farmworkers.

Perfecto Flores, a man in his seventies, and Petra, who is thirty-seven years younger, travel together with Petra's children, finding field work wherever they can. Estrella is Petra's eldest daughter; she is thirteen, and her voice controls much of the narrative.

The story is complicated by a young man named Alejo, who works in the same field as Estrella. He earns extra money by stealing fruit until he is accidentally sprayed with pesticides and becomes very sick. Petra tries all her healing methods, but nothing seems to work. Alejo gets sicker each day, but as he grows weaker, love between Alejo and Estrella grows.

Finally Estrella and her family take Alejo to the clinic. The nurse diagnoses Alejo with dysentery, tells Estrella that he must go to the hospital, and charges them ten dollars for the clinic visit. Unfortunately Perfecto only has eight dollars and some change, and their gas tank is empty. He attempts to barter with the nurse, telling her he can do chores for the clinic, but she insists that she cannot give him work. Perfecto reluctantly hands over their last nine dollars, and they leave the clinic, wondering what they are going to do. Finally Estrella takes out a tire iron, and walks back into the clinic. She smashes the tire iron against the nurse's desk and demands the nine dollars back. With the last of their money Perfecto fills the gas tank, and they drive to the hospital. Estrella is forced to leave Alejo in the emergency room knowing they cannot pay the bill but that the doctors will help him.

— *Angela Athy*

Perfecto's gentleness and concern for Petra contrast sharply with the kind of male characters that dominate *The Moths*. The novel focuses upon thirteen-year-old Estrella, whose life has been one of impermanence and loss. Though drained by exhaustion and poverty, Estrella finds the strength to fight the injustice of her life when her first love, Alejo, falls ill after being exposed to pesticides. After the family has spent all the money they have on a useless medical examination for Alejo, Estrella threatens a nurse with a crowbar, recovers the family's money, and enables Alejo to receive treatment at a hospital. The novel ends with Estrella perched on the roof of a barn she had longed to climb, an image that conveys her determination, heroism, and triumph.

— Maura Ives

Learn More

Carbonell, Ana Maria. "From Llarona to Gritona: Coatlicue in Feminist Tales by Viramontes and Cisneros." *MELUS* 24 (Summer, 1999): 53-74. Analyzes the representations of the Mexican goddess Coatlicue and the folkloric figure of the wailing ghost La Llorona in the works of Mexican American women writers Viramontes and Sandra Cisneros.

Castillo, Debra A., and María Socorro Tabuenca Córdoba. *Border Women: Writing from La Frontera*. Minneapolis: University of Minnesota Press, 2002. An analysis of writing by women living on both sides of the American-Mexican border, examining how these writers question accepted ideas about border identities.

Garza-Falcón, Leticia. *Gente Decente: A Borderlands Response to the Rhetoric of Dominance*. Austin: University of Texas Press, 1998. Garza-Falcón analyzes work by Viramontes and other writers of Mexican descent whose narratives counter the myth of the fearless white Anglo male settler bringing civilization to the American Southwest.

Green, Carol Hurd, and Mary Grimley Mason. *American Women Writers*. New York: Continuum, 1994. Includes a brief biographical sketch as well as an analysis of the short stories in *Moths*.

McCracken, Ellen. *New Latina Narrative: The Feminine Space of Postmodern Ethnicity.* Tucson: University of Arizona Press, 1999. Viramontes's work is included in this analysis of writing by Cuban American, Puerto Rican American, Mexican American, and Dominican American writers. McCracken explains how these writers have redefined concepts of multiculturalism and diversity in American society.

Moore, Deborah Owen. "La Llorona Dines at the Cariboo Cafe: Structure and Legend in the Works of Helena María Viramontes." *Studies in Short Fiction* 35 (Summer, 1998): 277-286. Contrasts the distant and close-up narrative perspectives in Viramontes's work.

Mujcinovic, Fatima. *Postmodern Cross-culturalism and Politicization in U.S. Latina Literature: From Ana Castillo to Julia Alverez.* Modern American Literature 42. New York: P. Lang, 2004. Viramontes's work is examined in this literary and cultural analysis of the work of Mexican American, Puerto Rican, Cuban American, and Dominican American women writers. Mujcinovic views these writers' work from a contemporary feminist, political, post-colonial, and psychoanalytical perspective.

Yarbo-Bejarano, Yvonne. Introduction to *The Moths, and Other Stories,* by Helena María Viramontes. Houston, Tex.: Arte Público Press, 1995. Discusses Viramontes's portrayal of women characters who struggle against the restrictions placed on them by the Chicano culture, the church, and the men in these women's lives.

Hugo Wast

Argentine novelist

Born: Córdoba, Argentina; October 23, 1883
Died: Buenos Aires, Argentina; March 28, 1962
Also known as: Gustavo Adolfo Martínez Zuviría

LONG FICTION: *Alegre*, 1905; *Flor de durazno*, 1911 (*Peach Blossom*, 1929); *Casa de los cuevos*, 1916 (*The House of the Ravens*, 1924); *Valle negro*, 1918 (*Black Valley*, 1928); *La corbata celeste*, 1920; *Pata de zorra*, 1924; *Desierto de piedra*, 1925 (*Stone Desert*, 1928); *Myriam la conspiradora*, 1926; *Lucía Miranda*, 1929.
NONFICTION: *Año X*, 1960 (history).

Gustavo Adolfo Martínez Zuviría, known in literature as Hugo Wast (HEW-goh vahst), was born in Córdoba, Argentina, in 1883. While still a university student he wrote his first novel, *Alegre*, published in 1905. Then he went on to become a doctor of laws, in 1907, and joined the University of Santa Fe as professor of economics and sociology. Politics also attracted

> *Sometimes she convinced herself that she was suffering for the wrongdoing of others, that she must have more than atoned for her own mistake, that the whole thing would never have occurred if the two families had been friends—or at least had not hated each other on account of those wretched pieces of land.*
>
> —from *Black Valley*
> (trans. Herman and Miriam Hespelt)

him, and he served several terms in the Argentine Congress. He was the longtime director of Argentina's National Library; later he served as minister of education.

After two juvenile attempts at novel writing, he published a serious novel about unmarried love, *Peach Blossom,* in 1911. Afraid that the critics of Buenos Aires would scorn any work of a provincial author, he signed it with an anagram of his first name, from which he made "Hugo Wast." The novel proved a success. During the next forty years, Wast published thirty-three books, many of them through a company that he organized. His books have appeared with Spanish and Chilean imprints in nearly three hundred editions, and nearly a million and a half copies have been sold. In addition, some seventy translations have appeared in eleven different languages.

W H A T   T O   R E A D

Black Valley

Gracian Palma was fourteen when his father died suddenly, and the boy, already motherless, became the ward of Senor Palma's old and trusted friend, Don Jesús de Viscarra. Don Jesús takes Gracian to Black Valley for the summer. Gracian soon begins to feel that there is a mystery at Black Valley that he does not understand.

Don Jesús is embroiled in a bitter boundary dispute with Don Pablo de Camargos, which is complicated by the love of his sister, Flavia, for Don Camargos (the father of her secret child). Years pass, and Gracian leaves to travel abroad, but when he returns he goes to see Flavia, who is taking care of Don Pablo, now a broken, sad man. There Gracian meets Flavia's daughter, Victoria, and the two are in love until Gracian reunites with his longtime friend Mirra and falls in love with her. The two plan to marry until Mirra learns that Victoria is expecting a child, and she sends Gracian away from Black Valley and back to Victoria.

Wast's best-selling novel, *The House of the Ravens,* won for him a prize from El Ateneo in 1915. For *Black Valley* he won the gold medal of the Spanish Academy, which later made him a corresponding member and enlarged its dictionary by the inclusion of words from his writing. *Stone Desert* was awarded the Grand National Prize of Argentine Literature for the year of its appearance.

Wast's novels can be divided into several groups. One series, for example, covers the history of his country from the earliest days of exploration and conquest, as told in *Lucía Miranda,* through the struggle for independence shown in *Myriam la conspiradora* (Myriam the conspirator), the period of the dictatorship dramatized in *La corbata celeste* (the blue necktie), and into the future in later novels.

Black Valley (1918) is subtitled *A Romance of the Argentine.* The romantic elements of the novel are readily apparent. A story of a primitive way of life and elemental emotions, the action has been staged against a background of wild natural beauty. Hugo Wast's settings are real, as are his people and the way of life he presents. The plot, although episodic in form, is well ordered, and the story moves forward with increasing emotional and dramatic interest as the writer unfolds the dual theme presented through the ill-fated love of Flavia and Don Pablo and the relationship of spoiled, weak Gracian and strong, devoted Mirra. The style is vigorous, precise, and pure.

Wast was educated by Jesuits just before the end of the nineteenth century. He felt that women were morally superior to men and excoriated cruelty, selfishness, and the flint-hearted rich. Atheism and Communism were attacked in his oceanic literary output, as were the excesses of the Catholic church.

Wast's early and prolonged popularity with Argentine readers stemmed not only from his nationalism but also from his knack for jerking urban readers out of their stifling settings with the rustic beauty of his novels. *Black Valley* promptly became a best-seller and won a gold medal from the prestigious Spanish Academy.

Wast's training in economics and sociology is apparent in his problem novels set in rural regions and in his fictional treatment of urban problems in others. He had young readers in mind for several novels, especially the amusing 1924 work *Pata de zorra*, named for a fortune teller who tries to help a university student pass his examination in Roman law. It is for the number of readers whom Wast's writings have attracted, rather than for any particular influence he has exerted on his contemporaries, that he merits a place in Argentine literature.

Learn More

Hespelt, E. H. "Hugo Wast, Argentine Novelist." *Hispania* 7 (1924). An analysis of Wast's work.

Magaldi, Juan Bautista. *En torno a Hugo Wast.* Buenos Aires: Ediciones del Peregrino, 1995. A Spanish-language critique of Wast's work.

Moreno, Juan Carlos. *Genio y figura de Hugo Wast.* Buenos Aires: Editorial Universitaria de Buenos Aires, 1969. In Spanish.

Sedgwick, Ruth. "Hugo Wast, Argentina's Most Popular Novelist." *Hispanic American Historical Review* 9 (1929). A profile of Wast.

Agustín Yáñez

Mexican novelist

Born: Guadalajara, Mexico; May 4, 1904
Died: Mexico City, Mexico; January 17, 1980

LONG FICTION: *Archipiélago de mujeres,* 1943 (novella); *Pasión y convalecencia,* 1943; *Al filo del agua,* 1947 (*The Edge of the Storm,* 1963); *La tierra pródiga,* 1960; *Las tierras flacas,* 1962 (*The Lean Lands,* 1968).

SHORT FICTION: *Espejismo de Juchitán,* 1940; *Esta es mala suerte,* 1945.

NONFICTION: *Genio y figuras de Guadalajara,* 1940; *Flor de juegos antiguos,* 1942; *Fray Bartolomé de las Casas, el conquistador conquistado,* 1942 (biography); *El contenido social de la literatura iberoamericana,* 1944; *Alfonso Gutierrez Hermosillo y algunos amigos,* 1945 (biography); *Yahualica,* 1946; *Don Justo Sierra, su vida, sus ideas y su obra,* 1950 (biography).

Even as a child and adolescent, Agustín Yáñez (ah-gews-TEEN yah-NYAYS) had what he later called a "rigorous critical sense" as well as a "sentimental temperament" so intense that it "could not but manifest itself, even exaggeratedly, and ended in coloring his life absolutely." The characteristics of seriousness, austerity, and preoccupation with artistic form shaped all his literary work.

Yáñez associated himself with other young writers of Guadalajara and founded a literary journal, *Bandera de Provincias* (provincial banner), the establishment of which was a national event. He received his law degree in Guadalajara and later moved to Mexico City, where he devoted himself to university teaching and writing and held several important public offices.

According to the aesthetic creed of Yáñez, the ideal of art is form. For him, the idea of literary form follows a movement inward, a theory of composition initiated by means of living the reality and then reliving it in the literary work until one completes it in the appropriate verbal form. "I never write—least of all when writing novels—with the intention of sustaining a premeditated thesis, committed to predetermined conclusions." After intuiting a form, he would develop it until it took on consistency; it was then necessary that he follow it, striving not to falsify characters, situations, and atmosphere.

Yáñez as a writer was very conscious and cognizant of his function. His style is elaborate, reflective, grave, and refined. His knowledge of contemporary philosophy, of the Spanish classics, and of the resources of the modern novel infuses his work. Almost all of Yáñez's works have reminiscence as a common ingredient. On the occasion of the commemoration of the fourth centennial of the founding of Guadalajara, he wrote two books: *Flor de juegos antiguos*, lyrical memories of his childhood and of the games of his province, and *Genio y figuras de Guadalajara*, in which he presents a brief description of this city in 1930 and character studies of its principal citizens throughout its history. In 1943 he published *Archipiélago de mujeres*, a collection of seven stories, each one called by the name of a woman who represents a step on the author's "ladder of adolescence": music, revelation, desire, beauty, folly, death, and love.

In *The Edge of the Storm* (the literal translation of the title is "to the edge of the water"), Yáñez produced his best novel and, according to many critics, one of the finest Mexican novels of the

---

"I tell you, Padre, it can't go on like this; sooner or later the worm will turn, and for better or worse, things will change. To be frank, it would be better if the gringos did come and teach us their way of life than for us to stay the way we are now, living no life at all. Who enjoys it? Tell me."

—from *The Edge of the Storm*
(trans. Ethel Brinton)

mid-twentieth century. In a prose that is dense, unhackneyed, and subtle, he presents the life of a typical pueblo of Jalisco. In the routine and monotony of everyday life, passion and religion are the two stimuli of these provincial small-town people. The dramas of conscience brought about by the conflicts of flesh and spirit are analyzed with subtle introspection.

Two other books complete his trilogy of novels about Jalisco, his native land—*La tierra pródiga* (the lavish land) and *The Lean Lands*. During the time he held the office of governor of Jalisco, he had the opportunity to obtain firsthand knowledge of the inhabitants of its coastal region. From this contact, *La tierra pródiga* was born as a portrait of the struggle between barbarism and civilization that results in humankind's finally overcoming nature. In *The Lean Lands* he re-creates the atmosphere of *The Edge of the Storm*, namely, the secluded, traditional life of small

W H A T   T O   R E A D

The Edge of the Storm

Al filo del agua (literally, "on the edge of the water"), the Spanish title for *The Edge of the Storm* (1947), has two meanings. It signifies the moment that the rain begins, and it also refers to something imminent. The imminent event in Agustín Yáñez's novel, the Mexican Revolution, was brought on by dissatisfaction with the dictatorship of Porfirio Díaz and by social unrest. The Roman Catholic church was deeply affected by the unrest; hence, the novel's emphasis on religion.

Yáñez has painted a series of character studies portraying the effects of a rigid and conventional life on different people, some of whom have had exposure to outside influences. In the eyes of the village, these influences are negative, and include bright clothing, strangers, uncensored writings, and fun. The fictitious but typical town in which the action takes place is set in the state of Jalisco, of which the author was a native.

Don Dionisio, the stern and upright but compassionate parish priest, touches in some way the lives of all the other characters in the book. Two other personalities who present a study in contrasts are María and Marta, Don Dionisio's orphaned nieces. Marta is contented with her work and children, but María is rebellious and joins the revolutionary army. Like all the characters who come in contact with the outside world, María's downfall is doubt, and she falls under the weight of a relentless social system that will tolerate no questioning.

The novel hints at a time near at hand in which many doubters will join together with enough force to rebel against Mexican society and force a crack in the wall of hypocrisy (hence the meaning of the title). The book is not a call to arms; rather, it presents an understanding, scathingly honest, and touching portrait of life in a Mexican town at the beginning of the twentieth century.

— *Linda Prewett Davis*

towns, with arid lands and a people unfazed by the appearance of technology.

Yáñez's studies of Mexican literature are well regarded. Particularly outstanding are those devoted to the chronicles of the Spanish conquest of Mexico and to the native myths of the pre-Hispanic epoch. Yáñez contributed to the modernization of the Mexican novel, and he is considered a forerunner of the Spanish American narratives of the 1960's that achieved world acclaim.

— *Emil Volek*

Learn More

Brushwood, John S. "The Lyric Style of Agustín Yáñez." *Symposium* 26 (1972). Discusses *Al filo del agua*.

Detjens, Wilma Else. *Home as Creation: The Influence of Early Childhood Experience in the Literary Creation of Gabriel García Márquez, Agustín Yáñez, and Juan Rulfo*. New York: Peter Lang, 1993. Detjens analyzes the relationship of childhood to the creative process in *The Edge of the Storm* and novels by other Latin American authors.

Harris, Christopher. *The Novels of Agustín Yáñez: A Critical Portrait of Mexico in the Twentieth Century*. Lewiston, N.Y.: E. Mellen Press, 2000. Argues that the novelist of the Mexican Revolution, who was also a member of the government, was dedicated to economic development, eradication of corruption, and freedom of artistic expression.

Longo, Teresa. "Renewing the Creation of Myth: An Analysis of Rhythm and Image in the 'Acto preparatorio' of Yáñez's *Al filo del agua*." *Confluencia* 4, no. 1 (Fall, 1988). Structure and myth in this novel are reconsidered.

Sommers, Joseph. "Genesis of the Storm: Agustín Yáñez." In *After the Storm: Landmarks of the Modern Mexican Novel*. Albuquerque: University of New Mexico Press, 1968. An excellent point of departure for a study of Yáñez.

Jose Yglesias

Cuban American novelist

Born: Tampa, Florida; November 29, 1919
Died: New York, New York; November 7, 1995

LONG FICTION: *A Wake in Ybor City*, 1963; *An Orderly Life*, 1967; *The Truth About Them*, 1971; *Double Double*, 1974; *The Kill Price*, 1976; *Home Again*, 1985; *Tristan and the Hispanics*, 1989; *Break-in*, 1996; *The Old Gents*, 1996 (novella).
SHORT FICTION: *The Guns in the Closet*, 1996.
DRAMA: *Chattahoochee*, pr. 1989; *The Dictatorship of the Proletariat*, pr. 1989; *You Don't Remember?*, pr. 1989; *New York 1937*, pr. 1990.
NONFICTION: *The Goodbye Land*, 1967; *In the Fist of the Revolution*, 1968; *Down There*, 1970; *The Franco Years*, 1977.
TRANSLATIONS: *Island of Women*, 1962 (pb. in England as *Sands of Torremolinos*); *Villa Milo*, 1962; *The Party's Over*, 1966.

Jose Yglesias (hoh-SAY eeg-LAY-see-ahs) is best known for being a prolific writer whose works are often about individual lives and hardship in Cuba and in Latin American countries affected by revolutions. Of Cuban and Spanish descent, Yglesias was born to Jose and Georgia Milian Yglesias in Tampa, Florida. He worked as a stock clerk and a dishwasher when he moved to New York City at age seventeen. Yglesias then served in the U.S. Navy from 1942 to 1945 during World War II; he received a naval citation of merit. After the war, he attended Black Mountain College in 1946. He married Helen Basine, a novelist, on August 19, 1950. Yglesias held numerous jobs during his lifetime, from assembly line worker to film critic, from assistant to a vice president of a pharmaceutical company to Regents Lecturer at the University of California at Santa Barbara in 1973.

Yglesias's birthplace greatly influenced his literary concern and career. He was born in the section of Tampa called Ybor

City. Until Ybor City, a cigar-making town, was founded by V. Martinez Ybor in 1885, there were not many Latinos in Tampa. As Ybor City and its economy grew, Cubans and other Latinos arrived and brought their own cultural activities and vibrant traditions. These aspects of life in Ybor City served as inspiration and material for Yglesias's plays and books. According to him, these events must be documented so that the history and cultural richness of that part of America will not be forgotten.

Descriptions of Ybor City and its history can be found in the pages of Yglesias's first novel, *A Wake in Ybor City*. The novel is a colorful and interesting depiction of Cuban immigrants in the Latin section of Tampa on the eve of the Cuban Revolution in 1958. The story deals with family dynamics, class envy, sexual intrigues, and cultural assimilation, along with machismo and matriarchal powers in conflict. This novel started his prolific writing career, in which he would move back and forth between fiction and nonfiction.

Being of Cuban and Spanish ancestry also greatly influenced Yglesias's second book, *The Goodbye Land*. The laborious energy required—as well as personal desire—to travel to the mountainside village of Galacia, Spain, in 1964 in order to trace his father's birth and death there proved to be worthwhile; the book

> *It was a stand-off. Tristan knew how to steer past the reefs of his parents' angers. He was not one to boast—quietude had been (until Nanao) his most dearly won companion—but to himself he could say that he had always picked his way between Mom and Dad with such care that no one was bruised. Especially himself. (He did not know if he had inherited this trait or had picked out for himself, as at a shop.)*
>
> —from *Tristan and the Hispanics"*

Arte Público Press

was a great success and was praised by many critics for its authenticity as a travel narrative.

Many of Yglesias's books since *The Goodbye Land* deal with personal statements and individuality amid the revolutionary experience. His nonfiction work *In the Fist of the Revolution* addresses individual lives and hopes amid political and social problems in the town of Miyari, Cuba. *The Franco Years* depicts the living conditions of the author's Spanish acquaintances under the Fascist regime of dictator Francisco Franco, who died in Spain in 1976. (Yglesias was in Spain at the time.) Again, many critics agreed that these two books demonstrate authentic social reporting because the author, while in Cuba and Spain interviewing people, experienced their hardships and turmoil. That authenticity reflects the critical talent and genuine objectivity of Yglesias, who went against the mainstream literary fashion of political and social analysis and moralizing.

Yglesias's talent and honesty in his literary desire to present emotions, aspirations, and disappointments unique to Latino émigrés in the United States led to success and critical acclaim in his novels as well as nonfiction works. His persistent interest in individual lives, the immigrant experience, and cultural assimilation can be seen in novels such as *The Kill Price*, *Home Again*, and *Tristan and the Hispanics*.

Mainly known for writing novels, nonfiction, and translation, Yglesias was also a talented dramatist. He wrote only four plays,

---

W H A T   T O   R E A D

The Truth About Them

Yglesias's *The Truth About Them* (1971) focuses on the family history of a Cuban American clan whose American experience dates from 1890, when the narrator's aristocratic grandmother first arrived in Tampa, Florida. Although much of their life in America is associated with the up-and-down fortunes of Florida's cigar industry, this working-class family displays a pride and cohesiveness that defy all obstacles. During the lean years of the 1930's, some members of the clan are forced to go north to New York City in search of jobs. Before long, however, they find themselves drifting back to Ybor City, owned and controlled by the cigar company. The narrator, much like Roberto of *A Wake in Ybor City*, is truly a Cuban American. Brought up in the very Latin atmosphere of Ybor City, he eventually becomes a left-wing journalist and learns to swim freely in America's traditionless mainstream. Eager to learn more about his Latin roots, however, he visits postrevolutionary Cuba.

Written in an episodic style (several adventures were first published separately in *The New Yorker*), this fictionalized family portrait with its rich and varied characters and its free-flowing style, offers a panoramic vision of a part of America generally unknown to non-Cuban Americans. Its detailed and loving depiction of Cuban culture suggests that America is greater for having accepted such resolute and distinctive communities.

— *Richard Keenan*

three of which—*Chattahoochee, The Dictatorship of the Proletariat,* and *You Don't Remember?*—form a trilogy set in Ybor City in 1912, 1920, and 1989, respectively. The fourth play, *New York 1937,* is an autobiographical comedy involving cigar making and the Great Depression, set in Manhattan's Washington Heights. In his plays, Yglesias's creative drive and imagination brings his characters to life upon the stage.

In addition to his efforts as novelist and dramatist, Yglesias contributed major articles for prestigious literary magazines, newspapers, and other periodicals. He was the patriarch of a literary family, which included his former wife and his son Rafael, also a novelist and screenwriter. Yglesias died of cancer in 1995. His body of work places him as one of the pioneers of modern American and Latino literature.

— *H. N. Nguyen*

Learn More

Baskin, Leonard. "Jose Yglesias." *Tampa Review* 13 (1996). This article examines Yglesias, the literary influence of his work, and his overall literary life.

Hospital, Carolina, and Jorge Cantera, eds. *A Century of Cuban Writers in Florida: Selected Prose and Poetry.* Sarasota, Fla.: Pineapple Press, 1996. Yglesias is one of the thirty-three writers whose work is included in this anthology of Cubans who have lived, or who are living today, in Florida. The introduction by the editors describes the historical importance of the Cuban connection to Florida's heritage.

"Jose Yglesias." In *Contemporary Novelists.* 6th ed. Detroit: St. James Press, 1996. This reference article provides an overview of Yglesias's significant work and highlights a few of his books.

Essays

Latino and Latin American Drama

A brief survey of Latin American drama cannot do justice to the more than five-hundred-year history of such a vast body of work, even if a skeptic might make short shrift of much of the dramatic literature of Latin America. From the Southern Cone to the Latino communities of North America, from the earliest mystery plays used by the Spaniards to convert and assimilate the indigenous peoples to the drawing-room comedies that have plagued serious critics and enthralled huge audiences throughout the past century, from the derivative experimentalism of arcane ensembles to the educational and agitprop methods of hundreds of revolutionary groups—all have made an impressive mark on theatrical performance.

Because of the historical importance of unscripted work (such as pre-Columbian religious rituals, colonial pageants, and "folk" theater) and of unpublished works of which only the gist and impact have been recorded, many recent scholars of Latin American theater study more than just texts that have been preserved as dramatic scripts and take into account a great deal of anthropological and even archaeological evidence to describe this complex and multifaceted history.

Aztec Precedents

Although many civilizations flourished in Central and South America thousands of years before the coming of the Spanish *conquistadores*, the history of pre-Columbian theater is poorly understood. There are many reasons for this gap, including the fact that few records from the ancient Mayan, Olmec, and Aztec civilizations survive, and those that do exist are difficult for modern scholars to interpret. The main records of the Aztec civilization come from Spanish monks who arrived in the New World to convert the Aztecs to Christianity. Naturally, these records are biased in favor of European civilization.

Performance art for the Aztecs was basically religious and demonstrated the central focus of Aztec theology: the great interconnectedness between humanity and the gods. The Aztec calendar had eighteen months, and each month was marked with a major festival paying homage to the gods: Many of these festivals involved spectacular dances of numbers of performers wearing elaborate and beautiful costumes honoring, for instance, the Aztec god of rain and wind, Quetzalcóatl. This is probably the origin of the traditional *quetzal* dance still performed annually in Mexico, in which dancers wear headgear of paper, silk, and feathers measuring up to 5 feet (1.5 meters) in diameter.

A major component of Aztec performance ritual was human sacrifice: For the Aztecs, this sacrifice demonstrated their connection to the divine, and sacrificial victims were thought to enjoy special privileges in the afterlife. One great theatrical ritual of the Aztecs was the ritual honoring the god Xipe Totec in the second month. In this ritual, prisoners reenacted sacred battles with Aztec warriors, similar to the Ta'ziyeh plays still performed in Arab countries. At the end of the battle, the prisoners were shot with arrows or had their hearts removed with flint knives. Their limbs were then eaten in a ceremonial stew at a special meal. In the fifth month ceremony, a young man who had spent a year spiritually impersonating the god Tezcatlipoca started a ritual of singing and dancing, and playing sacred instruments. At the end of the ceremony, he would climb the steps of a temple, breaking the instruments, and was seized by priests who swiftly removed his heart and head. In the eleventh month, the mother-goddess was honored by an old woman who impersonated the goddess by ritually reenacting spiritual events. Finally, she was decapitated and her flayed skin was worn by a male priest to demonstrate the unity of male and female in the divine plan.

Colonial Era

The Spanish conquest of the New World began in the 1490's, when the Aztec capital city of Tenochtitlán (now Mexico City) was one of the largest cities in the world. The Spaniards were impressed with the Aztec accomplishments: Hernán Cortés wrote to his king that the palaces of King Moctezuma (Montezuma) were grander than anything in Spain, and the Spanish soldiers believed the marketplaces of the city to be greater than those of Rome or Constantinople. However, the conquering Spaniards saw the indigenous Americans only as misguided savages despite their ancient and complex culture and their great achievements in architecture, art, weaving, and metalwork. To Spanish monks, the great Aztec gods were merely the devil in disguise, and converting the Aztecs to Christianity and destroying their culture became a primary mission of the conquering Spaniards.

Theater was one of the chief forms of entertainment of these newcomers, who often performed *actos, entreméses,* or even dramas to fill their leisure time. Thus in the explorers' chronicles there are reports that soldiers acted for fun in the late sixteenth century, in northwestern outposts that are now part of the southwestern United States, and in the 1760's, shortly after Spain acquired the Falkland Islands, off the coast of modern-day Argentina, from France, the local garrison put on a three-day festivity that included dramatic performances, with props and materials provided by the military governor.

Theater was from the beginning a proselytizing tool. Some of the earliest attempts by Spanish missionaries to convert the natives involved the Spanish equivalent of the Passion plays and miracle plays of Western Europe. The evangelical zeal of the conquerors went to extraordinary lengths, as evidenced by the willingness of the friars to learn native languages and to present religious doctrine (often through drama) in those languages, and by the cultural syncretism between Catholicism and Indian beliefs that appears even as late as the mid-seventeenth century, in an allegorical play by the famous Mexican writer Sor Juana Inés de la Cruz.

Plays brought as instruments of ideological control and religious persuasion became part of the heritage of the common people. Miracle plays can still be seen in Mexico (and in the former Mexican territories of the southwestern United States); villagewide reenactments of the Passion plays are still common

741

at Easter in many parts of Mexico and Central America; and the quasi-ritualistic *moros y cristianos* plays keep alive the allegorical struggle between Christians and the Moors, in mock battles and in full costume, throughout Latin America and even in the Philippines. Yet these traditional forms of Spanish theater survive primarily at the level of folk theater, and it was only in the late twentieth century that professional theater groups returned to them as sources of material and artistic expression, integrating them into a theater with a much wider audience.

Theater has served as a medium for satire or social protest in Latin America since the sixteenth century, but this was not a radical departure from one of the traditional functions of theater throughout the Middle Ages either. The earliest recorded case of a playwright being punished for writing such material was that of Cristóbal de Llerena, who in 1588 was banished to the Caribbean coast of South America from Santo Domingo for having published an *entremés* that satirized corruption and poor government in the colony.

Throughout the history of the colonies, theater played an important part in community entertainment, mainly at public holidays (such as the king's birthday) or in pageants and festivities welcoming a new viceroy or other dignitaries. There could be private performances of the latest plays from Spain, or of works by native authors, in the courtyards or ballrooms of distinguished residents, while in streets and plazas one often found plays presented by guilds and brotherhoods and performances by Indians or Africans that reflected the variety of ethnic influences already present in the colonies. Within the first half-century of Spanish rule, religious plays were being performed in colleges, and occasionally the students and scholars would introduce a secular play that might merit censorship because of its content.

The development of theatrical activity in the different colonies depended on the degree of encouragement or repression offered by the representatives of the crown and by the Church hierarchy. In some cases, an enlightened viceroy or captain-general would strike a deal with the bishop, by which the Church would lift its ban on theatrical performances, and box-office returns would go to a needy institution such as an orphanage, a women's hostel, or a hospital.

Theater was usually presented in improvised public spaces or in a *corral* owned by an entrepreneur, but by the end of the eighteenth century, most principal cities of the Spanish colonies had theater houses to cater to the mestizo elite and a rising bourgeoisie. Entertainment was not necessarily the priority only of liberal governments: One of the most impressive theaters was built in Havana by Captain-General Miguel de Tacón, who headed a repressive government during the Cuban War of Independence; the Paraguayan dictator José Gaspar Rodríguez Francia, who virtually sealed his country from the outside world, was a devotee of culture and built a beautiful theater.

The Era of Independence
Drama and theatrical activity played a minor albeit interesting role in the transition to independence and in nation building. The end of the eighteenth century brought the success of the *sainete* (a genre made popular in Spain by Ramón de la Cruz), the characters of which were drawn from everyday contemporary society and were often social types; these characters reflected the particular social makeup of a given colony, and in the unique ethnic origins, opinions, and speech patterns presented onstage, the colonized could begin to see their own distinctive national identity.

The patriotic theme was the subject of a few plays throughout Latin America, beginning in Chile, Peru, and Argentina between 1812 and 1820, then in Mexico around 1820, and eventually in Cuba and Puerto Rico beginning around mid-nineteenth century. *Abdala* (pb. 1869), by the Cuban patriot José Julián Martí, is an allegory of independence with an African hero, an early attack on colonialism, specifically Spanish domination of Cuba.

In Argentina, on the eve of independence, one could find some rural comedies and satires of Spanish theater. In Cuba, after the remainder of Latin America was free and long before Cuba's wars of independence (1868-1900), comedy developed through the fifty-year career of a brilliant actor and impresario,

Francisco Covarrubias, the author of several dozen comedies that laid the foundation of Cuban theater. (The texts were lost; only records of the performances remain.) *Costumbrismo* (comedy and drama that depict social types and customs) dominated the scene in most countries, and elements of it resurfaced even in the naturalist theater of the early twentieth century.

Romanticism flourished in the nineteenth century with several distinguished playwrights, such as Francisco Javier of the Dominican Republic, Alejandro Tapia y Rivera of Puerto Rico, Joaquín Lorenzo Luaces and Gertrudis Gómez de Avellaneda of Cuba, and Carlos Bello of Chile. A theater of ideas or social and political protest appeared occasionally: Juan Bautista Alberdi wrote his dramatic satire while in exile from Argentine dictator Juan Manuel de Rosas between 1838 and 1879, and Alberto Bianchi was jailed in Mexico in 1876 for criticizing the draft in *Los martirios del pueblo* (pr. 1876; the people's martyrdom).

The *teatro bufo* of Cuba, with its stock characters, spanned a quarter century and had its counterparts in Puerto Rico and the Dominican Republic. It, too, was an important spawning ground for impresarios, actors, musicians, and playwrights. It is interesting to note that although many of the plays elicited sympathetic responses from patriotic (anti-Spanish) audiences, many of the playwrights were opposed to independence, and that the early *teatro bufo*, with its comic sketches of unique freshness, gave way after independence (1900-1920) to burlesque and vaudeville similar to those of the United States.

Twentieth Century Drama
As the independent republics became relatively stable democracies with increasing industrialization and European immigration, the theater continued to develop along two main lines: "serious" drama that addressed grave questions and moral issues or the human condition, in a fairly traditional, formal structure; and popular theater that broached topical issues or questions of morality, lightly at best, in a satiric vein.

The first sophisticated social drama emerged in the early twentieth century, with the theme of national identity still prominent, either in response to a changing historical and political reality or as a new perspective on the same old problems of race and class. Historically, playwrights, like other Latin American artists and intellectuals, have been committed to their role as critics and are often involved, through their main profession (as teachers, journalists, and diplomats), in the affairs of their country. Many have used drama as a medium for expressing their commitment; a few good writers have made the stage a powerful forum for debates by characters that are often allegorical or stereotypical yet manage to move an audience and to challenge prejudice, outmoded behavior, and destructive systems.

José Antonio Ramos, a leading Cuban intellectual and a diplomat, analyzed his country's most basic conflicts, embodied in different family members whose future is tied to their large estate, in his play *Tembladera* (pr. 1917). The play explores intergenerational conflict and the roots of Cuba's economic crisis; American penetration of Cuba, especially after the Spanish-American War, and the remnants of loyalty to Spanish tradition; and the contradictions inherent both in cultural tradition and in progress.

Between 1903 and 1906, Florencio Sánchez in a similar naturalist vein attacked the prevailing assumptions about national identity and immigration in Argentina and Uruguay. His *Barranca abajo* (pr. 1905; *Retrogression*, also known as *Down the Ravine*, 1961) exposes the real condition of an old peasant: Changes in economic relations and control of the land strip him of his property and his dignity, leading him to suicide. *La gringa* (pr. 1904; *The Foreign Girl*, 1942) is about the daughter of Italian immigrants: Her marriage to a local youth promises a solution to the conflict between the value systems of the "old," rural Argentina (or Uruguay) and the different austerity imposed by the newcomers.

Antonio Acevedo Hernández, who was influenced by Florencio Sánchez and Russian author Maxim Gorky and by the ideas of Pyotr Kropotkin, detailed in a fairly brutal manner the degradation of the rural poor in Chile. He won the national theater prize four times in forty years with such plays as *Almas perdidas* (pr. 1917; lost souls, a play about the slums of Santiago), *La canción rota* (pr. 1921; the pauper song, about the indentured farm laborer), and *El arbol viejo* (pr. 1928; the old tree, about young people leaving their roots and their father to go to the city).

In Mexico, some of the strongest naturalist drama of the years before the revolution of 1910 was written by Federico Gamboa, who is better known as a novelist. *La venganza de la gleba* (pb. 1907; the revenge of the soil) is considered to be the first weighty criticism of the system that was crushing the Mexican peasant.

Historical drama finds its best voice, perhaps, in Rodolfo Usigli, who in a famous "antihistorical" trilogy challenges three historical myths of Mexico: the apparition of the Virgin of Guadalupe in *Corona de luz: La virgen* (pr. 1963; *Crown of Light*, 1971); the role of Doña Marina in Hernán Cortés's conquest of Mexico and the martyrdom of chief Cuauhtémoc in *Corona de fuego* (pr. 1960; crown of fire); and the madness of Carlota, after the execution, by a Mexican firing squad, of her husband, Emperor Maximilian, in *Corona de sombra* (pr. 1947; *Crown of Shadows*, 1946). In each of the dramas, the historical characters are at once fictionalized and humanized, thus becoming keys for a new, critical understanding of three crucial periods in the formation of the modern Mexican nation: the conquest and domination of the indigenous peoples; the merging of cultures; and the emergence of the liberal republic under Benito Juárez (the historical antecedent of the revolution of 1910).

An equally celebrated play of Usigli is *El gesticulador* (pr. 1947; the impostor), one of the earliest critiques of the political system that was established after the revolution. The play's protagonist, a history professor, enters politics by assuming the identity of César Rubio, a revolutionary hero who disappeared during the war, but the protagonist finds that he has entered a labyrinth of lies. The protagonist is murdered by the rival candidate, a corrupt politician who was responsible for the death of the original César Rubio, and the protagonist's death (blamed on a fanatic enemy of the revolutionary party) becomes the killer's ticket to victory. The analogy to Julius Caesar is obvious, as Usigli takes a historical referent that to this day epitomizes the ambiguity of power and of human motivation, adapting it to illustrate also the ambiguities of contemporary events. Usigli's younger contemporary Wilberto Cantón looks critically at a turning point in the revolution in *Nosotros somos dios* (pr. 1965; we are God).

Contemporary Drama

The final four decades of the twentieth century saw terrible upheavals in Latin America: poverty, disease, hunger, natural disasters, guerrilla fighting, oppression, torture, kidnappings, hijackings, strikes, riots, wars, and the appearance of death squads, drug cartels, and massacres of indigenous peoples, all of which incited a more widespread feeling of discontent with government across the continent. Social protest and dissent met with repression, including assassinations and disappearances. Playwrights and other theater artists have come to figure prominently as agents of social and political protest, combining aesthetics with what Paulo Friere called *conscientizaçao,* or "conscienticization." Building on the political theater writings of Bertolt Brecht, certain playwrights led a movement collectively known as the Theater of Revolt. So effective was this movement in challenging oppression that theater became the art form of those most frequently harassed by military governments. Playwrights were censored, arrested, and tortured; theaters were closed or even burned down by government forces. Around 1973, the year of the military coup in Chile and widespread continental unrest, theater in Latin America suffered a near-paralysis, which in some places persisted for years. Yet certain playwrights' works have managed to persist in these horrifying periods.

Socially conscious theater has flourished in Chile since the 1970's in the work of several outstanding playwrights. Among the forerunners in this century are María Asunción Requena and Isidora Aguirre, who have written about women's struggles, relations between whites and Indians, and class conflict; and the poet Pablo Neruda, with his *Fulgor y muerte de Joaquín Murieta* (pr. 1967; *Splendor and Death of Joaquin Murieta,* 1972), a re-creation of the tragic life of Chilean prospectors in the California gold rush. Since the 1950's, audiences have seen Egon Raúl Wolff's carefully choreographed invasions of the bourgeoisie's comfortable space by threatening creatures from the wrong side of town in *Los invasores* (pr. 1964; the invaders) and in *Flores de papel* (pr. 1970; *Paper Flowers*, 1971); Jorge Díaz Gutiérrez's neo-existentialist critiques of modern alienation, such as *Réquiem para una girasol* (pr. 1961; requiem for a sunflower), followed by a powerful piece on the miners of Chile, *El nudo ciego* (pr. 1965; the blind knot), and by the ferocious satire *Topografía de un desnudo* (pr. 1967; the topography of a nude), about the 1963 massacre of Brazilian peasants; and Alejandro Sievking's critical view of political oppression in Chile in *Pequeños animales abatidos* (pr. 1975; small downcast animals).

Social and political themes have been presented by equally sophisticated writers in other countries, especially in Argentina, which has produced some of the continent's leading playwrights. Three excellent examples are Osvaldo Dragún, Andrés Lizárraga, and Griselda Gambaro, whose works are proof of the possibility of achieving universal appeal along with very specific messages about history, social relations, and economic questions.

Dragún, active since the mid-1950's in popular theater, has dealt with some of his country's (and Latin America's) most difficult themes: class relations and the malaise of youth in *Y nos dijeron que éramos inmortales* (pb. 1962; and they told us we were immortal); the tendency to rely on formulaic ideas to solve problems that require an original, native solution in *Heroica de Buenos Aires* (pr. 1966); and the power of economic pressures that can turn one into a watchdog for hire, let one die of an abscessed tooth, or kill hundreds of Africans with tainted meat for the sake of a multinational corporation's profits in *Historias para ser contadas* (pr. 1957; *Stories for the Theatre*, 1976). Dragún has also handled a historical figure that has become a favorite of the Latin American stage, the Inca Tupac Amaru, who led a major rebellion against the Spaniards in the eighteenth century; in *Tupac Amaru* (pr. 1957), the tormentor is ultimately driven mad by the spiritual resistance of the physically broken and defeated hero.

Lizárraga has criticized the narrowness of provincial life, the hypocrisy of Argentina's social system, and the sentimentalization of history as a tool of social control. Some of his best work is contained in his trilogy about the wars of independence; one play in this trilogy, *Santa Juana de América* (pr. 1960), is an award-winning portrait of a female revolutionary figure, presented in a Brechtian style.

Griselda Gambaro's work is sometimes labeled Theater of Cruelty or Theater of the Absurd, because of its formal and structural similarity to European and North American works of those genres. Yet it is profoundly rooted in Argentine reality, and despite its possibilities as an art that dissects the most perverse aspects of human relationships, it points to the larger picture: that of a society whose collective psyche was already torn, by the mid-1960's, between "Cains," who took pleasure in asserting their power and their cruelty, and "Abels," who suffered passively, and sometimes foolishly, through deceit and betrayal. A good example is her *Los siameses* (pr. 1967; *The Siamese Twins*, 1967).

In *El campo* (pr. 1968; *The Camp*, 1970), Gambaro creates a brilliant piece of ambiguity (despite its almost mechanical workings): The title translates as "the countryside" (where the main protagonist, who controls the events, insists that the action is taking place) or as "the camp," that is, a military camp or a concentration camp, an interpretation suggested by most of the signs (the physical appearance of the main character in his uniform, the brutal behavior by guards toward the "guests," and the cries of pain). The irony of the play is that while its main referent is the Nazi experience of the 1930's and 1940's (with its possible relevance to Argentina, where so many Nazis fled after the war), its ideological structure is not entirely alien to Argentina: The climate of the "liberal democracy" shifted radically in the 1960's, and the polarization resulted in the excesses of the 1970's, when such concentration camps became a reality, and when the entire society began to function in ambiguous codes—the authorities denying their actions (much like the play's protagonist), and the victims (society at large) accepting the authorities' definition of reality.

In 1977 Gambaro's novel *Ganarse la muerte* (to earn one's death) was banned and Gambaro left Argentina to live in Spain and France, returning in 1980 and continuing her work as a playwright. Gambaro received a great deal of global attention with her 1973 play *Información para extranjeros* (wr. 1971; *Information for Foreigners*, 1992), which for many critics captures the spirit of "postmodernism" perfectly. The play, which is about incidents of state violence in Argentina, actually forces its audience to engage with the staged theater in a very powerful way. The play is staged in a house, with the audience broken up into small groups, each with a "guide." The guide moves the groups through the house, opening doors and witnessing scenes within rooms. As the groups progress, the boundaries between "performance" and "reality" blur until the audience is forced to question its role in both, and come to grips with its own culpability for allowing state violence to continue.

Among this generation of good writers, one should also include Eduardo Pavlovsky, a psychiatrist by profession, whose characters' psychological makeup (often one of twisted and perverse cruelty) is usually explored in a sociopolitical context, such as the Caribbean dictatorships of François Duvalier (Papa Doc) and Rafael Trujillo, as an allegory relevant to any country.

Strong social protest and revisions of history and myth are central to the works of the Colombian Enrique Buenaventura, whose plays can be a vicious indictment of class oppression, and whose *Los papeles del infierno* (pr. 1968; the papers of Hell) documents the terrible period of modern Colombian history known as "La Violencia" through a series of short plays about ordinary human beings caught in the whirlwind of political violence and repression.

In Venezuela, José Ignacio Cabrujas and Román Chalbaud have been leading contemporary authors who also see the stage as a vehicle for questioning history and politics. Cabrujas's work is more clearly one of protest, not merely against the corruption inherent in institutions, but also against the mechanisms that corrupt pure individuals who attain power. Although Cabrujas writes in the style of Brecht, Chalbaud has played with the soap opera, with games and rituals, and with eroticism and thus resists any easy label as a "protest" writer.

Sebastián Salazar Bondy of Peru wrote a series of social dramas, moving on in the early 1960's, immediately before his death, to a unique dramatic style all his own, filled with irony and with elements of farce and popular comedy. Manuel Galich of Guatemala, an exiled member of the Arbenz government deposed in the 1953 coup, persisted in a straight theater of denunciation, tempered only by sardonic humor; Galich's works are among the few to deal so specifically with United States involvement in Latin America.

Cuban theater has always been among the most active and progressive in the Americas, with many distinguished writers and directors. Individual playwrights such as Virgilio Piñera, José Triana, Manuel Reguera Saumell, and Carlos Felipe are typical of the best, and they all treat social themes through fairly solid texts and (with the exception of Triana) largely conventional techniques.

These four authors span the period immediately before and after the triumph of the revolution in 1959. Their main concerns are social; their main focus, the individual's interaction with his or her environment (family, a slum, the effects of the revolution, institutional corruption under Fulgencio Batista), and one even finds, in Felipe's *Réquiem por Yarini* (pr. 1960), a powerful portrait of a famous pimp.

Triana's works reflect society in a critical light. His chief works were created on the eve of the 1959 revolution and present darkly satiric visions of "sacred" institutions such as the Church and the family, using mythical allusion and ritual devices that sometimes make his work very reminiscent of that of French playwright Jean Genet. In fact, his award-winning *La noche de los asesinos* (pr. 1966; *The Criminals*, 1967), in which three young people enact their parents' murder, bears a strong resemblance to Genet's *Les Bonnes* (pr. 1947; *The Maids*, 1954).

Puerto Rican drama has found its finest expression in the works of a number of authors since the 1950's. Francisco Arriví tackled such difficult subjects as racism, the role of the intellectual (at a time when intellectuals were highly vulnerable because of their pro-independence views), and the complexes that beset the Puerto Rican psyche. Arriví's best-known work perhaps is his trilogy that includes *Vejigantes* (pr. 1957; mummers). René Marqués pursued political themes more aggressively, always obsessed with the nature of Puerto Rican identity as a culture and as a nation. His *La carreta* (pr. 1952; *The Oxcart*, 1969) has become a classic portrayal of the migration of Puerto Ricans, from the country to San Juan to New York and a life of continued economic hardship compounded by social problems such as drugs and prostitution.

Modern Genres and Themes

The great majority of theatergoers in Latin America continue to flock to lighter fare, to comedy, and to musicals. The tradition of the *género chico* is uninterrupted: The comedy of social customs, the farce, and the musical comedy or review have always been the mainstay. In the traveling *carpas* (tents) of Mexico and the southwestern United States and in the *sainete criollo* (Argentine version of the Spanish *sainete*, with tangos and social types from Buenos Aires), in the prolific production of the Alhambra Theatre of Havana (where some of Cuba's best playwrights and musicians exercised their profession), and of other locales around the continent where vaudeville coexisted with good, solid comic drama, and in far more reputable playhouses, such as the San Martín municipal theater of Buenos Aires, literally thousands of scripted plays have entertained millions. Many of the best playwrights still work in that style, while a great many also combine elements of this popular tradition with European conventions à la Georges Feydeau or Noël Coward (adapted to Latin American culture). Even in revolutionary Cuba, the *comedia musical* has thrived through the pen of such good playwrights as Héctor Quintero and José Brene.

Among authors who have worked on psychological drama or fantasy, certain popular names stand out: Conrado Nalé Roxlo and Carlos Gorostiza of Argentina; Celestino Gorostiza, Xavier Villaurrutia, Salvador Novo, Carlos Solórzano, Elena Garro, Maruxa Vilalta, Luisa Josefina Hernández, and Rafael Solana of Mexico; Isaac Chocrón of Venezuela; and Elena Portocarrero and Julio Ortega of Peru. Many, influenced by Eugene

O'Neill and Tennessee Williams, have sought to create characters of great psychological complexity, while others have created outright fantasies in which the characters play in dream-worlds.

Collective Creations and Political Performance

The 1960's brought with its revolutionary politics a corresponding movement in the theater. Much as the workers' theater of the 1930's and 1940's and the popular theater (the products of the Mexican revolution in the 1910's and Fray Mocho in Argentina in the 1950's) had gone out in search of their audience, many of the young actors, directors, and writers in the 1960's chose to place their craft at the service of the revolution.

Following the example of Fray Mocho and Augusto Boal in Brazil, and Enrique Buenaventura and Santiago García in Colombia, dozens of theater groups established themselves in strategic relationship to the communities that they wished to serve and to "conscientize" (educate toward liberation). The internal process of each group was revolutionized, with collective sharing of responsibilities and with collective creation becoming the most significant single change in playwriting in centuries.

Buenaventura, for example, gave up individual playwriting to become an equal member of the collective that he had founded in Cali. A number of groups (such as El Aleph of Chile, Libre Teatro Libre of Argentina, and Grupo Escambray of Cuba) produced quality plays through this method. In a few cases, groups of playwrights collaborated on a single play, the most famous example perhaps being *El avión negro* (pr. 1970), a satire about Juan Perón's return to Argentina, coauthored by Roberto Cossa, Carlos Somigliana, Ricardo Talesnik, and Germán Rozenmacher, all distinguished Argentine playwrights. Collective creation caught on particularly in the community-based theater groups, whose interest was mostly in theater as an instrument of education and social change; Latino theater groups in the United States (particularly in the Chicano groups through their association TENAZ) have been active promoters of the process to this day. Its limitations have been amply demonstrated, however, in the quality of the texts produced, and it has become clear that a good, strong playwright is necessary to produce the end product of a collective process.

Another of the "Three B's" of Latin American Theater (along with Brecht and Buenaventura) is Augusto Boal. Boal has explored the relationship between politics and performance possibly more intimately than any other contemporary theorist. In 1971, Boal was arrested, tortured, and exiled: Even during his imprisonment he continued writing, and his play *Torquemada* (pb. 1972) is an autobiographical account of those events, in which he compares his torturers to those who participated in the Spanish Inquisition. Boal's book *Teatro del oprimado y otras poéticas políticas* (1974; *The Theatre of the Oppressed*, 1979) is now included as standard reading for most advanced theater theorists. Boal as a director engaged in a variety of experiments to create the revolutionary theater he envisioned: These experiments blurred fantasy and reality, creating unexpected theater in unusual places, such as restaurants, to demonstrate the freedom of the individual.

Community-based groups continued to flourish in the 1980's despite political and economic difficulties. The movement has flourished in Cuba and Nicaragua in particular, where it receives considerable official support, with hundreds of amateur and semiprofessional groups from which talented individuals are routinely singled out for professional training.

Latino Theater in North America

Latino theater in the United States grew impressively during the last decades of the twentieth century, a result primarily of two factors: the immigration of large numbers of Cubans and Puerto Ricans to the New York area and the growth of community movements among the Chicano population. Many Cuban and Puerto Rican artists, actors, and writers moved to New York in the mid-1960's and assumed an active role in the cultural life of the city, founding theater groups and workshops and boosting the activity of such pioneering groups as the Puerto Rican Travelling Theatre. It became possible to attend different Spanish-language theater performances every night of the week in New York, ranging from Spanish classics to Latin American repertory to original works by local authors.

The Chicano movement in California in the 1960's grew out of the civil rights and the farmworkers' movements. El Teatro Campesino sprang directly from agitprop work with César Chávez's organization and from experience with the San Francisco Mime Troupe. Teatro de la Esperanza and, later, other community-based groups developed along similar lines. Teatro Nacional de Aztlán continues to exist, with more than one hundred member groups from all over the United States, with links to Mexican theater; in these links it has restored a relationship that had existed well into the twentieth century between the theaters of the United States and Mexico, through the Mexican companies that toured the American Southwest and California.

The Chicano and other community theaters tend to use original material or adaptations of repertory and classics, and some individual authors, such as Luis Miguel Valdez, have moved into the mainstream with works that deal with the Mexican American experience and culture. The work of Valdez with El Teatro Campesino, stunningly visual and powerful, reaches back to the performance rituals of pre-Columbian Aztec cultures, thus ideologically and politically separating itself from the European conquerors. In addition, his work clearly associates the Anglo-dominated U.S. government with the Spanish imperialists. The community theaters have established good working relationships with Chicano studies programs at various universities, through which Chicano theater has become legitimatized as a subject of research and scholarship.

Among the most popular of modern Mexican American theater artists since the 1990's is Guillermo Gómez-Peña, a poet and playwright as well as actor, and regular commentator on National Public Radio (NPR). His work, along with that of Coco Fusco, emphasizes the multiple ethnicities of American culture and attempts to dissolve borders between identities. His performances use modern imagery of supersophisticated technology combined with ancient Aztec iconography, creating bizarre hybrid characters like El Mexterminator, Cyber-Vato, and El Naftazteca.

Theater festivals continue to bring groups, directors, writers, and critics together. Now these festivals are held not only in Manizales, Colombia, in Havana, in Mexico, or in Caracas, but also in New York, in Montreal, and in other North American cities. Latin American theater has overcome the balkanization that plagued it for centuries, as it plagued all former Spanish colonies: Since the 1960's, writers and directors, companies, and scholars of different countries have met and shared their work and their experience. The historical tie between the Latino culture of the United States and the cultures of Latin America is being restored, thanks in part to the theater.

—Judith A. Weiss, updated by Michael M. Chemers

Learn More

Albuquerque, Severino J. *Violent Acts: A Study of Contemporary Latin American Theatre.* Detroit, Mich.: Wayne State University Press, 1991. Provides an extremely useful, if disturbing, model for uniting twentieth century Latin American "Theater of Revolt" across many countries and cultures by pointing out the recurring themes of riot, murder, assassination, and state-sponsored torture.

Allen, Richard F. *Teatro hispanoamericano: Una bibliografía anotada (Spanish American Theatre: An Annotated Bibliography).* Boston: G. K. Hall, 1987. Allen's guide is a good place to start when searching for materials on this subject. It is superior to some earlier versions because of the content and usefulness of its notations, which give the reader some idea of where a particular listing will lead.

Dauster, Frank N. *Historia del teatro hispanoamericano: Siglos XIX y XX.* Mexico City, Mexico: Ediciones de Andrea, 1966. An early work by one of the established writers of the field, this work is generally held to be a comprehensive history of the era, although now dated. An important text for pre-1960's drama but not to be considered alone, especially if researching pre-Columbian performance roots. In Spanish.

_____, ed. *Perspectives on Contemporary Spanish American Theatre.* Lewisburg, Pa.: Bucknell University Press, 1996. Dauster is one of the most respected writers in the field and here he has assembled some excellent essays to help provide several good models for analyzing recent Latino drama.

Gardner, Joseph L., ed. *Mysteries of the Ancient Americas.* Pleasantville, N.Y.: Reader's Digest Association, 1986. Assembled by the editors at *Reader's Digest,* this is a good first book for those who are just beginning to study pre-Columbian America. Full of lush photographs and artwork, this book has great information about the performance rituals of the Aztecs and other indigenous peoples, and explores how those traditions merged with medieval and modern ones under Spanish influence.

Gómez-Peña, Guillermo. *The New World Border: Prophecies, Poems, and Loqueras for the End of the Century.* San Francisco, Calif.: City Lights Books, 1996. Winner of the American Book Award, a collection of satirical dramatic texts as well as essays and poems by the border-busting artist. At turns funny and thought-provoking, Gómez-Peña is one of the most prominent inheritors and innovators of the Latino "Theater of Revolt" tradition, linking modern hip-hop Anglo-American culture and ancient Aztec religion in a fascinating mix.

Huerta, Jorge A. *Chicano Drama: Performance, Society, and Myth.* Cambridge, England: Cambridge University Press, 2001. Using informative biographies of playwrights and analyses of their plays, discusses the way in which Chicano and Chicana dramatists negotiate cultural differences.

Weiss, Judith A., and Leslie Damasceno. *Latin American Popular Theatre: The First Five Centuries.* Albuquerque: University of New Mexico Press, 1993. Focuses on such specific topics as the urban theater; popular forms, characters, and ideology; theater in the 1960's; and new trends in drama from the region.

Woodyard, George W., and Leon F. Lyday, eds. *Dramatists in Revolt.* Austin: University of Texas Press, 1976. Although this is an older book, it has taken its place as one of the fundamental texts for understanding antigovernment theatrical traditions in Latin America.

Latino Long Fiction

L atino fiction presents the experience and multiplicity of perspectives unique to Latinos—residents of the United States whose cultural, ethnic, and linguistic ties to Latin America connect them as members of a distinct yet multiethnic community. The principal Latino ethnic or cultural groups include Chicanos, or Mexican Americans; Puerto Rican Americans; Cuban Americans; and residents or citizens of the United States who trace their origins to other countries in Central or South America. Each of these constituent groups is distinct in its own right, with its own history, folklore, and traditions. However, they all share commonalities of language, culture, religion, experience, and values; these attributes distinguish Latino culture both from the dominant Anglo culture of the United States and from those of other immigrant populations. Much Latino long fiction is characterized by a sense of ethnicity and by the portrayal of ethnic experience.

Mexican American/Chicano Long Fiction

In 1848 the Treaty of Guadalupe Hidalgo ceded all Mexican territories north of the Rio Grande to the United States. One year later, all former citizens of Mexico who still resided in the area automatically became U.S. citizens. These people were a diverse group engendered principally from a mixture of European, Aztec, and Native North Americans; from each ethnocultural wellspring the group derived myths, values, religious and cultural traditions, laws, and literary models. In the ensuing years the overlay of Anglo influence enriched the mixture. The resulting culture came to call itself Chicano, a term used to designate the distinct history, culture, and literature of the American Southwest.

Chicano long fiction, like Chicano language and culture generally, derives from three distinct sociohistorical sources: Mexican Indian, predominant prior to 1519; Spanish Mexican, predominant from 1519 to 1848; and Anglo, emergent after the signing of the Treaty of Guadalupe Hidalgo in 1848. These sources provide a richness of myth, legend, history, and literary models and techniques, both oral and written, from which Chicano writers have drawn inspiration and material, the reactions to which have constituted the conflicts and tensions that drive all forms of Chicano literary expression.

Chicano long fiction is multilingual, employing Spanish, English, and Pocho, a hybrid blend of linguistic elements. Used together, these language options allow the Chicano novelist to express the full range of his or her experience, encompassing the dominant Anglo culture, the culture of origin, and the culture of the home and the *barrio*. Chicano novelists are conscious of their linguistic and ethnic heritage and depict a people proud of their history and culture, aware of their uniqueness, and committed to preserving their familial, social, and literary traditions. Their novels portray men and women who accept themselves as they are and resist pressures to become more closely aligned with the mainstream Anglo culture that threatens to Americanize them. Proximity to Mexico and movement both north and south across the border continually reinforce the Hispanic and mestizo ways, creating a cultural dynamic, unique to Chicano literature, which continues to influence the Chicano novel's vital, energetic, and creative momentum.

The first significant Chicano novelist was José Antonio Villarreal. His *Pocho* (1959) was the first Latino novel issued by a major publishing firm, and it is frequently regarded as the first work of real literary or historical value to reflect the Chicano experience. The protagonist is a boy who seeks self-discovery, but as a Chicano he also must decide which of the ideals, traditions, and attitudes of his parents to reject in favor of Anglo ones he likes. Though sometimes criticized for not placing appropriate emphasis on racial and cultural issues, *Pocho* remains an important work in Latino fiction. Richard Vásquez's *Chicano* (1970), like *Pocho*, has been criticized for its failure to depict the Chicano experience realistically, but in its portrayal of Chicano themes, the novel constitutes a seminal work. Raymond Barrio's *The Plum Plum Pickers* (1969) exposes the harshness of social and economic life for migrant Mexican and Chicano farmworkers in Southern California. Its literary excellence, the richness of its narrative technique, and its realistic depiction of the difficulties faced by Chicano laborers have earned it an important place in the evolution of Chicano fiction.

The novelists who represent the emergence into maturity and international acknowledgment of the Chicano novel include Rudolfo Anaya, Rolando Hinojosa, Ron Arias, and Sandra Cisneros. The critical acclaim accorded these novelists has established them as major twentieth century artists and has drawn attention to the genre of Latino fiction.

Rudolfo Anaya's *Bless Me, Ultima* (1972) uses dream sequences, Magical Realism, and mythological echoes to approach the fantastic. The novel's protagonist, through the agency of a folk healer named Ultima, achieves a level of spiritual and perceptual experience that awakens his awareness of the mythological figures of his Chicano heritage, teaching him respect for folk wisdom and custom and leading him to an alternate reality which, by extension, becomes available to the reader as well. The novel, widely read and critically acclaimed, established Anaya as a major force in American letters.

Rolando Hinojosa was the first Chicano writer to win an important international literary award. He was also the first U.S. citizen to be honored by the Casa de las Américas panel. His novel *Klail City y sus alrededores* (1976; *Klail City: A Novel*, 1987) was the second book in a trilogy that re-creates the reality, beliefs, and vision shared by generations of members of the Spanish-speaking community in south Texas, where Hinojosa was born. The other two volumes of the trilogy are *Estampas del valle, y otras obras / Sketches of the Valley and Other Works* (1973; English revision, *The Valley*, 1983) and *Claros varones de Belken* (1986; *Fair Gentlemen of Belken County*). Hinojosa creates a collage of points of view, personalities, landscape snapshots, spots of time, and events both trivial and sublime that establish a palpable, vital fictional world through which a powerful sense of identity and continuity surges. Hinojosa suggested that he wrote the trilogy to help himself keep alive a past that grew in importance as it became more remote; in doing so, he has also made the Latino experience immediate and accessible to a broad spectrum of readers.

Ron Arias's *The Road to Tamazunchale* (1975) reveals the influence of contemporary international literary currents. The emphasis on the subjective, internal reality of his protagonist, rather than on the exterior world of objects, is consistent with the emphases of many other modern novelists. The effect of this emphasis on alternative reality is to diminish the narrative distance between writer and reader by smearing the distinctions within the novel between illusion and reality. Arias's mastery of contemporary literary technique and his emphasis in the novel on the *barrio* experience, the problems of illegal Mexican immigrants in the United States, and the rejection of victimhood in favor of empowerment make *The Road to Tamazunchale* unique in the body of Latino fiction, perhaps setting a new standard for the Chicano novel.

Sandra Cisneros is one of an emerging group of Chicano writers who have graduated from a creative writing program; her novel *The House on Mango Street* (1984) was completed during her tenure as a National Foundation of the Arts Fellow, and it received the Before Columbus American Book Award in 1985. Employing fragmentation and montage, she depicts not only the Chicano experience from the unusual perspective of growing up in the Midwest among predominantly Puerto Rican Americans but also the emergence of her self-awareness as a writer and creator. Like Hinojosa, Cisneros admits a need to recapture the past in order to fulfill the needs of the present.

Puerto Rican Long Fiction
The population of Puerto Rico is a blend of the cultures and races of Europe, Africa, and the Americas. From 1493 until 1898, Puerto Rico was a Spanish colony. Puerto Rican fiction assumed a mestizo identity, in opposition to Spanish pressures to assimilate; this emphasis evolved to reflect a more Latin American character in the twentieth century, when Puerto Rico became a U.S. territory. After World War II, almost a third of the island's population immigrated to the United States, dispersed to points as far apart as Hawaii and New York. This distribution complicated the process whereby Puerto Ricans sought to define and protect their cultural and literary identity. Furthermore, by physically separating family and community members,

the immigration reduced the efficacy of the oral tradition as a means of propagating values and traditions, making long fiction the culture's principal mechanism for articulating its vision of its own reality.

The language of the Puerto Rican American novel reflects the diversity of Puerto Rican ethnic and linguistic origins, a product of the melding of European (Spanish, French), African, and Native American cultures overlaid with an American patina. Puerto Rican American fiction has retained diverse elements of myth, culture, and value structures. Most Puerto Rican American fiction is bilingual, and it employs grammatical elements and vocabulary of the Caribbean patois and the Native American elements of its linguistic heritage.

The development of Puerto Rican literature has been constituted in part by a series of reactions. The reaction of nineteenth century Puerto Rican artists to Spanish dominance was to create a sense of identity that emphasized the values and linguistic elements of the indigenous, African, and mestizo aspects of its cultural heritage. From 1898 to about 1940, Americanizing pressures prompted Puerto Rican writers to emphasize the Spanish language itself and to use Latin American models in their efforts to define and protect their identity as a separate culture. Finally, since the end of World War II and in reaction to the new assimilating forces following the surge in emigration of the 1940's and 1950's, the efforts to preserve their cultural autonomy have increasingly led Puerto Ricans away from idealized depictions of the island and toward settings in New York, Chicago, and other enclaves of Puerto Rican American cultural influence.

The long fiction of the late twentieth century, written by the children of first-generation working-class immigrants, criticizes the complacency of an Americanized middle class as well as the oppressive dominance of Anglo culture. Typical of this class is Pedro Juan Soto's novel *Spiks* (1956), which emphasizes the anguish of the impoverished immigrants and looks wistfully back to an idyllic past. Another novelist who focused on the oppression and alienation of the Puerto Rican American in New York was José Luis González, with *En Nueva York y otras desgracias*

(1973; in New York and other disgraces). Critics have come to regard these novels as reactionary, creating a distorted, idealized view of the reality that existed before American involvement in Puerto Rico and reflecting a skewed, one-dimensional image of Puerto Rican American life, focusing only on the tragedy, alienation, and exploitation of immigrants at the mercy of a cold and greedy America.

New York Puerto Rican writers of the late twentieth century were writing mostly in English and had inherited a popular tradition heavily influenced by Hispanic folklore and the multifaceted culture of one of the world's largest cities. Thematically and structurally their work has much in common with African American, Third World, and other Latino writers seeking identity through recognition of their multiethnicity rather than through acquiescence to pressures to assimilate. Nicholasa Mohr, one of the most productive and critically acclaimed Puerto Rican American novelists, deemphasizes the theme of alienation, creating characters who are not overly conscious of cultural conflict or crises of identity. *Felita* (1979) and *Rituals of Survival: A Woman's Portfolio* (1985) are examples of this fiction of self-determination.

Cuban American Long Fiction

Cuban literary influence in the United States can be traced to the early 1800's, when José Martí and other patriots worked from the United States for Cuban independence. After Fidel Castro's 1959 victory in the Cuban Revolution and the large-scale emigration that followed, however, Cuban Americans emerged as a major contributing force to Latino culture and literature. Unlike Puerto Ricans, Cubans came as refugees rather than immigrants. Furthermore, although Cuba had been a U.S. protectorate since 1898, it was never a political colony of the United States in the same sense as Puerto Rico. At the time of the Cuban Revolution, then, Cuban writers, having felt no assimilationist pressure, had developed no literary expressions of defiance or protection against the imposition of mainstream American culture onto Cuban American identity. In fact, because it was sparked by a political and social revolution, the emigration involved a cross-section of Cuban society: workers, middle-class service personnel, professionals, intellectuals, and the wealthy. Many subsequently adapted to and became a part of U.S. and Hispanic mainstream culture.

The fiction of Cuban Americans in the 1960's was primarily written in Spanish. One reason may be that the audience targeted by these first-generation exiles was primarily Spanish-speaking, either Cuban or Latin American. Another reason may be found in the essentially political, often propagandistic nature of the material. The themes were less concerned with discovery and preservation of an ethnic, cultural, or literary identity than with criticizing Cuba's communist economic and political system. Therefore, the Cuban American novel of the 1960's was almost devoid of the kinds of ethnic and linguistic self-consciousness that marked Chicano, Puerto Rican, and other minority ethnic fiction.

Fiction written by Cuban American novelists of the 1970's was less preoccupied with exile and looking back to the island past than with meeting the demands of the Cuban American communities then flourishing in the United States. Their novels were dominated by English, although code-switching (changing languages when expression in one seems richer or clearer than in the other) became more frequent, as did representation of a Cuban dialect heavily influenced by American idioms. Cuban American novelists of the late twentieth century have more in common with other Latino writers than did their forerunners of the 1950's and 1960's, having sought solidarity with the Latino community of writers and thinkers rather than returning to another, or remaining distinct as exiles. Immigration from Cuba continues to reinforce the dynamic nature of this evolution, however, and to provide an impetus resisting assimilation.

The first Cuban American novels, which began to be published in 1960, almost exclusively attacked Marxist doctrine in general and the political manifestation of it in the Cuban Revolution in particular. The first such novel, *Enterrado vivo* (1960; buried alive), written by Andrés Rivera Collado, was published in Mexico; the ensuing decade saw similar novels, published in the United States and abroad. At worst, these works were openly propagandistic and inflammatory, while at best they were unrealistically and ineffectively nostalgic in their idealization of prerevolutionary Cuba.

A change in direction for Cuban American fiction was initiated by Celedonio González, whose focus in *Los primos* (1971) was on Cuban life and culture in the United States. The thematic emphasis in González's subsequent novels, *Los cuatro embajadores* (1973; the four ambassadors) and *El espesor del pellejo de un gato ya cadáver* (1978; the thickness of the skin of a cat that is already a cadaver), is on the cultural and social conflicts experienced by Cuban Americans in a predatory economic system that keeps immigrants disadvantaged and alienated in order to exploit them. Like other Latino fiction, these novels depict a people not fully Americanized but clearly unable to return to or participate fully in their land or culture of origin.

Cristina García's work seeks resolution of the tensions between first and subsequent generations of Cuban Americans; born in 1958 in Havana, she grew up in New York City and was educated at Barnard College and The Johns Hopkins School of Advanced International Studies. Her first novel, *Dreaming in Cuban* (1992), earned favorable critical reception and became widely popular. Neither strident nor nostalgic, the novel avoids romantic excess, depicting a search for cultural and personal identity.

In the novels of Oscar Hijuelos, the evolution of Cuban American fiction moved even closer to integration in the American mainstream. He was born in New York in 1951, and neither Hijuelos nor his parents were exiles. Their experience, and his, is more consistent with that of Chicano and Puerto Rican American writers who lack the political agenda of writers in exile and whose thematic emphasis is on discovery and preservation of the integrity of their cultural and linguistic legacy. His first novel, *Our House in the Last World* (1983), is autobiographical, though often classified as a novel. He won the 1990 Pulitzer Prize for fiction; further evidence of his acceptance by mainstream America was the adaptation of his second novel, *The Mambo Kings Play Songs of Love* (1989), for film by Warner Bros.

— *Andrew B. Preslar*

Learn More

Baker, Houston A., Jr., ed. *Three American Literatures: Essays in Chicano, Native American, and Asian American Literature for Teachers of American Literature.* New York: Modern Language Association of America, 1982. A collection of critical essays for students and general readers, offering historical and traditional critical perspectives. Overview essays direct students to subjects of further study. Chapters include notes and references.

Behar, Ruth, ed. *Bridges to Cuba/Puentes a Cuba.* Ann Arbor: University of Michigan Press, 1995. For students and general readers with literary interests, this collection of essays, poems, drawings and stories by Cuban and Cuban American writers and scholars explores issues of culture, language, and national identity. Excellent resource for understanding the Latino search for ideological solidarity.

Christie, John S. *Latino Fiction and the Modernist Imagination: Literature of the Borderlands.* New York: Garland, 1998. Examines the works of Cuban Americans, Mexican Americans, and Puerto Ricans, among others. Includes thirteen pages of bibliographical references, as well as an index.

Gish, Robert Franklin. *Beyond Bounds: Cross-Cultural Essays on Anglo, American Indian, and Chicano Literature.* Albuquerque: University of New Mexico Press, 1996. An insightful exploration of the interrelationships of myth, language, and literary traditions of the overlapping cultures of the American Southwest.

Horno-Delgado, Anunción, et al., eds. *Breaking Boundaries: Latina Writings and Critical Readings.* Amherst: University of Massachusetts Press, 1989. Focusing on the experience of Hispanic female writers from all ethnic and cultural backgrounds, this collection of critical essays on fiction, poetry, and linguistics offers explanatory, introductory, and analytical studies of issues relating to all aspects and genres of Latina literary production. Scholarly but accessible, with notes and a bibliography.

Marqués, René. *The Docile Puerto Rican.* Translated with an introduction by Barbara Bockus Aponte. Philadelphia: Temple

University Press, 1976. Essays written for young Puerto Ricans to help them understand their cultural, ideological, and historical legacy. Treats issues of national identity directly and clearly, focusing on language, art, and literature. Endnotes offer explanation but are not intrusive or obscure; index and bibliography direct the student to further reading.

Robinson, Cecil. *Mexico and the Hispanic Southwest in American Literature.* Tucson: University of Arizona Press, 1977. Appropriate for a general audience, this book offers an excellent historical perspective on the evolution of culture and literature in the American Southwest. An introduction and prologue provide context and focus. Contains illustrations, an epilogue, unobtrusive references by chapter and page, a bibliography, and an index.

Shirley, Carl R., and Paula W. Shirley. *Understanding Chicano Literature.* Columbia: University of South Carolina Press, 1988. An introduction helps focus the material of the chapters following: poetry, theater, the novel, short fiction, and more, with notes, bibliography, index, and a list of suggested readings. Dense with information; appropriate for high school seniors and above.

Steele, Cynthia. *Politics, Gender, and the Mexican Novel, 1968-1988: Beyond the Pyramid.* Austin: University of Texas Press, 1992. A thoughtful study of contemporary Mexican long fiction. Discusses politics, social problems, sex roles, and female characters.

Latin American Long Fiction

Inherent in the ideology underlying the conquest and colonization of Latin America were certain factors that severely retarded the development of the novel there. Notable among them was the Church's view that the novel form was harmful to morals, coupled with the vision of Latin America as a mission field, from which such negative influences could and should be excluded. Thus, in 1531, it was forbidden for books such as *Amadís de Gaula* (1508; *Amadis of Gaul,* partial translation, 1567, 1803; better known as *Amadís*) to be imported. While it is true that from 1580 on, all sorts of fiction did enter the region—and it even appears that a sizable portion of the first edition of Miguel de Cervantes's *El ingenioso hidalgo don Quixote de la Mancha* (1605, 1615; *The History of the Valorous and Wittie Knight-Errant, Don Quixote of the Mancha,* 1612-1620; better known as *Don Quixote de la Mancha*) came to the New World—the law is indicative of an attitude that, in the Spanish-speaking regions, successfully prevented the production of anything that might properly be called a novel until 1816.

In Brazil, the attempt to exclude the form was not so successful. It was, in fact, a churchman who produced the first novel there. Four years after the publication of John Bunyan's *The Pilgrim's Progress from This World to That Which Is to Come* (1678, 1684; more commonly known as *The Pilgrim's Progress*), the Jesuit Alexandre de Gusmão (1628-1724) published *História do predestinado peregrino e seu irmão Precito* (1682). Also in the allegorical mode is the *Compêndio narrativo do peregrino da América* (1728), by Nuno Marques Pereira (1652-1728), and in 1752, Teresa Margarida da Silva e Orta published *Aventuras de Diófanes.* These attempts to turn the form to the service of morality left no progeny, and when the Brazilian novel returned, it was in the fullness of the Romantic movement.

The outstanding Brazilian novelist of the Romantic period was José de Alencar (1829-1877), whose early work consists of a series of sentimental novels of adventure, dealing particularly with the idealized Indian, modeled on Chateaubriand's noble savage, who predominated throughout Latin American literature in this era. Alencar's more mature works, including *Lucíola* (1862), *Iracema* (1865; *Iracema, the Honey-Lips: A Legend of Brazil,* 1886), and *Senhora* (1875; *Senhora: Profile of a Woman,* 1994), are more concerned with the portrayal of urban society, as is the notable *Memórias de um sargento de milícias* (1854; *Memoirs of a Militia Sergeant,* 1959), by Manuel António de Almeida (1831-1861), which concentrates on Rio de Janeiro. At the same time, Bernardo Guimarães (1825-1884) was dealing with nationalistic themes.

The Nineteenth Century
The first novel of Spanish America, as well, appeared within the politically liberal orientation of nascent Romanticism. With the accession of the Bourbons to the Spanish throne in 1700, considerable French influence began entering the colonies, and the Enlightenment left its mark on their literature. José Joaquín Fernández de Lizardi (1776-1827), known as "The Mexican Thinker," was fundamentally a pamphleteer and essayist who traveled with a portable printing press, turning out material in support of the war of independence. His first novel, *El periquillo sarniento* (1816; *The Itching Parrot,* 1912), was, appropriately, a statement of reason at the same time that it led to a current of Romantic novels in the region. Although the picaresque genre in Spain had been an instrument of the Church, useful in the preaching of morality, Lizardi's picaresque novel is brutally anticlerical even while its entertaining narrative is marred by lengthy sermons. This tendency toward essay in the novel perhaps had its roots in the missionary traditions of the colonies and has continued to the present day, particularly in the fiction of the Mexican Carlos Fuentes. In the Mexican novel, there is also a tendency to employ circular structures, which are already visible in Lizardi's work. Each episode presents the reader with a turn of the Wheel of Fortune, as the protagonist becomes successful only to end in desperate straits again.

The vast majority of Latin America's nineteenth century novels appeared in the second half of that century, although one notable work spans nearly a half century in itself: *Cecilia Valdés* (first part 1839, completed 1882; *Cecilia Valdés: A Novel of Cuban Customs*, 1962), by the Cuban author Cirilo Villaverde (1812-1894). Like nearly all fiction following the attainment of independence by most of Latin America (although not yet by Cuba), *Cecilia Valdés* is Romantic in character; following the example set by Lizardi, Villaverde's is a political Romanticism, relatively unconcerned with nature.

The Latin American short story has its roots in the celebrated narrative "El matadero," by Esteban Echeverría (1805-1851). Another work of doubtful genre in the same era, *Vida de Juan Facundo Quiroga* (1845; *Facundo: Life in the Argentine Republic in the Days of the Tyrants: Or, Civilization and Barbarism*, 1868), by Domingo Faustino Sarmiento (1811-1888), exercised considerable influence on the course of the novel for decades to come. A combination of biography, novel, and essay, it establishes with its subtitle the theme of the struggle between the relatively sophisticated, often Europeanized, cities of Latin America and the more barbaric outlying areas, be they the Argentine pampas or the Venezuelan llanos. In general terms, the novel of the nineteenth century tends to contrast the refinement of Europe with the crudeness of the New World. The sons of Brazilian planters, for example, received the finest education that Europe could offer, often returning to bewail their homeland's lack of culture.

The most prominent of a number of novels written in opposition to the Argentine dictator Juan Manuel de Rosas was *Amalia* (first part 1851, second part 1855; *Amalia: A Romance of the Argentine*, 1919), by José Mármol (1817-1871), who learned his craft from Sir Walter Scott and Alexandre Dumas, *père*. In his struggle against injustice, Mármol's Daniel Bello is the prototype of the Romantic hero, while the heroine Amalia is representative of European refinement surrounded by New World vulgarity. In this era, many novels were serialized in newspapers, among them *Amalia*, which exhibits the episodic character of this type of composition.

Probably the most widely read Latin American novel of the nineteenth century was *María* (1867; *María: A South American Romance*, 1890), by Jorge Isaacs (1837-1895). At this stage, the Romantics were generally more concerned with nature, and the heroine of Isaacs's novel appears to be almost a projection of the landscape of Colombia's Cauca Valley. The tale is typical of the novels of its day, involving an encounter of soul mates who are separated and then reunited at the conclusion, only to learn that fate has made their marriage impossible. In this case, the couple are brother and sister by adoption, and her death prevents their marriage. A variation on the theme appears in *Cumandá* (1879), by the Ecuadoran Juan León Mera (1832-1894): After the lovers have overcome many obstacles, the proposed marriage is prevented by the revelation that the couple are brother and sister, separated in infancy. In *Cumandá*, Mera lays the foundations for the modern novel of protest against the inhuman treatment of Indians, concerning whom he has solid documentary knowledge. In 1889, the same type of novel, overlaid with European sentimentalism and full of fateful coincidences and melodramatic surprises, including the usual impossible marriage of siblings, appeared in Peru under the title *Aves sin nido* (*Birds Without a Nest: A Story of Indian Life and Priestly Oppression in Peru*, 1904). The author, Clorinda Matto de Turner (1852-1909), wrote a preface within the tradition of the moralistic essay, declaring that her purpose in writing was to exhibit the unjust treatment of the Peruvian Indian and argue for the marriage of priests. It is a prime example of the nineteenth century Romantic novel in that it is far more concerned with theme than with technique. Nevertheless, it exercised a powerful influence in Latin America.

Cuban-born Gertrudis Gómez de Avellaneda (1814-1873) published her novel *Sab* (English translation, 1993) in 1841, with a black slave as protagonist, anticipating by nearly a century the handful of novels that would attempt to set black people's situation in relief. More significant is her *Guatimozín* (1846; *Cuauhtemoc, the Last Aztec Emperor: An Historical Novel*, 1898), a well-researched historical novel dealing with the conquest of Mexico and one of the two most important of that genre in the century, the other being *Durante la reconquista* (1897), by Alberto Blest Gana (1831-1920).

French literary influences gradually gained momentum throughout Latin America in the nineteenth century, and critics are often hard-pressed to identify the tendency to which a given writer or work belongs. It is preferable to point out that while Romantic tendencies underlie nearly all the novelistic production of the region until 1880 or so, writers were beginning to feel the influence first of Honoré de Balzac and Émile Zola and then of the Parnassian and Symbolist movements, and to experiment with them. In Brazil, *Inocência* (1872; *Innocencia: A Story of the Prairie Regions of Brazil*, 1889), by Alfredo de Escragnolle Tarmay (1843-1899), represents something of a transition from the dominance of Romanticism to realism in that country. The well-known *Martín Rivas* (1862; English translation, 1916), by Blest Gana, is illustrative of his desire to become the Balzac of Chile, although at its base it is still a Romantic work rather than a realistic one. It has, in fact, been termed the best example of "Romantic realism" in Latin America, and it exhibits the typical polarity that is so evident in the novels of this period: city against country, reality against appearances, good characters against evil ones.

The Mexican writer Ignacio Manuel Altamirano (1834-1893) attempted to raise the quality of the Latin American novel by urging his fellow authors to read widely in order to gain a more universal literary vision, something that Lizardi and others had already been doing. Although an Indian himself, and desirous of making the novel more realistic, he tended to produce romantically stereotyped characters, Indian or otherwise, and failed to plead the Indian's case strongly. His *Clemencia* (1869) and *La Navidad en las Montañas* (1870; *Christmas in the Mountains*, 1961) are worthy novels, but his considerable ability to tell a good adventure story is best displayed in *El Zarco: Episodios de la vida Mexicana en 1861-1863* (1901; *El Zarco, the Bandit*, 1957), in which he attempts to break with Romanticism yet employs as an omen an owl in the tree where his title character is to be hanged. There are two couples, one positive and the other negative, the one illustrating what is good for Mexico and the other illustrating what threatens to destroy it.

About 1880, the call of writers such as Altamirano bore fruit, for there was at that time a considerable increase in both the quantity and the quality of Latin American fiction, corresponding, perhaps coincidentally, to the emergence of naturalistic tendencies. These were mixed with what remained of Romanticism and realism, the best of which led to the regionalist novel as the writer became increasingly preoccupied with accurately describing the circumstances on the land. *Costumbrismo,* as the term indicates, involves the more or less superficial portrayal of types and customs in a given region. The term *criollismo* is related, but the *criollista* writer is more deeply involved in the subject of study. In the last two decades of the century, these tendencies became mixed with the emerging *Modernismo,* whose most powerful impetus was provided by the publication in 1888 of *Azul,* a collection of short stories and poems by Rubén Darío (1867-1916). *Modernismo* in the Spanish-speaking countries (in contrast to the modernism of Brazil) was a truly indigenous movement, the roots of which, however, were in French Parnassianism and Symbolism. *Modernismo* is a movement characterized by refined sensibilities, even hyperaestheticism, and in contrast to *criollismo*'s desire to come to grips with Latin American reality, its aim in general was to rise above it in a manner of escape. It left its mark on prose fiction in a greater concern on the part of the writer for sound artistic accomplishment and in an increase in the use of imagery in prose style, issuing ultimately in some novels that must be read almost as poetry on account of the intensity of their language.

In the Spanish-speaking countries, the leading exponent of naturalism is probably Eugenio Cambacérès (1843-1890), whose *Música sentimental* (1884), while clearly influenced by Zola, still exhibits realistic tendencies. In Mexico, the most prominent of those deeply influenced by naturalism was Federico Gamboa (1864-1939), a careful artist whose most important works are *Suprema ley* (1896) and *Santa* (1903). The latter was more successful than any Mexican book up to its time and strongly influenced the later prominent Mexican novelist Mariano Azuela (1873-1952). Gamboa's principles are drawn from French naturalism, but his work serves as a bridge between the Romantic realism of the nineteenth century and the regionalism of the twentieth. Another Mexican novelist, Emilio Rabasa (1856-1930), was the first to come to grips with the social issues leading to the

Mexican Revolution of 1910, and as such anticipates the novel of that revolution. The Cuban Carlos Loveira (1882-1928) produced a late example of the naturalist novel, *Juan Criollo* (1927), whose protagonist, reared in a family of higher social class, is nevertheless condemned to a life of misery by his lower-class birth.

In Brazil, the most prominent writers in the realist-naturalist camp were Aluísio Azevedo (1857-1913), whose best works are *Casa de Pensão* (1884) and *O cortiço* (1890; *A Brazilian Tenement*, 1926; also as *The Slum*, 1999), and Adolfo Caminha (1867-1897), whose *Bom crioulo* (1895; *Bom-Crioula: The Black Man and the Cabin Boy*, 1982), concerning homosexuality in the Brazilian navy, produced a national scandal. Among the Brazilian writers whose novels defy classification are Euclides da Cunha (1866-1909), whose *Os sertões* (1902; *Rebellion in the Backlands*, 1944), regarded as one of the masterpieces of Brazilian literature, deals with war in the backlands and is similar to Sarmiento's *Facundo* in its mixture of genres, and Raúl Pompéia (1863-1895), whose *O Ateneu* (1888) employs a boys' boarding school as a microcosm of society.

Equally difficult to classify is the man generally considered to be Brazil's greatest writer, Joaquim Maria Machado de Assis (1839-1908), whose principal model was Laurence Sterne. Machado de Assis ignored naturalism to explore the psychological dimensions of alienation. Although he is considered a pioneer of psychological realism, his major concern is not with character development but with novelistic technique, so that his work both fits into the emerging aestheticist tendencies of the Spanish-speaking countries and anticipates the later Latin American novel's preoccupation with language as such, in the handling of which he is an acknowledged master. His first work of excellence is *Memórias póstumas de Brás Cubas* (1881; *The Posthumous Memoirs of Brás Cubas*, 1951; better known as *Epitaph of a Small Winner*, 1952), but it was only with *Quincas Borba* (1891; *Philosopher or Dog?*, 1954; also as *The Heritage of Quincas Borba*, 1954) and *Dom Casmurro* (1899; English translation, 1953) that his greatness was generally recognized.

A significant novel later retrieved from critical oblivion was important in the development of technical excellence in the late nineteenth century: *Mitío el empleado* (1887), by the Cuban Ramón Meza (1861-1911), is characterized by what has been described as a picaresque *costumbrismo* similar to that of Emilio Rabasa. It exhibits a Wheel of Fortune structure somewhat similar to that of *The Itching Parrot*, as the hero experiences a rise, a fall, and finally what is presumably a permanent rise in Mexico. The work's picaresque qualities, rooted in the Cuban *choteo*—the Trickster-like practice of mocking everything—anticipates a persistent humorism in the modern Spanish American novel.

Known as one of the foremost *Modernista* poets, the Colombian José Asunción Silva (1865-1896) produced *De sobremesa* (1896), a lesser-known novel of some importance for the understanding of the direction the genre was taking around the end of the nineteenth century. Rooted in the aesthetic decadentism that was one of the primary characteristics of urban Latin American culture at that time, it presents a protagonist whose values are emphatically those of the *Modernistas*, just as the earlier Colombian writer Jorge Isaacs's Efraín (in Isaacs's novel *María*) is the quintessential Spanish American Romantic hero. The *Modernista* concern for aesthetic values as opposed to those of pragmatism is delineated in an essay by the Uruguayan José Enrique Rodó (1871-1917), *Ariel* (1900; English translation, 1922), a work perfectly placed for psychological impact at the opening of the new century. In it, Rodó insists that the developing culture of Latin America, while taking advantage of the admirable advances of technology in North America, reject its materialistic values in favor of those of the spirit. *Ariel* profoundly influenced an entire generation of Latin American intellectuals.

The Early Twentieth Century
In the novel at this time, there is an increasing commitment to technical quality, along with an attempt at a more skillful analysis of the regions in which the authors lived. Regionalist tendencies were accentuated in the first decades of the twentieth century by the relative isolation of national capitals from one another, and added to the geographical isolation was the almost worshipful attention paid by authors in each region to what was

taking place in Europe, so that a writer in Lima and one in Santiago might each be far more aware of the literary scene in Paris than in the other's city. Therefore, the regionalist tendency became strong within a general *criollista* current.

One of the most skillful of the regionalist writers was Tomás Carrasquilla (1858-1940), whose novels, including *Frutos de mi tierra* (1896), *Grandeza* (1910), *La marquesa de Yolombó* (1928), and *Hace tiempos* (1935), are set in the city and countryside of Colombia's Antioquia, a region of difficult access before the advent of air travel. Correspondingly, the circumstances of Carrasquilla's characters are static, as is generally the case in the early regionalist novels of Latin America. Characterization for Carrasquilla is largely by way of regionalistic speech.

In Chile, Blest Gana had a successor in Luis Orrego Luco (1866-1949), whose *Casa grande* (1908) was the first novel to analyze in depth the life of the Chilean upper classes. Orrego Luco's concern, that of the psychological penetration of a social sphere that interests him, using a calm, controlled, polished language, is typical of Chilean fiction, from its inception to the present day, and is especially evident in the work of José Donoso. Orrego Luco is something of a transitional figure, standing between nineteenth century realism and twentieth century *criollismo*. Another transitional figure is Manuel Gálvez (1882-1962), who straddled the gap between Romanticism and *Modernismo*, producing books of unbridled subjectivism, a quality associated with both schools. As typically Argentine as Orrego Luco was Chilean, Gálvez sought to analyze his nation's reality in terms of his own ongoing spiritual crisis, to produce an opus illustrative of his and Argentina's anxiety and hope for the future. His *La maestra normal* (1914) is a prime example of the *costumbrista* novel, but in its agonized introspection it anticipates the novels of Eduardo Mallea as well as the call for social reform and women's rights.

Among the Brazilian regionalists, the most prominent was Lima Barreto (1881-1922), who, like Machado de Assis, was black. Unlike Machado de Assis, however, Barreto reacted violently against the racism that he felt even in his relatively easygoing country, becoming a militant anarchist. His bitter parodies of the Brazilian mainstream caused the critics of his day to ignore him.

Out of the wave-interference pattern of sometimes contradictory literary movements, there emerged some novels of clearly definable *Modernista* character, while others whose *Modernista* aesthetic is discernible, such as *El embrujo de Sevilla* (1922; *Castanets*, 1929) and *El gaucho florido* (1932), by the Uruguayan Carlos Reyles (1868-1938), betray the melodramatic character of the old Romanticism. Among the better *Modernista* novelists was the Chilean Augusto d'Halmar (1882-1950). In 1902, Manuel Díaz Rodríguez (1871-1927) published *Sangre patricia* (English translation, 1946), in which he struggled to force psychological penetration beyond the limits of *Modernismo*'s usual superficiality. In it, however, even the protagonist's suicide becomes a positive aesthetic event. Another tour de force is *La gloria de don Ramiro* (1908; *The Glory of Don Ramiro*, 1924), by Enrique Larreta (1875-1961), which employs a historical setting in Toledo as the basis for a transformation of that reality into a sensorial experience—a process betraying *Modernismo*'s roots in Symbolism, in which the object perceived is gradually metamorphosed into a representation of the observer's psychic state. Some critics have mistakenly placed Rafael Arévalo Martínez (1884-1975) and his works, such as *El hombre que parecía un caballo* (1916), in the naturalist camp because his characters are often compared to animals. In fact, this process in his stories is also an example of Symbolist transformation.

The advent of modern communications eventually began unifying Latin America to the extent that authors came to have freer access to one another. There are some modern authors who have commented that, as their centuries-long insularity finally gave way, they became aware of their common goals, and several have even spoken of "the novel that we are all writing," which has issued in Carlos Fuentes's attempt, in *Terra nostra* (1975; English translation, 1976), to pick up the quests of the heroes of several novels written by his peers and complete them, even bringing a number of those heroes together at the conclusion of his novel. This attitude stands in contrast to that of many nationalistic leaders of the individual countries, who at times insist that there is no real Latin America—that each individual nation is an entity in itself and impossible to classify with others.

As the authors of Latin America came to an increasing awareness of their common experience and concerns, regionalist tendencies gradually became less important, and the focus came to be upon America as a problem. While European literary currents continued to exercise a strong influence, a complex series of events moved the Latin American novel into the channels it was to follow. Rodó's plea for a continuing stress on Latin American cultural identity was very much in the minds of these writers, as they wrote in the *costumbrista* and *criollista* modes. This Latin American identity was reinforced in 1910 by the centennial of the outbreak of the wars for independence from Spain. Intellectuals became preoccupied with what Latin America had become in those hundred years, and their stress on America as a viable, powerful entity in itself, rather than a stepchild of Europe, became known as *mundonovismo*.

Because little had changed with independence save the replacement of Spanish-born political leaders by governors of Spanish descent born in the New World, in many cases government had deteriorated into dictatorship. One of the worst of these governments in terms of its emphasis on progress at the expense of the cynical exploitation of the poor was that of Porfirio Díaz in Mexico, and in another instance of timing with considerable symbolic value, in the centennial year of 1910, a true revolution (as opposed to the typical Latin American replacement of one dictator by another) broke out there. Latin Americans, already profoundly concerned with the direction to be taken by their region, watched closely as, in the midst of the Mexican Revolution, World War I broke out, and then, before either war was concluded, the Russian Revolution took place. Sociopolitical upheaval was clearly the order of the day, and Latin America already had a well-established tradition of writers influencing the course of such events.

This confluence of currents produced, among other effects, a subgenre of the regionalist novel, that of the Mexican Revolution, the first example of which appeared in the course of the fighting. *Los de abajo* (1916; *The Underdogs*, 1929) is most notable

for the ability of its author, Mariano Azuela (1873-1952), to transform living experience into fiction as it occurred. The work has
the typically Mexican circular structure, the protagonist dying at
the same location at which he begins his successful career in the
revolution. While this has been termed an epic structure, it may
also be viewed as another turn of the Wheel of Fortune, indicative not only of the nature of one revolutionary's fortunes but
also of the lot of the nation as a whole as its revolution was to
lead to new forms of death-dealing oppression. *The Underdogs*
was largely ignored until 1925, when journalists discovered it
and brought it to the public's attention.

Martín Luis Guzmán (1887-1976) also published a work
linked to journalism, *El águila y la serpiente* (1928; *The Eagle and
the Serpent*, 1930), which is a novel of the sort that a war correspondent might be expected to write; it nevertheless contains
some of the best prose of its day. The next year, he produced *La
sombra del caudillo* (1929), in which he, like Azuela, views the
Mexican people as being swept inexorably along by the revolution. For him, its story is one of *caudillos*, the petty regional dicta-
tors whose story was to emerge in its most powerful form in a
work by Juan Rulfo (1918-1986), *Pedro Páramo* (1955; English
translation, 1959). Gregorio López y Fuentes (1897-1966), in
his *El indio* (1935; English translation, 1961), bridges the gap between the novel of the Mexican Revolution and the Indianist
(*indigenismo*) novel, examining the role played by Indians in the
conflict and questioning their treatment since that time. In doing so, he moves away from the traditional narrative technique
of Mexico's novel involving the common people, treating them
as masses rather than as individuals. Many other authors turned
to a portrayal of the Indian plight during the 1920's and 1930's.
If America was a problem, then at its roots was the situation of its
aboriginal peoples, who had been raped, slaughtered, enslaved,
and generally exploited throughout the centuries since the conquest.

John S. Brushwood pointed out that three stages should be
recognized in the development of Indian-oriented fiction in
Latin America. The first has its roots in some of the earliest writings of the region, in works such as *Arauco domado* (1596; *Arauco*

779

Tamed, 1948), by Pedro de Oña (1570-c. 1643). In this epic poem, the aboriginal American is glorified and made to conform to European ideals of language, behavior, and even physical appearance. Later, under the influence of French writers such as Chateaubriand, these conceptions were reinforced in the "noble savage" mode, as in Avellaneda's *Guatimozín* or Mera's *Cumandá*. The second stage involves a view of Indians as a problem, describing and protesting against social injustice and dealing with them in terms of what has been called social realism, as in *El indio*. Finally, there are novels such as *Los ríos profundos* (1958; *Deep Rivers*, 1978), by José María Arguedas (1911-1969), and *Oficio de tinieblas* (1966; *The Book of Lamentations*, 1996), by Rosario Castellanos (1915-1974), in which the author actually writes from the Indians' viewpoint, revealing their vital experience from within. These works belong to a period of more universal concerns in the novel in general.

In the regionalist mode of the second stage, one of the important novels is that of the poet César Vallejo (1892-1938), *El tungsteno* (1931; *Tungsten*, 1988), dealing with the agelong problems of Indians in the mines of Latin America. In other Indianist novels, the stress is on the unjust distribution of land, not merely for the purpose of pointing out the problem of economic exploitation but because of the Indians' need for a sense of belonging. In this connection, it should be stressed that to the extent that Marxist concepts entered Latin American thinking in this area, they tended to be received in terms not so much of their economic import as of their cultural import, which is in part the result of the fact that these writers derived their Marxist ideals from Nikolay Berdyaev rather than the more economically oriented theoreticians.

Thus, while the Indians in these second-stage novels are generally portrayed as masses, they are never simple adjuncts to an economic theory, but rather a people in quest of ethnic wholeness. An early example by Alcides Arguedas (1879-1946), *Raza de bronce* (1919), deals with the impossible position in which Indians find themselves, even while the author fails to call for any radical change. Jorge Icaza (1906-1978), in his *Huasipungo* (1934; *The Villagers*, 1964), chose to employ scenes of unspeakable atrocity to shock the reader into indignation, while the Mexican Mauricio Magdaleno (1906-1986) makes use of astronomical metaphors to depict the Indians' situation in *El resplandor* (1937; *Sunburst*, 1944), reflecting the preconquest belief of the people in a destiny set in the heavens. The last significant novel in this stage, by the Peruvian Ciro Alegría (1909-1967), was *El mundo es ancho y ajeno* (1941; *Broad and Alien Is the World*, 1941), in which the Indians are dispossessed by the greed of white people. The novel is most notable for its creation of a powerful individual, the chief Rosendo Maqui, a sign of hope as in his human qualities he towers over his oppressors in their venality.

One of the issues that greatly intrigued the regionalists was the response of Americans to a nature that was often perceived as overwhelming. During the 1920's, this concern resulted in a series of landmark novels, each dealing with the issue in a different manner. The novelist of the Colombian jungle, José Eustacio Rivera (1889-1928), wrote of how "men disintegrate like worms and nature closes implacably over them." His *La vorágine* (1924; *The Vortex*, 1935) treats the jungle as an irresistible destructive force, reducing human beings to pitiful shells and then swallowing them. Sarmiento's civilization-versus-barbarism theme was transferred to the plains of Venezuela by Rómulo Gallegos (1884-1969), who later was to become president of his country. His *Doña Bárbara* (1929; English translation, 1931), complete with allegorical names, portrays the victory of city-based enlightenment over superstition and the raw lust for power found in the outlying regions.

In Sarmiento's Argentina, however, what appeared in *Facundo* as an ambivalent Romantic attitude toward the gaucho is transformed into a *Modernista* presentation of him as, paradoxically, the Romantic ideal of humans in harmony with nature in both suffering and triumph: *Don Segundo Sombra* (1926; English translation, 1935), by Ricardo Güiraldes (1886-1927), is a sort of *Bildungsroman* for Argentine youth, in which the hero is drawn from his effeminate civilized surroundings into the gaucho world, eventually to return as a landowner. The cycle of major novels dealing with humans and nature is completed, as humans have been viewed as dominated by nature, dominant over it, and in harmony with it. Each of the novels deals with the problems of a specific region, even while creating an experience to which all Latin Americans can relate. The fact that the three can be seen almost as a loose sort of unwitting trilogy on humans and nature is indicative of the growing tendency of Latin American writers to write on the same topics in ways that indicate shared experiences and concerns.

The 1920's and 1930's
There has been an unfortunate critical tendency to treat the situation of prose fiction in the 1920's and 1930's as if the only significant works were of the regionalist variety, whether they dealt with the Mexican Revolution, social issues of some other sort, or more general Latin American themes. For this reason, many have viewed later Latin American novels as if they had been created *ex nihilo* or pieced together from foreign sources. The fact is that there had been a more or less steady and consistent development of the vanguardist novel, parallel to those works preoccupied with sociopolitical issues. The most important link between the two lay in the profound rejection of existing social values in virtually all the novels of this period. From that point on, there was a divergence, some writers, as in the nineteenth century, being more concerned with their message than with the language in which it was couched, while others were primarily concerned with their novels as works of art. In the mid-1910's, the Chilean poet Vicente Huidobro (1893-1948) produced his "Creationist Manifesto," in which he rejected the demand that the artist reproduce external reality to make mimetic art, asserting instead the right to invent new realities, in an art involving genetic processes. Huidobro's view is that the poet is "a little god," so that each literary work is a new creation in the world. In the full flush of social commitment, his cries were ignored by a considerable percentage of writers, but many more followed his lead and those of other influential writers, among whom Marcel Proust, James Joyce, and the Peninsular author Benjamín Jarnés are the most frequently mentioned. In the 1920's, these theories were displayed most prominently in a series of often short-lived literary magazines.

At this time, vanguardist writers experimented with such techniques as antichronological development and interior monologue. In the fiction of this period, characterization is radically interiorized, and there are often variations in the narrative point of view. There is an increasing concern with visual effects and the use of startling imagery, along with an interest in playing with typography. Underlying it all, there is the conviction that the author is under no obligation to reproduce visible reality. *El café de nadie* (1926), by Arqueles Vela (born 1899), is heavy with radical innovations, including the concept of a fictional space within which the plot develops, and some early experiments with Surrealism.

Even when a novel of this time bears a regional cast, the increasing interest in a psychological penetration of the characters often places the universal orientation of an author in bold relief. The best examples in this period are two works of the Chilean Eduardo Barrios (1884-1963): *El niño que enloqueció de amor* (1915; *The Little Boy Driven Mad by Love*, 1967), in which a young boy falls in love with his mother's friend, and *El hermano asno* (1922; *Brother Ass*, 1922), a study of the emotional torment of a saintly monk. In the same decade, *La educación sentimental* (1929), by Jaime Torres Bodet (1902-1974), focuses on interior experience to such a degree that there is virtually no action. In the Argentine tradition of novels dealing with anguished characters obsessed with questions concerning the meaning of an alienated existence is *Los siete locos* (1929; *The Seven Madmen*, 1984), by Roberto Arlt (1900-1942), in which the revolutionary impulse has motives solely of personal gain. The Nietzschean will to power figures largely, as does Joycean interior monologue. In Chile, what Fernando Alegría terms the "deathblow to *criollismo*" was produced in two stages. In 1934, María Luisa Bombal (1910-1980) published *La última niebla* (*The Final Mist*, 1982; previously published as *The House of Mist*, 1947), which deals in a cool and elegant style with both the universal human condition and specifically feminine psychology. It was not until 1951, however, that Manuel Rojas (1896-1973) completed the process with *Hijo de ladrón* (*Born Guilty*, 1955), a completely secular novel—something virtually unknown before this time in

Latin America—that examines the life of a modern people in the cosmopolitan vein.

Modernism

In Brazil, the regionalist tendency was first challenged by that country's version of modernism, which represents a combination of vanguardist currents. Modernism suddenly appeared on the scene in 1922 and had the effect of making poetry dominant until 1930, when a series of neorealistic novels of a social orientation began appearing, among them *Vidas sêcas* (1938; *Barren Lives*, 1965), by Graciliano Ramos (1892-1953), a novel of psychological realism in the tradition of Joaquim Maria Machado de Assis focusing on character development rather than plot.

Still another major contribution to the complex set of influences on the Latin American novel was made by Jorge Luis Borges (1899-1986), who never wrote a novel himself but whose short stories serve as the primary impetus of what Seymour Menton calls *cosmopolitismo*. In the work of Borges, who wrote in Buenos Aires, prose fiction tends to move away from rural, regional concerns and into more urbane, universal settings, with the result that in the last several decades of the twentieth century there was a curious split in the best Latin American novels, some, such as *Rayuela* (1963; *Hopscotch*, 1966), by Julio Cortázar (1914-1984), with settings in the great cities of Europe and America, and others, most notably *Cien años de soledad* (1967; *One Hundred Years of Solitude*, 1970), by Gabriel García Márquez (born 1928), set in remote rural areas but nevertheless universal for it. Borges's major scholarly interests lie in medieval Northern Europe and England, and Nordic mythology therefore plays a role in his stories. He is known for his play with mythic and philosophical concepts, and his stories are rife with paranormal events, which differ from those of writers interested in the African and indigenous traditions mainly in having their roots in European mythologies and philosophies.

In Borges, the author's demand for the right to invent his or her own reality comes to full fruition. His *Ficciones, 1935-1944* (1944; English translation, 1962) and *El Aleph* (1949, 1952; translated in *The Aleph, and Other Stories, 1933-1969*, 1970) appeared at exactly the right moment, as the Latin American novel was ready to move into a new phase and take its place as one of the most creative and active in the world. Even before Borges's landmark works, however, Juan Filloy (1894-2000) had produced a radical piece of fiction entitled *Op Oloop* (1934, 1967) in the Joycean tradition, particularly in its innovative language. In 1941, Macedonio Fernández (1874-1952) published *Una novela que comienza*, insisting in the text that if he can locate a certain woman he has seen and incorporate her into the work, the novel can get under way. In this period, throughout Latin America, the general inclination to express dissatisfaction with social values was giving way to a cultural internationalism on the one hand and political liberalism on the other. *Adán Buenosayres* (1948), by Leopoldo Marechal (1900-1970), presents a character attempting to re-create Buenos Aires through language in order to make it conform to such ideals.

The Surrealists took a deep interest in inner landscapes. As painters, they portrayed visions supposedly arisen from the unconscious mind, while the poets, following André Breton's model of "the chance occurrence, upon a dissecting table, of a sewing machine and an umbrella," wanted to be the first to join two words together. Such a preoccupation with the unconscious and the seemingly irrational involves a flight from normal, supposedly logical, visions of reality that merge with several other concerns of the Latin American novelists of this era, among them an interest in penetrating beneath the surface of the Indians' world into their often radically different vision of the cosmos. The word "primitive" began to lose its negative connotations as archaeologists and anthropologists revealed that the pre-Columbian civilizations had been vastly superior in many aspects to that of the Europeans who conquered them. Latin American writers came to the realization that the myths, folktales, and rituals of even the modern descendants of the Mayas and Incas could not be dismissed as inferior, childish attempts to be civilized in the European sense.

Contributing to this change in attitude was the decreasing influence of the Church, which had condemned such myths and rituals as pagan and therefore satanic. Furthermore, Europe was experiencing yet another resurgence of interest in its own ancient mythologies, which were proving to be fascinatingly similar to those that anthropologists were collecting around the world. One result, in a world in which it appeared that the values of Western civilization were leading only to war and chaos, was a sense that the concepts that had aided in structuring the ancient societies of a region should be examined in search of their possible values for the same region in the twentieth century. Writers such as Joyce appeared to be searching for significance in their characters' acts by relating them to the archetypal deeds of the heroes of the past. Joyce, whose influence has been considerable in the Latin American novel, early went to Odysseus as a model and later seemed to allude to the Irish hero Finn MacCool and the expectation of his return to life in *Finnegans Wake* (1939).

Much of Latin America had placed its hope in European values. Sarmiento, having reluctantly rejected the gauchos (who were mainly mestizos) as a viable social force, called for European immigration as the salvation of Argentina. Civilization must prevail over the barbarity of the plains, and Gallegos echoed the cry from Venezuela eight decades later. Yet by 1929, with Arlt's *The Seven Madmen*, it was becoming evident that Sarmiento's theories were not working in the most important area, that of the human spirit.

Other voices had been heard, although they had been overwhelmed for a considerable length of time. Eugenio María de Hostos (1839-1903), active in education in the Caribbean, declared in an essay entitled "El cholo" that the hope of America lay in the fusion of the three major racial groups: Caucasian, African, and Indian. Later, in *La raza cósmica* (1925; *The Cosmic Race*, 1979), José Vasconcelos (1882-1959), a Mexican writer, expressed the theory that Latin America had the unique opportunity to reunite those racial groups, drawing on the strengths of each to build a great new society.

In order to do so, the intelligentsia would have to examine and come to a comprehension of the roots of the thinking of those groups, as expressed in Latin America. One early attempt was made by the brilliant Cuban Alejo Carpentier (1904-1980), in *¡Ecué-Yamba-O! Historia Afro-Cubana* (1933), an examination of the Afro-Cuban religious cults. Later, the author was to repudiate the work, having realized that he had been far from any true understanding of the premodern thought of the people involved. The Nobel Prize winner from Guatemala, Miguel Ángel Asturias (1899-1974), was the first to make a serious attempt to deal adequately with Indian mythology, with his *Leyendas de Guatemala* (1930), in which he recovers as much as possible of the thought of the Mayas as it survived in their descendants. Asturias serves as something of a transitional figure, for his social commitment is abundantly clear in his attacks on Latin American dictatorship and the United Fruit Company in works such as *El Señor Presidente* (1946; *The President*, 1963) and *Hombres de maíz* (1949; *Men of Maize*, 1975), while at the same time he laid the foundation for what was to become known as Magical Realism in Latin American prose fiction (not to be confused with the movement of the same name in North American painting). In *Men of Maize*, he revealed the continued effect of the *Popol Vuh* on the life of the Central American Indian.

Magical Realism

The term "Magical Realism" is nebulous, and many authors and critics prefer *lo real maravilloso*, which is based loosely on the French Surrealists' concept of *le merveilleux*. Magical Realism is fundamentally a reflection of the twentieth century's departure from what has been perceived as bourgeois categories. Psychology and sociology have shown that rational categories are not necessarily dominant in determining the course of the life of a person or society, and even physics has departed from the Newtonian model, with its more or less mechanistic bias. While the nineteenth century realist wanted to show life as it was actually lived, the Magical Realist believes that true reality is that which underlies the ordinary events of daily life. In this sense, the term "realism" is accurate, for writers in this vein believe that, once found, reality will always prove to have a paranormal, magical cast to it. Typically, in this type of fiction, supernatural occurrences are narrated in a matter-of-fact manner, as if they formed a part of normal daily life.

Demetrio Aguilera Malta (1909-1981) had been experimenting with such alternative realities in the early 1930's, along with writers such as Carpentier and Asturias. His *Don Goyo* (1933; English translation, 1942, 1980) reveals an early animistic tendency to personify nature that was to contrast sharply with the views of Alain Robbe-Grillet, whose *Pour un nouveau roman* (1963; *For a New Novel: Essays on Fiction*, 1965) contains a fierce repudiation of the pathetic fallacy of the Romantics. Aguilera Malta commented that if the works that he and others were writing in this vein during the 1930's had been received more enthusiastically, they would have continued writing them, but the Socialist Realist tendency nearly swamped the other. Only in 1970 did he return with one of the best examples of the novel of Magical Realism, *Siete lunas y siete serpientes* (*Seven Serpents and Seven Moons*, 1979), with its eerie, brooding evocation of the Ecuadoran jungle. People are transformed into animals or appear to be manifestations of otherworldly beings, and even the narrator is unsure of whether to believe what he has recounted. By the time he provides the reader with a rational explanation, the reader is not persuaded that it is valid.

In the context of the same great pre-Columbian culture, the Peruvian José María Arguedas, while, like most of these authors, not an Indian himself, lamented the inadequacy of the Spanish language to express the realities experienced by the descendants of the Incas, for his native language was the Quechua of the Indian household servants among whom he spent his first few years. His powerful *Yawar fiesta* (English translation, 1985) was published in 1941.

In the same period, however, there was another current in Latin American fiction, based in the Río de la Plata (often referred to as River Plate) region, which has experienced little influence from indigenous groups. The Argentine Eduardo Mallea (1903-1982) was extremely influential in the years between 1934 and 1940, and in 1941, his *Todo verdor perecerá* (*All Green Shall Perish*, 1966) was published. It is a vaguely existentialist work of human alienation, angst, and the impossibility of meaningful communication between people, yet it lacks the existentialist's concept of self-affirmation through struggle. The works of the

Uruguayan Juan Carlos Onetti (1909-1994) are in much the same vein. His *Tierra de nadie* (*No Man's Land*, 1994) also appeared in 1941, and his later works, such as *El astillero* (1961; *The Shipyard*, 1968), present the same dismal atmosphere of hopelessness. The Argentine Ernesto Sábato (born 1911) deals with psychological and sociological issues. In *El túnel* (1948; *The Outsider*, 1950; also known as *The Tunnel*) he, too, presents the case of people together physically but spiritually isolated from one another. Later, in *Sobre héroes y tumbas* (1961; *On Heroes and Tombs*, 1981), he makes use of the Borgesian labyrinth as his hero descends to the network of sewers underlying Buenos Aires. His *Abaddón, el exterminador* (1974; *The Angel of Darkness*, 1991) focuses on the Argentine apocalyptic motif, seen earlier in Arlt's short story "La luna roja" and in Mallea's work.

There appeared a number of novels that might be considered transitional between the older regionalist and vanguard tendencies and the explosive *nouveau roman*, or New Novel. In them, there is what Fernando Alegría calls a thirst for universality, along with a further development of the long-standing movement to move from mimetic to genetic forms. If the Impressionist artist had demanded the right to portray his or her subjective reactions to the perceived, and Huidobro had insisted that the poet is a creator rather than an imitator, Borges would absorb such theory and delight in creating a mixture of philosophy, fantasy, and play elements. The novelists accepted his spirit of inventiveness, using language to draw the reader into a new sort of participatory experience. Among the important transitional novels is *Al filo del agua* (1947; *The Edge of the Storm*, 1963), by Agustín Yáñez (1904-1980), a work regional in its setting but more concerned with the interpersonal and intrapersonal conflicts of the characters and with the use of whatever narrative techniques the author believes are most effective in presenting them. Another experimenter is the aforementioned Asturias, whose *The President* uses vanguard techniques to re-create the atmosphere of dread that characterizes the Latin American dictatorship. In 1949, Carpentier published *El reino de este mundo* (*The Kingdom of This World*, 1957), introducing in it his preoccupation with the cyclical nature of tyranny and revolution, employing a highly cerebral style. In *Los pasos perdidos* (1953; *The Lost Steps*, 1956), Carpentier experimented with time, at the same time laying hold of the ongoing American fascination with the marvelous qualities of the land. In it, the protagonist is able to travel backward in time by departing from a modern city into the ever more primitive wilderness. Ten years later, Carpentier's masterful *El siglo de las luces* (1962; *Explosion in a Cathedral*, 1963) was to ring the historical novel firmly into the stream of the new fiction.

The Mexican novel, with its rich tradition leading from *The Itching Parrot* through the works of its revolution and those of Yáñez, began to come to full maturity in Rulfo's *Pedro Páramo*. Like much of Mexican fiction, it is preoccupied with death, and the reader eventually learns that all the characters, including the narrator, are dead. In a sense, this, too, is a transitional work, in that its setting is regional and it deals with the *caudillo* system and the revolution, but in it the act of making art is the controlling factor, and the predominant impression gained by the reader is one of the magical atmosphere into which the protagonist descends as he visits the town of his birth, an atmosphere made up of classical mythology, pre-Columbian ideologies, and even voodoo.

In his first novel, *La región más transparente* (1958; *Where the Air Is Clear*, 1960), Carlos Fuentes (born 1928) deals with the betrayal of the Mexican Revolution in a generally realistic manner, while frankly admitting the influence of Joyce, John Dos Passos, and several other foreign writers where technique is concerned. He attempts to incorporate an element of *lo real maravilloso* in the form of a character known as Ixca Cienfuegos, a sort of incarnation of Mexico's indigenous heritage, who, as a quasi-mythic being, is not very well integrated with the other characters. In his later novels, Fuentes moved more fully into the mythic mode, with the exception of *Las buenas conciencias* (1959; *The Good Conscience*, 1961) and *La muerte de Artemio Cruz* (1962; *The Death of Artemio Cruz*, 1964); in them and his short stories, he was refining the themes and techniques he was to use in his massive *Terra nostra*, which represents an attempt to mythologize the history of the West for the past two thousand years. In its extremely free handling of time, multiple reincarnations, appearances of supernatural beings such as Satan, and other features, it represents a manifestation of Magical Realism carried to the limit. While *Terra nostra* is his most important novel, his best technical achievement remains *The Death of Artemio Cruz*, a masterpiece of novelistic construction in which another character guilty of betraying the Mexican Revolution is viewed at the time of his death. Narration is variously in the first, second, and third persons, and in the present, future, and past tenses, respectively.

The New Latin American Novel
Fuentes's works are central to the related but separate phenomena known as the "New Latin American Novel" and the "Boom." The former refers to what most critics would call the coming of age of the Latin American novel, a gradual process that was accelerated in the 1950's. At that time, the prose fiction of the area was worthy of moving into the realm of world literature and exercising a good deal of influence of its own. On the other hand, the Boom, somewhat difficult to define at best, is fundamentally a phenomenon of the 1960's and early 1970's involving a more general recognition of the quality of the novels of a limited group of authors, some of whom believe that the Boom was essentially a phenomenon of public relations and economics, in that a few authors became celebrities and were at last able to make a living from their writing and closely related activities: Fuentes, García Márquez, Cortázar, Rulfo, Carpentier, Guillermo Cabrera Infante, Donoso, and Mario Vargas Llosa, among others. Donoso (1924-1996) wrote its story in his *Historia personal del "boom"* (1972; *The Boom in Spanish American Literature: A Personal History*, 1977), while Fuentes produced an excellent analysis of the larger movement, entitled *La nueva novela hispanoamericana*, in 1969.

The Chilean Donoso's novelistic production represents an advance in the novelist's art in his country at the same time that it continues that country's tradition of examining a segment of society by the use of carefully controlled language. His *Este domingo* (1965; *This Sunday*, 1967) dissects the wealthy class of Santiago, while the shorter *El lugar sin límites* (1966; *Hell Has No Limits*, 1972) deals with the underclass. His best novel, *El obsceno pájaro de la noche* (1970; *The Obscene Bird of Night*, 1973), employs more radical techniques.

The work of Julio Cortázar presents a major example of the movement of the Latin American novel into the universal sphere. The novel that first attracted the world's attention to him was *Hopscotch*. Moving from the sterile atmosphere of most of the Argentine novels of his generation, he presents a far more authentic existentialist hero in Horacio Oliveira (although author and character would deny the latter's adherence to the existentialist philosophy), who converses with others in Buenos Aires and Paris and almost reaches them. The essential point is that Oliveira is a person in motion, creating a persona, however defective, as he moves. There is humor in the work, the title of which presents the reader with a child's-play version of Borges's characteristic labyrinth. The chapters are not presented in any prescribed order; Cortázar only suggests a hopscotch order in which the reader might approach them. One of his important contributions to the New Novel is his insistence that the reader participate in the creative act with him. Five years after *Hopscotch*, speculating on the possibility of constructing a novel on the basis of "found" materials, including chapter 62 of the earlier novel, he produced *62: Modelo para armar* (1968; *62: A Model Kit*, 1972). Among Cortázar's other novels is *Libro de Manuel* (1973; *A Manual for Manuel*, 1978), a handbook for a child growing up in a world of radical change.

The Cuban exile Guillermo Cabrera Infante (1929-2005) produced two novels based on humor—especially puns and other forms of wordplay—and, as in *Hopscotch*, the frenetic search for creativity in chaotic language. *Tres tristes tigres* (1967, 1990; *Three Trapped Tigers*, 1971) challenges its reader to discover a meaningful structure, which emerges only on the level of a nebulous mythology created by language as it disintegrates. After a series of books of essays and short stories, in 1979 Cabrera Infante brought forth *La Habana para un infante difunto* (*Infante's Inferno*, 1984), a *Bildungsroman* dealing with the sexual initiation of a young would-be Don Juan in pre-Castro Havana.

Another explosive experiment with language and mythology in Cuba was *Paradiso* (1966; English translation, 1974), by the premier poet of that country, José Lezama Lima (1910-1976), a novel that in a sense constitutes his poetics. A dense atmosphere is created as the author overlays his characters' words and deeds with metaphor, in one expression of what the critics have termed the Cuban neobaroque. Lezama Lima, too, appears to be attempting to lend significance to his characters' acts by comparing them to the archetypal deeds of heroes.

Another major writer of the Cuban baroque tendency is Severo Sarduy (1937-1993), who wrote a number of novels characterized by an explosive language and humor, among them *De donde son los cantantes* (1967; *From Cuba with a Song,* 1972) and *Cobra* (1972; English translation, 1975). Reinaldo Arenas (1943-1990), forced to leave Cuba in 1980 as one of the boat people, combined features of Magical Realism with a baroque style in *El mundo alucinante* (1969; *Hallucinations: Being an Account of the Life and Adventures of Friar Servando Teresa de Mier,* 1971) but generally withdrew from both in his more important *El palacio de las blanquísimas mofetas* (1975; *The Palace of the White Skunks,* 1990).

Carpentier, who had done much to provoke the baroque movement in Cuba by his use of a self-consciously erudite style, in 1974 published *El recurso del método* (*Reasons of State,* 1976), which is one of a number of Latin American novels appearing in various countries in the space of a few years to deal with the subject of dictatorship. One of the persistent themes of the Latin American novel for more than a century had been the "shadow" of the dictator, the man depersonalized and viewed more as a malevolent force, as in *Amalia* or, a century later, in *The President,* but in some of the new novels of dictatorship there is a tendency analogous to the new presentation of Indians from their own perspective, as the reader now finds himself or herself inside the dictator's palace and, in some cases, inside his mind. Carpentier creates a powerful effect by the use of interior monologue to characterize his *Primer Magistrado.* In *Hijo de hombre* (1960; *Son of Man,* 1965), by the Paraguayan Augusto Roa Bastos (born 1917), the emphasis is still on the action of the people against tyranny as exemplified by the individual dictator, while Aguilera

Malta had moved into a radically mythic vision with *Seven Serpents and Seven Moons* in 1970 only to descend to an often ludicrous level through an excess of Magical Realism in *El secuestro del general (Babelandia,* 1985) in 1973. The novel of this tendency that has received the most attention is *El otoño del patriarca* (1975; *The Autumn of the Patriarch,* 1975), by Gabriel García Márquez, a personal view of the perennial dictator in decline. Exaggerating the already incredible events typical of such a dictator's rule, he attempts to re-create the stifling atmosphere of tyranny, an atmosphere that unfortunately is communicated to the text itself.

García Márquez had previously dealt with the towns of the Caribbean coast of Colombia, in that often seemingly regional focus of the New Novel that nevertheless takes on universal appeal in the nature of the experience created in the text. His *La hojarasca* (1955; *Leaf Storm, and Other Stories,* 1972) and *El coronel no tiene quien le escriba* (1961; *No One Writes to the Colonel,* 1968) had already established his reputation when he published *One Hundred Years of Solitude* in 1967. This is the Latin American novel that has had the greatest impact worldwide, and it won for García Márquez the Nobel Prize in Literature in 1982. The novel is the history of a fictional town called Macondo and of the Buendía family within it. Reversing normal values so that the commonplace appears marvelous and vice versa, and exercising the storyteller's right to exaggerate and embellish, García Márquez has created another prime example of Magical Realism, one in which the atmosphere is the private property of author and reader, bearing little relationship to reality outside the text.

It subsequently became difficult to establish trends and tendencies in other Latin American fiction. There has been a wide variety of subjects and treatments, ranging from the Argentine Manuel Puig's tongue-in-cheek satires on pop culture in such works as *La traición de Rita Hayworth* (1968; *Betrayed by Rita Hayworth,* 1971) and *Pubis angelical* (1979; English translation, 1986) to the dense, brooding works of José María Arguedas, most notably his *Deep Rivers.* One of the foremost novelists of the period is the Peruvian Mario Vargas Llosa (born 1936), much of whose work has to do with the military establishment, prostitution, or a combination of the two. With *La ciudad y los perros*

(1962; *The Time of the Hero*, 1966), his credentials were established, and *La casa verde* (1965; *The Green House*, 1968) and *Conversación en la catedral* (1969; *Conversation in the Cathedral*, 1975) continued in the vein of almost bitter analyses of Peruvian society. With *Pantaleón y las visitadoras* (1973; *Captain Pantoja and the Special Service*, 1978), however, he was drawn in spite of himself into a humorous treatment of the military and prostitution themes, and this approach continued in *La tía Julia y el escribidor* (1977; *Aunt Julia and the Scriptwriter*, 1982), a masterful example of the New Novelist's concern with revealing in his or her work the process involved in its composition. His *La guerra del fin del mundo* (1981; *The War of the End of the World*, 1984) is a long, difficult, and powerful novel based on the same historical incident that inspired Euclides da Cunha's *Rebellion in the Backlands*.

In Brazil, around 1960, there came about a rejection of the emphasis on the social message of the novel in favor of a concentration on the craft of the writer. The most prominent novelists of this generation have been João Guimarães Rosa (1908-1967) and Clarice Lispector (1925-1977). The former's interest in universalizing local experience leads to a concentration on the mythic and folkloric traditions of the Brazilian outback, expressed in a Joycean language rich in neologisms and regional speech. His work culminates in *Grande Sertão: Veredas* (1956; *The Devil to Pay in the Backlands*, 1963). Lispector's mentor was Lúcio Cardoso (1912-1962), whose *Crónica da casa assassinada* (1959) is considered one of the best of modern Brazilian novels. Lispector herself departs from Guimarães Rosa in emphasizing thematic development over technique, in works such as *A maçã no escuro* (1961; *The Apple in the Dark*, 1967). One of Brazil's most popular novelists is Jorge Amado (1912-2001), whose works contain some of the finest treatments of the feminine experience in Latin American literature.

The Late Twentieth Century

After the Boom generation, the 1980's inaugurated a new era in which women, gays, and Afro-Hispanics were finally allowed into the literary canon. While a Boom novel typically portrayed the earnest search of the protagonist for the meaning of life, the post-Boom novel was more likely to describe a journey of this kind with parodic humor; pastiche was its favored trope. It is true that the Boom writers continued to publish during the 1980's—García Márquez wrote *Crónica de una muerte anunciada* (1981; *Chronicle of a Death Foretold*, 1982); Fuentes, *Gringo viejo* (1985; *The Old Gringo*, 1985); and Vargas Llosa, *¿Quién mató a Palomino Molero?* (1987; *Who Killed Palomino Molero?*, 1987)—but this era was especially characterized by a group of new writers.

Luna caliente (1983; *Sultry Moon*, 1998), by the Argentine Mempo Giardinelli (born 1947), tells the story of a young man, Ramiro Bermúdez, recently returned to Buenos Aires from Paris, who has a distinguished career before him but whose life swiftly disintegrates once he becomes fascinated with Araceli, the thirteen-year-old daughter of a doctor friend, whom he rapes and kills (or so he thinks). The novel parodies the genre of the *novela negra* (hard-boiled crime novel) to produce a gripping plot, combined with a Cortazarian sense of the uncanny that unexpectedly explodes that world from within. *Ardiente paciencia* (1985; *Burning Patience*, 1987), by the Chilean Antonio Skármeta (born 1940), centers on the love affair and eventual marriage of Mario Jiménez and Beatriz González. In order to win Beatriz's heart, Mario seeks the help of the famous Chilean poet, Pablo Neruda, for whom he works as the postman. In a playfully parodic way, literature is depicted in the novel as a cultural reservoir which plays a direct formative role in the everyday lives of ordinary people. *Gazapo* (1965; English translation, 1968), by the Mexican Gustavo Sainz (born 1940), tells the story of a group of adolescent boys living in Mexico City who share their tales of sexual and criminal exploits with each other. The novel suggests that the telling of the stories is more important than the events that they supposedly relate, all of which gives the novel a playful feel.

It was the novels of the female authors of the post-Boom that caught the public's attention. While there were earnest political novels written by women during this period—*Conversación al sur* (1981; *Mothers and Shadows*, 1986) by Marta Traba (1930-1983) was the prototype—it was the way in which *La casa de los espíritus*

(1982; *The House of the Spirits,* 1985) by Isabel Allende (born 1942) mixed politics with Magical Realism that captured the readers' imagination in Latin America and Europe. The novel traces the political struggle in twentieth century Chile between the Left (symbolized by Pedro García; his son, Pedro Segundo; and his grandson, Pedro Tercero) and the Right (personified by Esteban Trueba). Whereas the Left is presented in terms of continuity through family lineage, the Right is shown finally to be issueless, since Esteban Trueba's male progeny either become Marxists (Jaime) or dropouts (Nicolás) and his female progeny fall in love with revolutionaries.

Allende's novel is ultimately a positive—as well as playful—affirmation of the value of solidarity in the face of evil and political oppression. *Como agua para chocolate: Novela de entregas mensuales con recetas, amores, y remedios caseros* (1989; *Like Water for Chocolate: A Novel in Monthly Installments with Recipes, Romances, and Home Remedies,* 1992), by the Mexican novelist Laura Esquivel (born 1950), redolent of the television soap (a great favorite in Mexico), is, in essence, a feminist counterversion of the Mexican Revolution, offering a kitchen's-eye view of those turbulent years that is at odds with the masculinist rhetoric of the history books. This novel was one of the best to emerge in the post-Boom era, and its humor and metaphoric flair were successfully carried over into the 1992 movie version, which was a box-office hit in the United States as well as Mexico.

The most significant Hispanic gay writer, the Argentine Manuel Puig (1932-1990), had published his major works in the 1970's—his masterpiece *El beso de la mujer araña* (*Kiss of the Spider Woman,* 1979) came out in 1976—and these set the scene for the acceptance of gay writing in the following decade. *Otra vez el mar* (1982; *Farewell to the Sea,* 1986) by the Cuban Reinaldo Arenas is written from the perspective of a young Cuban couple who are spending a holiday on the beach. There is a plot of sorts (a woman moves with her son into the cabin next door, and the latter, mysteriously, is found dead later on that day), but more striking is the novel's Joycean rejection of the limitations of Euclidean space and time and its playful use of language. *La nave de los locos* (1984; *The Ship of Fools,* 1989) by the Uruguayan-

Spanish writer Cristina Peri Rossi (born 1941) is a postmodern, gay text that rewrites the alphabet of Christian culture. It describes the misadventures of a character, whose name is simply a letter of the alphabet, equis (that is, *X*), in a variety of urban settings; the novel includes episodes describing sordid sexual encounters, far-fetched dream sequences, and Equis's philosophizing about life and the universe with his companions, Vercingetorix and Graciela.

Like gay writing, Afro-Hispanic literature also created space for itself in the new literary canon of the 1980's, and here the major work is *Changó, el gran putas* (1983) by the Colombian Manuel Zapata Olivella (born 1920), which has five parts, each of which traces successive historical eras in which the Africans struggled against oppression in the New World. Zapata Olivella's novel expresses a wake-up call for all Americans of African descent to take up the fight for the right to own their own culture.

— William L. Siemens, updated by Stephen M. Hart

Learn More

Boland, Roy C., and Sally Harvey, eds. *Magical Realism and Beyond: The Contemporary Spanish and Latin American Novel.* Madrid: Vox/AHS, 1991. Explores Latin American authors' use of Magical Realism in modern long fiction.

King, John, ed. *Modern Latin American Fiction: A Survey.* London: Faber and Faber, 1987. An excellent collection of first-rate, readable essays on all the major novelists of the Boom, including Gabriel García Márquez, Carlos Fuentes, Mario Vargas Llosa, and Julio Cortázar.

Martin, Gerald. *Journeys Through the Labyrinth: Latin American Fiction in the Twentieth Century.* London: Routledge, 1989. An elegantly written overview of the development of the Latin American novel in the twentieth century. Highly recommended.

Shaw, Donald L. *The Post-Boom in Spanish American Fiction.* Saratoga Springs: State University of New York Press, 1998. An authoritative, hard-hitting survey of the main figures of the post-Boom novel written by an acknowledged expert.

Sommer, Doris. *Foundational Fictions: The National Romances of Latin America.* Berkeley: University of California Press, 1991. The best study of the Latin American nineteenth century novel. Separate chapters treat *Amalia, Sab,* and *Iracema,* examining the interplay between the path toward nationhood and the journey of love in those novels.

Swanson, Philip. *The New Novel in Latin America: Politics and Popular Culture After the Boom.* Manchester: Manchester University Press, 1995. Authoritative overview of the work of the post-Boom novelists. Contains separate chapters on Manuel Puig and Isabel Allende, among others.

Williams, Raymond L. *The Modern Latin American Novel.* New York: Twayne, 1998. Part of Twayne's Critical History of the Novel series, this is an excellent introduction to long fiction in Latin America.

Latino Poetry

In the 1960's and 1970's, poets and other writers of Mexican, Puerto Rican, and Cuban descent formed three discrete groups in literary response to various social, historical, and cultural impulses in the United States at that time. The Civil Rights movement inspired literary Chicanos and Puerto Ricans (especially the Nuyoricans, as Puerto Ricans in New York were known) to write about their experiences in their own voices, which frequently were excluded from mainstream publications. The Cuban American poets of this period wrote primarily in Spanish and in response to the historical circumstance of their exile from Cuba. Chicanos, Puerto Ricans, and Cuban Americans still comprise the largest groups of Latino poets in the United States, although the field has grown to include writers of other backgrounds.

Literary Magazines and Anthologies

The literary magazines and small press publications of the burgeoning Chicano, Nuyorican, and Cuban American literary culture are an essential source of information on the initial development of Latino poetry. Among the magazines of varying regional or national renown, significance, and circulation were the Chicano periodicals *De Colores* (Albuquerque, New Mexico), *El Grito* and *Grito del Sol* (Berkeley, California), and *Tejidos* (Austin, Texas); the Puerto Rican diaspora magazine *The Rican* (Chicago); and the Cuban American review *Areíto* (New York). Some of these small journals were edited by leading poets, such as *Maize* (San Diego), by Alurista, and *Mango* (San Jose), by Lorna Dee Cervantes. These and numerous other journals, whether interdisciplinary or purely literary in focus (and many of them highly ephemeral), provided a necessary publishing outlet for the alternative voices erupting throughout the United States during the 1960's and 1970's. These publications have recorded a momentous turning point in American literature.

No serious study of the origins and development of Latino literature of any genre can be undertaken without considering

Revista Chicano-Riqueña (1973-1985) and its continuation in *The Americas Review* (1986-1999). A long-running literary magazine founded by the historian and scholar Nicolás Kanellos, the journal focused on creative writing, with interviews, literary essays, scholarly articles, book reviews, and visual art complementing each issue. Beginning with the premier issue, the work of most of the major Chicano, Nuyorican, and, as coverage quickly expanded, other Latino poets appeared in the pages of these magazines, in many cases marking the first appearance of a writer on the literary radar. Tino Villanueva, Alurista, Lorna Dee Cervantes, Victor Hernández Cruz, Gary Soto, Ricardo Sánchez, Tato Laviera, Sandra María Esteves, Jimmy Santiago Baca, and Pat Mora—to indicate only a few—figure among the Chicano and Nuyorican poets featured. In addition, the magazines published the poetry of writers better known for different genres, such as Rolando Hinojosa, Carlos Morton, Miguel Piñero, and Tomás Rivera. Many of these poets and other writers helped shape and influence the journal by doubling as contributing editors or editorial board members. Special or monographic issues focused on particular topics within U.S. Hispanic literature. The celebrated *Woman of Her Word: Hispanic Women Write*, edited by Chicana poet Evangelina Vigil (volume 11, nos. 3/4, 1983) anthologizes the finest Latina writing of that time. Several issues emphasize the Latino writers active in various regions of the United States, including Chicago (volume 5, no. 1, 1977), Wisconsin (volume 13, no. 2, 1985), Houston (volume 16, no. 1, 1988), and the Pacific Northwest (volume 23, nos. 3/4, 1995). The tenth and twentieth anniversary anthologies (1982 and 1992) provide a selection of the major poetical works published in the *Revista* and the *Review* during those decades. *The Americas Review* ceased publication in 1999, but Kanellos's singular mission to promote and publish Hispanic literature of the United States would continue through the ongoing publications of Arte Público Press (founded in 1979) and the activities of the Recovering the U.S. Hispanic Literary Heritage project (established in 1992).

 The Bilingual Review/La Revista Bilingüe (founded in 1974) is another long-standing periodical fundamental to the study of Latino literature. Primarily an academic journal of scholarly articles, book reviews, and interviews relating to bilingualism and to U.S. Hispanic literature, *The Bilingual Review* has not published the same volume of creative writing as did *Revista Chicano-Riqueña* and *The Americas Review*, despite a stated focus as a literary magazine. Even so, poetry appears in almost every issue (Gustavo Pérez Firmat, Martín Espada, and Judith Ortiz Cofer are among the poets represented) and is the subject of some of the research and interviews. More significant to the study of Latino poetry is Bilingual Press/Editorial Bilingüe, the press established by the journal in 1976. The extensive poetry backlist includes not only Chicanos of early distinction (Alurista, Alma Luz Villanueva, Tino Villanueva, and Bernice Zamora), but also Latinos of later periods (Marjorie Agosín, Elías Miguel Muñoz, Virgil Suárez, and Gina Valdés, for instance). Several anthologies published or distributed by the press, along with monographic issues of *The Bilingual Review*, contain representative Latino poetry in a variety of specialized categories. These include poets in New York (*Los paraguas amarillos: Los poetas latinos en New York*, 1983), poetry for or about young adults (*Cool Salsa: Bilingual Poems on Growing Up Latino in the United States*, 1994), and women poets (*Floricanto Sí! A Collection of Latina Poetry*, 1998). Such collections afford easy and important access to the vast and ever-flourishing numbers of Hispanic poets who have not gained the national prominence of the proportionately few better-publicized writers.

Anthologies, like literary magazines, are an invaluable primary source of Chicano, Nuyorican, and Cuban American poetry. Early anthologies like Luis Valdez and Stan Steiner's *Aztlán: An Anthology of Mexican American Literature* (1972) and Alurista's *Festival de Flor y Canto: An Anthology of Chicano Literature* (1976) indicate that Chicano literature, including poetry, was already under critical consideration by the early 1970's. (Virginia Ramos Foster annotates more than twenty-five such compilations from that decade in the Mexican American literature chapter of *Sourcebook of Hispanic Culture in the United States*, 1982, edited by David William Foster.)

Several early anthologies of Puerto Rican and Nuyorican literature share the distinction of bringing together island and mainland writers, in seeming recognition of the ongoing aesthetic and literary historical connections between "the two islands," Puerto Rico and Manhattan. (This concern exists to the present day for some scholars and compilers.) These compilations include Alfredo Matilla and Iván Silén's *The Puerto Rican Poets/Los poetas puertorriqueños* (1972), María Teresa Babín and Stan Steiner's *Borinquen: An Anthology of Puerto Rican Literature* (1974), and Julio Marzán's *Inventing a Word: An Anthology of Twentieth-Century Puerto Rican Poetry* (1980). Roberto Santiago has taken the same composite approach to Puerto Rican literature in *Boricuas, Influential Puerto Rican Writers: An Anthology* (1995). On the other hand, Miguel Algarín and Miguel Piñero's landmark *Nuyorican Poetry: An Anthology of Puerto Rican Words and Feelings* (1975) documents exclusively the initial period of creativity and so is the best starting point for any retrospective study of Nuyorican poetry.

The first Cuban American literature anthologies also emphasize the connections between writing in the United States and the homeland, Cuba. For example, several poets who write in Spanish in exile appear in Orlando Rodríguez Sardiñas's *La última poesía cubana: Antología reunida, 1959-1973* (1973; the latest Cuban poetry: an anthology) and exile poets are the exclusive focus of Angel Aparicio Laurencio's *Cinco poetisas cubanas, 1935-1969* (1970; five Cuban women poets); both collections were published in the United States. By the same token, an early critical dictionary, *Bibliografía crítica de la poesía cubana (exilio: 1959-1971)* (1972; critical bibliography of Cuban exile poetry), by exile writer Matías Montes Huidobro with Yara González, confirms that virtually all the poetry books of the decade under discussion were written in Spanish. The poetry in Silvia Burunat and Ofelia García's *Veinte años de literatura cubanoamericana: Antología 1962-1982* (1988; twenty years of Cuban American literature: an anthology) illustrates the tendency throughout two decades of exile and immigration to explore issues of identity within the context of the nascent Cuban American experience (and, in the 1970's as in the preceding decade, in Spanish). Ultimately, the study of the Chicano, Nuyorican, or Cuban American poetry in the foregoing and similar anthologies provides a synopsis both of individual poets and of each discrete group, at specific moments as well as over time.

Early Chicano Poetry

Many of the poets featured in the early Chicano anthologies or in other publications continued to publish or to appear in later anthologies, suggesting their ongoing significance in Chicano literary history even as others emerged. These include Alurista, Angela de Hoyos, José Montoya, Luis Omar Salinas, Raúl Salinas, and Tino Villanueva. Rodolfo Gonzales's *I Am Joaquín/Yo soy Joaquín* (1967) and the poetry of Ricardo Sánchez are especially representative of this early period. The bilingual *I Am Joaquín/Yo soy Joaquín*, by Denver-based activist and writer Gonzales, may be the single best-known Chicano poem of any period. It has been widely read, reproduced, and distributed by newspapers and magazines, students and teachers, performers, labor organizers, and Chicano organizations and organizers in every possible educational, cultural, political, and social milieu. *I Am Joaquín* is as much a historical commentary as a modern epic poem, and intentionally so. An early popular edition (Bantam Pathfinder, 1972) even supplemented the poem with paintings depicting historical events and a chronology of Mexican and Mexican American history. Also, as Gonzales himself states in the informative fact list that prefaces the poem, "*I Am Joaquín* was the first work of poetry to be published by Chicanos for Chicanos and is the forerunner of the Chicano cultural renaissance." Gonzales combines the poetic sensibilities of Walt Whitman's "Song of Myself" and Allen Ginsberg's "Howl" (1956) as Joaquín, a Chicano Everyman, explores himself and the history of the Chicano people—from the pre-Columbian and colonial periods, through independence and revolution up to the present day:

> I am Joaquín,
> lost in a world of confusion,
>
> .   .   .   .
>
> and destroyed by modern society.

Repetition, enumeration, and parallelism dominate the poem's short lines and long stanzas. The liberal use of displaced lines and capitalized words emphasizes key concepts, such as "MY OWN PEOPLE," "THE GROUND WAS MINE," and, in the prophetic and self-affirming final lines of the poem, "I SHALL ENDURE!/ I WILL ENDURE!"

The late Ricardo Sánchez also began writing in social protest. The lines that frame "In Exile" (from Sánchez's first book, *Canto y grito mi liberación*, 1971; I sing and shout my liberation) exemplify several of the salient characteristics of his poetry: the typographic hodgepodge and free verse, the sensation of getting out as much as possible in a single breath, and the vociferous sense of both self and people.

> it is by way of definition that i
> now write this short introduction of myself,
>
> . . . .
> and
> i write of my people, LA RAZA!

Elsewhere in this collection as in all his subsequent books, Sánchez frequently writes in Spanish or a mixture of Spanish and English, experiments with word formation ("soul/stream"; *piensasentimientos*, or *"mindfeelings"*; *mentealmacuerpo*, or mindsoulbody), inserts expository or poetic prose texts, and articulates his aesthetic and political visions. The enthusiasm and immediacy of his Beat-inflected voice readily draw the reader into the experience. Even the titles of Sánchez's books and poems emphasize this aesthetic of spontaneity: "This of Being the Soul/ Voice for My Own Conscienceness Is Too Much (Petersburg, Virginny)," *Hechizospells: Poetry/Stories/Vignettes/Articles/Notes on the Human Condition of Chicanos and Pícaros, Words and Hopes Within Soulmind* (1976) and *Eagle-Visioned/Feathered Adobes: Manito Sojourns and Pachuco Ramblings October 4th to 24th, 1981* (1990). Sánchez's poetry has enjoyed wide circulation in both small and university presses, and has even been published in a private edition (*Amerikan Journeys = Jornadas americanas*, 1994, in Iowa City by publisher and longtime Sánchez associate Rob Lewis). The publication of *Chicano Timespace: The Poetry and Politics of Ricardo Sánchez* (2001), a scholarly monograph by Miguel R. López, establishes in no uncertain terms Sánchez's position in the canon of Chicano—and, by extension, Latino and American—poetry.

Nuyorican Poetry: 1970's

The beginnings of Nuyorican poetry were equally strident. The anthology edited by Miguel Algarín and Miguel Piñero, *Nuyorican Poetry: An Anthology of Puerto Rican Words and Feelings* (1975), introduced a wide audience to the recent poetry that was coming out of the experience of being Puerto Rican in New York City. Even the title of the anthology captures the emotive lyricism that underlies the use of an ethnic-specific lexicon ("Puerto Rican words") to document a group experience ("[Puerto Rican] feelings") in poetry inspired by a place ("Nuyorican poetry"). Several of the featured writers went on to distinguish themselves in poetry beyond the anthology, including Sandra María Esteves, José Angel Figueroa, Pedro Pietri, and the compilers themselves. (Two poets active in the early 1970's, Victor Hernández Cruz and Tato Laviera, are not in the Nuyorican anthology.) The late Piñero, known more for the play *Short Eyes* (pr. 1974) than for his poetry, made a significant contribution nonetheless. The selections in the anthology exemplify his savage irreverence. In "The Book of Genesis According to Saint Miguelito," for instance, Piñero derides the God who created ghettos, slums, lead-based paint, hepatitis, capitalism, and overpopulation. A later work, the much-anthologized "A Lower East Side Poem" (*La Bodega Sold Dreams*, 1980), covers similar ground as the poet contemplates dying among the pimping, shooting, drug dealing, and other unsavory activities of the neighborhood. The perverse but catchy refrain "then scatter my ashes thru/ the Lower East Side" affirms both Piñero's allegiance to his barrio roots and the musical rhythms that inspire many Nuyorican poets.

While social reality is a thematic interest and protest a dominant tone throughout *Nuyorican Poetry*, Algarín and Piñero clearly were committed to promoting diverse voices. The "dusmic" poetry of the third and final section of the book, for example, proposes the possibility of finding love, positive energy, and balance. Esteves's "Blanket Weaver" exemplifies this impulse: "weave us a song of many threads/ that will dance with the colors of our people/ and cover us with the warmth of peace." (Some of Esteves's later poems, such as those in *Bluestown Mockingbird Mambo* (1990), indicate a similarly broad array of preoccupations and interests; these include a touching elegy for the artist Jorge Soto, numerous love poems, and strong but poetic statements against brutal regimes in Guatemala and South Africa.) Also, Algarín's introduction to the anthology, "Nuyorican Language," constitutes an indispensable discussion of the poet and poetry in the Nuyorican context, in both theory and practice. Algarín, in fact, is located squarely in the mainstream of contemporary poetry and poetics. He has translated into English the poetry of Pablo Neruda, he has written extensively on poetics, and he has taken his literature classes from Rutgers University to the Passaic River and Paterson Falls to enhance his students' study of William Carlos Williams's *Paterson* (1946-1958). The Nuyorican Poets Café, a cultural-arts venue Algarín founded in 1974, has broadened considerably the scope of its poetry and performance activities.

One of many remarkable books to come out of the Nuyorican movement is Pedro Pietri's *Puerto Rican Obituary* (1973), published by the progressive Monthly Review Press. In the title poem (which had achieved underground cult status long before its initial publication), the generic Puerto Ricans Juan, Miguel, Milagros, Olga, and Manuel trudge repeatedly through the daily routines in "Spanish Harlem" that only bring them closer to death and, ultimately, burial on Long Island. In the final analysis, only the afterlife and Puerto Rico offer respite from the poverty and discrimination suffered in New York: "PUERTO RICO IS A BEAUTIFUL PLACE/ PUERTORRIQUENOS ARE A BEAUTIFUL RACE." Pietri is at his best with the antiestablishment rhetoric with which he parodies religious and civic mainstays like the Lord's Prayer and the Pledge of Allegiance, as in "The Broken English Dream," in which he pledges allegiance "to the flag/ of the united states/ of installment plans." The contrast between New York and Puerto Rico—and between English and Spanish—underscores the irony of the political status of Puerto Ricans vis-à-vis the racial discrimination and linguistic choices awaiting them as they pursue the elusive American Dream.

Cuban American Poetry: 1960's-1970's

Spanish, not English, was the language of record for Cuban exile poets and Cuban American poets during the 1960's and 1970's, so language choice per se was not a conscious issue of either form or content, as it was for many Chicano and Nuyorican writers at that time. In fact, in contrast to the Nuyorican example, Cuban poetry in the United States of this early period often was seen as part of Cuban literature or Cuban exile literature elsewhere, not as a nascent branch of American ethnic literature. (Naomi Lindstrom analyzes this problem in the chapter on Cuban American and mainland Puerto Rican literature in *Sourcebook of Hispanic Culture in the United States.*) Even so, a number of individual poems anthologized by Silvia Burunat and Ofelia García in *Veinte años de literatura cubanoamerica: Antología, 1962-1982* (1988; twenty years of Cuban American literature) illustrate the tendency to explore issues of identity within the context of Cuban exile in the United States.

Uva Clavijo often defines her exile, as she does here in "Declaración" (declaration), in highly specific spatiotemporal terms:

> I, Uva A. Clavijo,
>
> . . . .
>
> declare, today, the last Monday in September,
> that as soon as I can I will leave everything
> and return to Cuba.

The enumeration of what she is prepared to give up—a house in the suburbs, credit, a successful husband and beautiful family, perfect English (in short, all the trappings of the American Dream)—presents a striking contrast to the specificity and simplicity of this declaration. In "Al cumplir veinte años de exilio" (upon completing twenty years of exile), Clavijo commemorates that anniversary as any other, pondering the growth and development of a Spanish-speaking, Cuban self formed "before confronting/ an immigration official/ for the first time." By the same token, Clavijo frames "Miami 1980" with very precise markers that pinpoint her loneliness and isolation: "Here, Miami, nineteen/ eighty, and my loneliness. . . .// And my astonishing loneliness." The simplicity of Clavijo's expressive and emotional needs in these poems might explain why she favors relatively short lines. In the Miami poem, for example, three especially significant lines succinctly capture the essence of the poem and the poet: "and hatred," "in the distance," and "loneliness."

For some Cuban American poets, the confrontation with New York is not unlike that of the Nuyoricans. In "Caminando por las calles de Manhattan" (walking through the streets of Manhattan), Alberto Romero meets with drug addicts, prostitutes, go-go dancers, and other marginal characters who people the streets of New York. Yet a sense of order and belonging pervades his search for God amid this riffraff:

> in the Jews of Astoria, in the Italians
> of Flatbush . . .
> in the Dominicans of 110th Street, in the South
> Americans
> of Queens, in the Cuban refugees.

Place influences identity for Lourdes Casal, too, who is "too much a Habanera to be a New Yorker,/ too much a New Yorker to be, . . . / anything else" ("Para Ana Veldford"). Despite some suggestive parallels with the Puerto Rican and Chicano experiences, however, the early Cuban American poetry written in Spanish was inaccessible to a broad readership of Latino literature. Moreover, the language factor has precluded the inclusion of these poets in English-language college textbooks like *The Prentice Hall Anthology of Latino Literature* (2002, edited by Eduardo del Rio).

Chicano, Puerto Rican, and Cuban American Poetry: 1980's-1990's

By the 1980's and 1990's, the diverse body of Latino literature by Chicano, Puerto Rican, and Cuban writers in the United States was receiving considerable critical, popular, and pedagogical attention. As current compilers are quick to point out, Latino poets—including those trained in graduate writing programs— were being recognized more widely through national fellow- ships, prizes, and other honors and awards. They, like other American writers, were publishing in mainstream literary maga- zines like *The American Poetry Review, The Kenyon Review, Parnas- sus,* and *Poetry.* U.S. Latino literature in English was being in- cluded in general anthologies of American literature and in American literature curricula in North American colleges and universities.

Gary Soto, Lorna Dee Cervantes, and Jimmy Santiago Baca are some of the Chicano poets of broad acclaim and distribu- tion at the beginning of the twenty-first century. Soto is not only one of the most prolific Latino poets but also probably the best known outside the confines of Chicano and Latino poetry. His sense of humor, the accessibility of his poetic language, and his sensitive portrayal of youth also have contributed to his success as a writer for young adults and children. (For many years Soto was virtually the only Chicano writing for the important young- adult market.) Like Soto, Chicana writer Pat Mora is a prolific poet and children's author. She counts several books of poetry among her works in various genres, including *Chants* (1984), *Borders* (1986), *Communion* (1991), *Agua Santa = Holy Water* (1995), and *Aunt Carmen's Book of Practical Saints* (1997). From her perspective as a woman and a Latina, Mora writes elo- quently about diverse topics, including marriage, family life, and children; traditional and modern Latino and Mexican In- dian culture; the Catholic devotion of saints; women; and the southwestern desert. In "Curandera" (folk healer) from *Chants,* for example, Mora interweaves several of these interests. When the villagers go to the healer for treatment, "She listens to their stories, and she listens/ to the desert, always to the desert." In many other poems, Mora similarly portrays the nurturing quali- ties of the southwestern desert, as in "Mi Madre" (my mother), also from *Chants,* "I say teach me. . . . / She: the desert/ She: strong mother." Like the traditional healer and the desert- mother, the many women who populate Mora's poems (the grandmothers, mothers, daughters, and granddaughters, the famous and the humble alike) tend to be strong, wise, and nurturing. That is not to say these women are uncritical, though. Extending the desert-woman metaphor in "Desert Women" (in *Borders*), Mora writes: "Don't be deceived./ When we bloom, we stun."

The 1975 publication of Algarín and Piñero's anthology *Nuyorican Poetry* helped pave the way for a later compilation of Puerto Rican writing, Faythe Turner's *Puerto Rican Writers at Home in the USA: An Anthology* (1991). Turner includes poets of both generations and recognizes the significant expansion of the Puerto Rican literary diaspora outside of New York. The newer generation includes poets Martín Espada, Judith Ortiz Cofer, Rosario Morales, and Aurora Levins Morales. Espada's poetry is informed variously by his own Puerto Rican heritage, experiences in the Latino enclaves of the United States, and radical causes in the United States and Latin America. Ortiz Cofer's *The Latin Deli: Prose and Poetry* (1993) invites the reader to negotiate a challenging but engaging combination of stories, essays, and poems that "tell the lives of barrio women." Similarly experimental in composition is Morales and Levins Morales's *Getting Home Alive* (1986), a mother-daughter collaboration of mixed genre (including poetry, poetic prose, and memoir), further distinguished by the intermingling of texts written by either mother or daughter. Significantly, the last piece, "Ending Poem," is itself a collaborative product (as indicated by the distinct typefaces):

> I am what I am.
> *A child of the Americas.*
> A light-skinned mestiza of the Caribbean.
> *A child of many diaspora, born into this continent at a*
>   *crossroads.*

These Caribbean women are not exclusively African or Taíno or European: "We are new . . . / *And we are whole.*" And their measured celebration of multiculturalism contrasts markedly with the earlier antipoetic angst of the Nuyorican experience.

Unlike their predecessors, the new Cuban American poets write in English and as part of American, not Cuban, literature. Dionisio D. Martínez, for example, appears in the 1996 edition of *The Norton Anthology of Poetry*. In *Little Havana Blues: A Cuban-American Literature Anthology* (1996), Delia Poey and Virgil Suárez have identified a corpus of sixteen recent poets, several of whom appear in many other groupings of canonical Latino or Cuban American poetry (among them Carolina Hospital, Ricardo Pau-Llosa, Pablo Medina, and Gustavo Pérez Firmat). The poetry of scholar and writer Gustavo Pérez Firmat offers a good example of the new Cuban American poetry. As he explains in his memoir, *Next Year in Cuba: A Cubano's Coming-of-Age in America* (1995): "Born in Cuba but made in the U.S.A., I can no longer imagine living outside American culture and the English language." Much of Pérez Firmat's English-language and bilingual poetry in *Carolina Cuban* (pb. in *Triple Crown: Chicano, Puerto Rican, and Cuban-American Poetry*, 1987) and *Bilingual Blues: Poems, 1981-1994* (1995) supports this notion. For example, he calls the Spanish-language preface to *Carolina Cuban* "Vo(I)ces," in deceptively simple recognition of an anglophone self (*I*) located in between Spanish (*voces*) and English (*voices*). In the verse dedication to the same collection he ponders the paradox of writing in a language to which he does not "belong," at the same time belonging "nowhere else,/ if not here/ in English." Pérez Firmat explores the equivalence of language and place further in "Home," in which home is as much a linguistic as a geographic construct: "[L]et him have a tongue,/ a story, a geography." Bilingual wordplay at the service of identity is Pérez Firmat's forte, as in "Son-Sequence": "Son as plural being./ Son as rumba beat./ Son as progeny." Suggestively, the confluence in this poem of language (*son*, "they are," from the Spanish verb of being *ser*), culture (the Cuban *son*, a musical form), and ancestry (the English *son* or offspring) acknowledges some of the time-honored preoccupations of many Latino poets.

End of the Twentieth Century
In the 1980's and 1990's, the changing demographic patterns of Spanish-speaking immigrants combined with an ever-increasing

interest in multicultural literature in both the marketplace and the classroom to bring broader recognition for Latino literature. Anthologies with a pan-Latino approach not only have brought together Chicano, Puerto Rican, and Cuban American writers but also have introduced new writers from other Latino backgrounds. Certainly Julia Alvarez, a Dominican born in New York City, is the most prominent of these writers (if for her fiction more than her poetry). As in her fiction, though, she has examined various problems of language and identity in her poetry (*The Other Side/El otro lado* [1995], *Homecoming: New and Collected Poems* [1996], and *Seven Trees* [1998]). Of special interest in Alvarez's poetry and poetics is the interplay of identity, form, and the poetic tradition as she proposes new ways to approach set forms (the sonnet, the villanelle, and the sestina) that reflect her identity as a woman poet, a bilingual poet, and a Latina poet.

The example of Alvarez underscores some significant developments in the field of Latino poetry since the publication of foundational works like *I Am Joaquín* and *Puerto Rican Obituary*. Latina poets, of course, receive more attention now than ever before. In addition, however, Latinas are included in the context of women poets in general. Similarly, anthologies and research have brought together Latinos and other poets on the basis of broad multicultural considerations. Some Latino poets also write for a young adult or children's audience. Other configurations have incorporated Latino poetry into American diaspora literature, Jewish letters, border writing, or gay and lesbian literature. Perhaps the most sweeping trend is the approach championed by the research activities of the Recovering the U.S. Hispanic Literary Heritage project: the inclusion of all Hispanic literature written in the United States, of all periods and in Spanish as well as in English. The project's anthology *Herencia: The Anthology of Hispanic Literature of the United States* (2002, edited by Nicolás Kanellos) reflects this objective. In fact, in this body of literature, Latino literature written in English is incorporated within the broader parameters of U.S. Hispanic literature.

         — *Catharine E. Wall (including original translations)*

Learn More

Cruz, Victor Hernández, Leroy V. Quintana, and Virgil Suarez, eds. *Paper Dance: Fifty-five Latino Poets.* New York: Persea, 1995. Notable for the inclusion of bicultural poets from numerous backgrounds, primarily Chicano and Mexican, Dominican, Cuban, and Puerto Rican, but also Colombian, Ecuadorian, and Guatemalan.

González, Ray, ed. *After Aztlan: Latino Poets of the Nineties.* Boston: Godine, 1992. Prolific anthology editor González collects thirty-four "poets coming into their own in the eighties and nineties," mostly Chicanos but also the leading Puerto Rican poets (Martín Espada, Victor Hernández Cruz, and Judith Ortiz Cofer).

Kanellos, Nicolás, ed. *Herencia: The Anthology of Hispanic Literature of the United States.* New York: Oxford University Press, 2002. This multigenre anthology, which begins with the Spanish American colonial period, has an indispensable introduction and biobibliographical synopses of each of the more than 150 authors or anonymous works. Reflects the current status of the Recovering the U.S. Hispanic Literary Heritage project and of Kanellos's own contributions to the field.

Lomelí, Francisco, ed. *Handbook of Hispanic Cultures in the United States: Literature and Art.* Houston, Tex.: Arte Público and Instituto de Cooperación Iberoamericana, 1993. An essential source with discrete essays (and extensive bibliographies) by experts on Puerto Rican, Cuban American, and Chicano literature; Hispanic aesthetic concepts; Latina writers; literary language; and Hispanic exile in the United States. The first of a four-volume set; the other three cover history, sociology, and anthropology.

Milligan, Bryce, Mary Guerrero Milligan, and Angela de Hoyos, eds. *¡Floricanto Sí! A Collection of Latina Poetry.* New York: Penguin, 1998. Brings together forty-seven both established and previously unknown or emerging Latina poets, including a few who write primarily in Spanish. These San Antonio-based writer-publishers had featured some twenty-five of the same writers in a previous compilation, *Daughters of the Fifth Sun: A Collection of Latina Fiction and Poetry* (1995). The insightful introductions to both collections elucidate aesthetic, thematic, critical, and bibliographic issues of Latina poetry and poetics in the 1990's.

Poey, Delia, and Virgil Suárez, eds. *Little Havana Blues: A Cuban-American Literature Anthology.* Houston, Tex.: Arte Público, 1996. Features sixteen poets (mainly second-generation Cuban Americans) writing principally in English and from within the boundaries of American literature, as distinct from their literary forebears. A brief but informative introduction to the multigenre anthology outlines historical, chronological, aesthetic, and thematic considerations.

Revista Chicano-Riqueña (1973-1985), continued by *The Americas Review* (1986-1999). These reviews published poetry (among other genres), scholarly articles and book reviews, interviews, and visual art. The foundational journal of Latino literature in both breadth and depth of coverage.

Sánchez González, Lisa. *Boricua Literature: A Literary History of the Puerto Rican Diaspora.* New York: New York University Press, 2001. Although this study focuses on narrative genres rather than on poetry, it illuminates the literary historical, cultural, and intellectual framework within which Nuyorican poetry has flourished.

Latin American Poetry

The panorama of Latin American poetry spans five hundred years, from the sixteenth to the twenty-first centuries.

From Encounter to the Colonial Era

The first "Renaissance" in the New World (1492-1556) was the era of discovery, exploration, conquest, and colonization under the reign of the Spanish monarchs Ferdinand and Isabela and later Carlos V. The origins of Latin American literature are found in the chronicles of these events, narrated by Spanish soldiers or missionaries. The era of colonization during the reign of Philip II (1556-1598) was a second Renaissance and the period of the Counter-Reformation. During this time, Alonso de Ercilla y Zúñiga (1533-1594) wrote the first epic poem, *La Araucana* (1569-1589). The native saga narrated the wars between the Spanish conquistadors and the Araucano Indians of Chile. This is the first truly poetic literary work with an American theme.

During the period of the Austrian Habsburg kings (1598-1701), this Renaissance was gradually replaced by the Baroque era. While the Golden Age of Spanish letters was declining in the Old World, Sor Juana Inés de la Cruz (1648-1695) reigned supreme as the queen of colonial letters. She was the major poet during the colonial era. The autodidactic nun, who wrote plays and prose as well as poetry, was known as the tenth muse, *la décima musa*. Her poetic masterpiece, the autobiographical *Primero sueño*, combines Baroque elements with a mastery of Spanish and classical languages and her unique style. Her shorter poems capture popular Mexican culture, with its lyrical verse phrasing and native themes. Some of her most famous sonnets are "Este que ves, engaño colorido" (what you see [is] dark deception), "¿En perseguirme, mundo, qué interesas?" (in pursuing me, world, what interests you?), "Détente, sombra de mi bien esquivo" (stop, shadow of my elusive love), and "Esta tarde, mi bien, cuando te hablaba" (this afternoon, love, when I spoke to you). Her most recognized *redondillas* (or "roundelays," stanzas of four octosyllabic lines rhyming *abba*) are "Este amoroso tormento" (this tormented love) and "Hombres necios, que acusáis" (stupid men, you accuse). Her charm and brilliance won her many wealthy and royal patrons. While she initially accepted their admiration, she died a recluse after rejecting her literary career and denouncing her precocious fame and vain pursuits.

During the Wars of Independence (1808-1826), Neoclassicism and other French influences dominated literary production. Andrés Bello (1781-1865) is better known for his prose, but he was also a prolific verse writer who followed the European Neoclassical movement. He wrote the poems "Alocución a la poesía" and "La agricultura en la zona tórida" with American themes and European style. José María Heredia (1803-1839) was a Cuban exiled in Mexico and the United States who wrote about the beauty of the countries that adopted him. Romanticism characterized his poems about Niagara Falls, "Niágara," Aztec ruins, "En el Teocalli de Cholula," and other wonders such as a storm in "En una tempestad." His ode "Himno a un desterrado" relates his experience as an exile in adopted nations.

Gertrudis Gómez de Avellaneda (1814-1873) left Cuba to write in Spain because of the greater freedom she could enjoy there as a female poet. Romanticism influenced her poems about love, God, and her homeland, such as "Noche de insomnio y el alba" (night of insomnia and dawn), "Al partir" (upon leaving), and "Amor y orgullo" (love and pride).

José Hernández (1834-1886) wrote about the Argentinean gauchos in *El Gaucho Martín Fierro* (1872; *The Gaucho Martin Fierro*, 1935) and *La vuelta de Martín Fierro* (1879; *The Return of Martin Fierro*, 1935). His Romantic verses followed the structures and lyrical rhythms of popular songs that romanticized the gauchos as a dying breed in the wake of industrialization.

Modernismo

By 1875, the roots of a poetic movement had grown into a new poetic era. The Latin American *Modernistas* were innovators and critics of the conservative thematic and stylistic structures that persisted from the colonial period. In Latin American society, global industrialization, capitalism, North American cultural and economic imperialism, and Spain's loss of all its colonies had a significant impact on artistic development.

A definitive moment in the progress of the movement resulted from José Julián Martí's publication of *Ismaelillo* in 1882. The poet and hero, who died fighting for Cuban independence (1853-1895), wrote *Versos libres* during this period, a collection that preceded *Versos sencillos*, published in 1891. All three collections characterized the existential angst of the era as they experimented with new lyrical forms and themes. Martí approached language as a sculptor approaches clay and molded words into new forms. His innovations have allowed him to be considered the first great visionary Latin American poet as he sought to define *Nuestra América,* a Latin American identity struggling for artistic as well as political and economic independence. Throughout the movement, the anguish, emptiness, and uncertainty of modernity provided a unifying thread for poets seeking innovation.

The Mexican modernist Manuel Gutierrez Nájera (1859-1895), was a journalist renowned for his prose writings in his own time. He founded *La Revista Azul,* a literary review that promoted *Modernismo* throughout Latin America. His contemporary Rubén Darío (1867-1916), however, defined the *Modernista* poetic. Darío's poetry was a reaction to the decadence of Romanticism in which he sought a unique voice while reinvigorating the Spanish language. He led a movement that borrowed themes popularized by the European Romantics and stylistic models of the French Parnassian movement. Darío not only was an instigator and initiator of the vindication of his language, but also served as a bridge to the second stage of *Modernismo.* His *Azul* (1888; blue), *Cantos de vida y esperanza, los cisnes, y otros poemas* (1905; songs of life and hope, the swans, and other poems), and *Poema de otoño y otros poemas* (1910; poem of autumn and other poems) represent Darío's dynamic style, respect for beauty, search for harmonious words, and celebration of pleasure. Despite the decadence of his later poetry collections, Darío maintained confidence in the saving power of art and its use to protest against social and historical injustices and resolve existential enigmas. The *Modernistas* defended humanism in the face of economic progress and international imperialism, which devaluated art. They elevated art as an end in itself.

Leopoldo Lugones (1874-1938) was the major Argentinean *Modernista* poet. His poems "Delectación morosa," "Emoción aldeana," and "Divagación lunar" lament ephemeral beauty captured and immortalized by perfectly placed words. Alfonsina Storni (1892-1938) was influenced by postmodernist tendencies. Her intense verse experimented with Symbolism and other twentieth century innovations. Her vivid sensual poems include "Tú me quieres blanca," "Epitafio para mi tumba," "Voy a dormir," "Hombre pequeñito," and "Fiera de amor." The Uruguayan Delmira Agustini (1886-1914) wrote intensely emotional and erotic poems that highlighted the dualities of human nature. Pleasure and pain, good and evil, love and death create and maintain verbal tension. These opposites struggle for dominance in poems such as "La musa," "Explosión," and "El vampiro."

All of these individual elements come together in these poets' faith in the artistic power of the word. This autonomous aesthetic power opposed the *fin de siglo* (turn of the century) angst resulting from industrialism, positivism, and competing ideologies. While reflecting on their predecessors, the *Modernistas* created original verse with unique usage of sometimes archaic or exotic words. The language was sometimes luxurious and sensual, adapting classical and baroque usage, from elements of the Parnassians to those of the Pre-Raphaelites to the Art Nouveau and European Symbolist movements and tendencies of decadent Romanticism. The symbolic impact of words characterized the movement as a whole. This all-encompassing factor defines the movement and its existential nature. This poetry is the living expression of an era of spiritual crises, personal and societal anguish, and uncertainty about the future of art as well as humanity's direction as it embarked upon the twentieth century.

Postmodernism and the Vanguard

No exact date marks the transition from Latin American Modernism to postmodernism or to a vanguard movement. A combination of historical and societal factors influenced the artistic development of individual Latin American countries. In the first two decades of the twentieth century, World War I and the Mexican Revolution interrupted artistic and literary exchange between the Old World models and the New World innovators. The urban bourgeoisie, who were patrons of the arts, were displaced. The United States had gradually replaced the European masters in science and industry as well as politics, and its dominance permeated all levels of Latin American society.

Altazor (wr. 1919, pb. 1931), by Chilean Vicente Huidobro (1893-1948), marks a break with the past. Huidobro originated stylistic practices never seen before in Latin American poetry. In *creacionismo*, his personal version of creationism, he sought to create a poem the way nature made a tree. His words, invested with autonomous linguistic and symbolic significance, reinvent themselves by creating a world apart from other words. They are antilyrical, intellectual, and disconnected from emotional and spiritual experience. Nevertheless, Huidobro's world, created by his unique use of words, was a human creation because in it the poet experiences alienation and existential angst. Huidobro's poems "Arte poética," "Depart," and "Marino" voice his despair in isolation.

Huidobro had a significant influence on younger poets, particularly in his development of a school of thought that centered on the theory of *Ultraísmo*, which attempted to construct alternative linguistic choices to those offered by the external world. *Ultraísmo* synthesized Latin American with Spanish and European tendencies. Among those influenced by *Ultraísmo* were Jorge Luis Borges (1899-1986), and in fact Borges became its main proponent. While his short stories have repeatedly caused him to be nominated for the Nobel Prize in Literature, his poetry reveals a linguistic expertise and lyrical genius unparalleled by his contemporaries. He believed that lyricism and metaphysics united to justify the means of the poetic process. This fusion provides the genesis of his most representative poems, "Everything and Nothing," "Everness," "Laberinto," "Dreamtigers," and "Borges y yo."

The Peruvian César Vallejo (1892-1938) developed a unique and distinctive poetic voice. His *Los heraldos negros* (1918; *The Black Heralds*, 1990), *Trilce* (1922; English translation, 1973), and *Poemas humanos* (1939; *Human Poems*, 1968) demonstrate the impossibility of mutual communication and comprehension, the absurdity of the human condition, and the inevitability of death.

In 1945, Gabriela Mistral (1889-1957) was the first Latin American writer to receive the Nobel Prize in Literature. Her verses echo the folksongs and traditional ballads of her native Chile, the Caribbean, and Mexico. They naturally blend native dialects with Castilian in a lyrical fusion. Some of her best poems include "Sonetos a la muerte," "Todos íbamos a ser reinas," "Pan," and "Cosas."

Mistral's countryman Pablo Neruda (1904-1973) also won the Nobel Prize in Literature, in 1971. During his formative years he was influenced by *Modernismo*, experimenting with various styles while serving as an international diplomat. The last stage of his poetry was marked by didacticism and political themes, and he was exiled for his activity in the Communist Party. Neruda sought to create a forum for "impure" poetry that encompassed all experience. His *Canto general* (1950) voiced his solidarity with humanity in his political and poetic conversion. *Odas elementales* (1954; *The Elemental Odes*, 1961) continued his mission of solidarity with the humblest members of creation. Other landmark collections include *Los versos del capitán* (1952; *The Captain's Verses*, 1972) and *Cien sonetos de amor* (1959; *One Hundred Love Sonnets*, 1986). Neruda believed that America and clarity should be one and the same.

The Mexican literary generation known as the *Taller* was led by Octavio Paz (1914-1998). He was awarded the Nobel Prize in Literature in 1990 for his brilliant prose and poetry that defined the Mexican culture and connected its isolation and universality to other cultures. His landmark analysis of poetic theory is proposed in *El arco y la lira* (1956; *The Bow and the Lyre*, 1971). The poetic evolution of linguistic progression considered "signs in rotation" culminated in *Piedra de sol* (1957; *Sun Stone*, 1963) and synthesized all twentieth century poetic theories into a highly original yet distinctly Mexican work. Representative poems include "Himno entre ruinas," "Viento entero," and "La poesía."

The Chilean poet Nicanor Parra (born 1914) developed a unique yet popular style. He called his poems *antipoemas* for their super-realism, sarcasm, self-criticism, and humor. Parra's poetry speaks to the masses and rejects pretension, as the poet revitalizes language and innovates with words in action. His masterwork, *Poemas y antipoemas* (1954; *Poems and Antipoems*, 1967), epitomizes antirhetorical and antimetaphorical free verse. "Soliloquio del individuo" and "Recuerdos de juventud" are representative.

The work of Sara de Ibañez (1910-1981) represents the antithesis of fellow Uruguayan Delmira Agustini. Her intellectual and metaphysical themes and neoclassical style allude to the poetry of Sor Juana Inés de la Cruz and Golden Age masters such as Spain's Luis de Góngora y Argote. Love and death are analyzed in "Isla en la tierra," "Isla en la luz," "Liras," and "Soliloquios del Soldado."

The "impure" poetry of Ernesto Cardenal (born 1925) unites political ugliness and the beauty of the imagination. It is characterized by *exteriorismo*, a technique that incorporates propaganda, sound bites, advertisements, and fragments of popular culture into poetry that seeks to convert and enlighten. The aesthetic value of these poems is not overshadowed by their political and spiritual message. Representative collections include *La hora O* (1960), *Salmos* (1967; *The Psalms of Struggle and Liberation*, 1971), *Oración por Marilyn Monroe y otros poemas* (1965; *Marilyn Monroe and Other Poems*, 1975), and *Cántico cósmico* (1989; *The Music of the Spheres*, 1990; *Cosmic Canticle*, 1993).

Rosario Castellanos (1925-1974) is best known for her novels and essays about social injustice in her native Chiapas. Because she focused on the status of women within the Mayan culture, as well as within Mexican society as a whole, she was considered a feminist. Her poetry and prose are concerned with the human condition, not only with the plight of women. Her most representative poems are "Autorretrato," "Entrevista de Prensa," and "Se habla de Gabriel."

Thematically and stylistically more militant and radical, Rosario Ferré (born 1938) writes overtly feminist poetry utilizing elements of symbolism and irony. Her poems include "Pretalamio," "Negativo," "La prisionera," and "Epitalamio." As editor of a literary journal, Ferré introduced feminist criticism to Latin American literature.

Movements on a smaller national scale characterize present-day poetry. They are characterized by experimental, politically and socially conscious efforts. The twenty-first century heralds the work of *los nuevos*, the new poets whose work is linked to national as well as international issues.

Individual postvanguard poets do not identify with particular ideologies. The poetry of Argentineans Mario Benedetti (born 1920) and Juan Gelman (born 1930) deals with personal exile as well as the universal experience of exile. Since the 1980's, women have emerged with empowered poetry that serves as liberation from oppression. Poets including Alejandra Pizarnik (1936-1972), Rosario Murillo (born 1951), Giaconda Belli (born 1948), Claribel Alegría (born 1924), Juana de Ibarbourou (1895-1979), and Ana Istarú (born 1960) have given voice to the silent struggles of women striving to realize their potential in a male-dominated society.

Poetry written during the last twenty years of the twentieth century focused on oppression and exile. The focus upon the withdrawal from history as a condition for the poetry of Octavio Paz has shifted to the poet belonging in the historical moment so that poetry has a public place and common concern. Contemporary Latin American poetry has become the process of naming the word and rewriting history in a lived world. The making of that world is the creative act that celebrates the word.

— *Carole A. Champagne*

Learn More

Agosín, Marjorie. *These Are Not Sweet Girls: Latin American Women Poets.* Fredonia, N.Y.: White Pine Press, 1994. Agosín is a prolific and influential poet as well as a distinguished professor and literary critic. This volume from the Secret Weavers series focuses on the poetic production of Hispanic women since the advent of feminism as expressed through their work, written predominantly during the last thirty years of the twentieth centurty. Agosín edited the collection and translated the poems in this bilingual volume.

Gauggel, Karl H. *El cisne modernista: Sus orígenes y supervivencia.* New York: Peter Lang, 1997. This study examines an icon of Latin American *Modernismo*: the swan, and its multitude of connotations. Gauggel examines its manifestations in the work of Darío, Lugones, Julio Herrera y Reissig, and Ricardo Jaimes Freyre, among other poets. He explores their roots in the Renaissance and the Spanish Golden Age, as well as neo-classical poets. Gauggel illustrates how poetic traditions were maintained by Sor Juana Inés de la Cruz and other New World poets. This is a fascinating literary adventure spanning several centuries of literary history. In Spanish.

Gonzalez, Mike, and David Treece. *The Gathering of Voices: The Twentieth Century Poetry of Latin America.* New York: Verso, 1992. This study addresses a wide range of topics. The contradictions of Latin American *Modernismo* are explored, including its elements of shock and despair that distinguished it from its predecessors. The roots of the Vanguard movement are examined, and the enduring poetry of Neruda is discussed in detail. Special topics are discussed, such as Brazilian *Modernismo* and the Guerrilla Poets of Cuba. The work concludes with studies of Postmodernism in Brazil and Spanish-language poets in exile. The collaboration between Gonzalez and Treece offers a wide variety of topics and approaches to over a century of poetry.

Green, Roland Arthur. *Unrequited Conquests: Love and Empire in the Colonial Americas.* Chicago: University of Chicago Press, 1999. This volume offers insight into Spanish colonialism, European imperialism, and their influences upon literature. Colonial love poetry is analyzed within its sociopolitical and historical contexts. Chapters are devoted to Sor Juana's fascinating life and works. This illustrated volume provides an extensive list of bibliographical references.

Jiménez, José Olivio, ed. *Antología crítica de la poesía modernista hispano-Americana.* Madrid: Ediciones Hiperión, 1985. This critical anthology discusses the corpus of the most prominent *Modernista* poets. Jiménez is recognized as an authority on Latin American poetry. While Darío's poetry is the primary work, Martí, Lugones, Herrera y Reissig, and Agustini are highlighted. Jiménez lays the groundwork for a thorough understanding of *Modernismo* with a substantial introduction and detailed presentations of each poet. In Spanish.

_____. *Antología de la poesía hispanoamericana contemporánea, 1914-1970.* Madrid: Alianza Editorial, 1984. This anthology continues where Jiménez left off by describing the decadence of *Modernismo* and the origins of several vanguard movements. The first movement was initiated by Vicente Huidobro, and the second stage was characterized by Neruda. Jiménez also discusses several postvanguard developments in the evolution of Latin American poetry. This collection is one of the most complete anthologies of postmodernist poetry. In Spanish.

Ortega, Julio, ed. *Antología de la poesía latinoamericana del siglo XXI: El turno y la transición.* México: Siglo Veintiuno Editores, 1997. Ortega gathers together some of the newest voices in Latin American poetry, including writers who bridge the gap between the postmodernist era and the present. These poets carry on the poetic tradition while breaking with their predecessors stylistically and thematically. Ortega admits that the endurance of their poetry will be tested by time and circumstance. In Spanish.

Rowe, William. *Poets of Contemporary Latin America: History and the Inner Life.* New York: Oxford University Press, 2000. This study discusses contemporary Latin American poets who bridge the centuries, including Nicanor Parra, Carmen Ollé, and Ernesto Cardenal. Rowe explores two major influences on late twentieth century and early twenty-first century poetry: the avant-garde movement and politically motivated poetic writing. He examines these roots from contextual and historical perspectives.

Smith, Verity. *Encyclopedia of Latin American Literature.* Chicago: Fitzroy Dearborn, 1996. This reference of nearly one thousand pages contains essays of at least fifteen hundred words on major poets, novelists, dramatists, other writers, movements, concepts, and other topics relating to South American, Central American, and Caribbean (including Spanish, French, and English) literatures. Overview essays cover literatures of individual countries, eras, and themes (such as science fiction, children's literature, and indigenous literatures), as well as the literatures of the major U.S. Latino communities: Cuban, Mexican, and Puerto Rican.

Sonntag Blay, Iliana L. *Twentieth-Century Poetry from Spanish America: An Index to Spanish Language and Bilingual Anthologies.* Lanham, Md.: Scarecrow Press, 1998. Three indexes provide access to more than twelve thousand Latin American poems from seventy-two anthologies: an author index, a title index, and an index of first lines. An important reference for serious scholars.

Spooner, David. *The Poem and the Insect: Aspects of Twentieth Century Hispanic Culture.* San Francisco: International Scholars Publications, 1999. This study examines the historical and literary contexts of poetic work spanning several continents, from Spain to South and Central America, then to Mexico and the United States. Spooner first discusses the work of Federico García Lorca, Antonio Machado, Pedro Salinas, and other Spanish poets. He connects the Old World to the New with analyses of Pablo Neruda and Octavio Paz. Spooner also discusses the innovative work of less well known poets, including Delmira Agustini. He offers some original ideas about some familiar poems.

Tapscott, Stephen, ed. *Twentieth-Century Latin American Poetry: A Bilingual Anthology.* Austin: University of Texas Press, 1996. This is the first bilingual collection of the most important Latin American poets. Portuguese as well as Spanish poems are translated, and the selections cover the full range of the century, from the *Modernistas* to the postmoderns, the vanguardists, and contemporary political and experimental poetry. Tapscott provides background material and introductions to eighty-five poets in a well-organized volume with excellent translations.

Unruh, Vicky. *Latin American Vanguards: The Art of Contentious Encounters.* Berkeley: University of California Press, 1994. This study focuses on the context and the character in the vanguard movements throughout Latin America. Unruh believes that the *Vanguardia* was a form of activity rather than a set of poems with similar characteristics. She demonstrates how the vanguard movement emphasized action in art and how vanguard poetry served as creative action. This perspective sheds new light on the poets' lives as well as their creative acts.

Yurkievich, Saúl. *Suma crítica.* Mexico City: Fondo de Cultura Económica, 1997. Yurkievich is one of the most highly regarded critics of Latin American literature. His analyses have provoked critical response and thoughtful discussion since the 1980's. He delves into the work of the *Modernistas,* including Darío, Lugones, Ramon López Velarde, and Gabriela Mistral. His analyses of *vanguardista* poetry address the work of Huidobro, Vallejo, and Neruda. He then demonstrates how the poetry of Borges and Paz goes beyond the limits of the vanguard movement. Yurkievich is a consistently brilliant literary critic. In Spanish.

Latino Short Fiction

While the popularity of short fiction in the twentieth century has been evidenced in the sheer volume of story anthologies, literary magazines, and copious production of collections by major artists, such as Joyce Carol Oates, John Updike, and Donald Barthelme, the short fiction of Latinos rarely made an appearance before the late twentieth century. Large presses generally carried few or no works by Latino writers; mainstream and smaller literary magazines—primarily located on the East Coast and attuned to literature by Anglo men—believed there was no market for Latino stories. In fact, there was little appearance of Latino short fiction until mid-century; the genre began to create inroads into the Latino community (in fact, creating its own readership) only in the late 1960's and 1970's, and the publication of short stories by Latino authors became robust in the 1980's.

With the establishment of journals such as *The Americas Review* (formerly *Revista Chicano-Riqueña*) and of presses such as Arte Público in Texas, which focused on writing by Latinos, a tradition of publication and distribution of short fiction began. As a result, the latter two decades of the twentieth century saw an explosion in the writing and publication of short fiction by Latinos and an exponential interest on the part of the public at large. Several works of Chicano and Latino fiction found their way into major literary anthologies and onto required reading lists in high school and college English classes. However, despite the evidence of greater accessibility and acceptability by the literary world at large, Latino fiction is still, in many ways, separated from Anglo-American, or "mainstream," literature and literary studies. Latino fiction merits study as a serious field now, and with the emphasis on multicultural studies and the examination of historical and sociopolitical forces in literature, it can be informative and valuable to look at works from an ethnic perspective in order to see how specific ethnic or cultural identification affects literary trends and themes.

Latinos are forecast to be the largest minority group in the United States in the twenty-first century. As literary production in the Latino community blossoms and as the U.S. Latino population has increased, there has been a significant increase in attention to "border" studies within the larger fields of American literature and cultural studies. Scholars and critics have begun to pay attention to the cultural dynamics of the U.S.-Mexican border, noting the exchange of influences and ideas. Prominent American studies and English professors such as José David Saldívar, Lois Parkinson Zamora, and Amy Kaplan have argued that scholars cannot consider the category "American literature" without taking into account all the Americas—North, South, and Central. At the same time, academic interest in the field of postcolonial studies requires a consideration of the relationship between the United States and its Caribbean neighbors, in terms of considering both the territory of each as colonized land following New World settlement and the participation of the United States in neocolonial relation to Puerto Rico, the Dominican Republic, and other Caribbean island nations. Among the results of this new focus is a fresh approach to a wide field of literature, including fiction by Chicanos and Latinos living in the United States.

What Is Latino Fiction?
In the sense discussed in this essay, "Latino" fiction includes works by writers in the United States who have either migrated from Latin America or are descendants of Latin Americans. Further, it can be argued that Latino writers are distinct in their linguistic, cultural, historical, and political sensibilities, and that their concerns frequently echo those of the community to which they belong. Still, the terms at times overlap and a word on usage is in order. While the term "Latino" is inclusive, meaning those from Mexico, Central and South America, and the Caribbean, the term "Chicano" is frequently employed when discussing those of Mexican or Mexican American heritage; Chicano/Latino is used when being both inclusive and mindful of distinctions therein. This article will avoid using the common term "Hispanic," which designates those whose linguistic origin

is Spanish. This term is controversial, since many Latino groups claim that it is an outgrowth of U.S. governmental policies of foreign and domestic containment, overlooking the cultural diversity of the different Latino nations, and that, further, it inaccurately lays its claim in Spain and the Iberian peninsula, thereby eliding the history of colonization and its subsequent cultural manifestations. Therefore, "Latino" and the feminine form "Latina" are preferred by many, being a reference to geographic origin, Latin America. While it is always problematic to assign a single term to a group that is far from homogeneous, it is the work of the scholar to locate the similarities that justify its usage, all the while attending to the cultural differences inherent in the field. Below, the aim is to do just that by tracing common themes, investigating their origins, and looking at particular authors and works that are notable for illustrating those themes.

The Latino Short-Story Form
Though not traditionally the dominant genre—novels and poetry have been more prevalent—the short-story form is particularly expressive for Chicano and Latino writers. The dramatic diversity and hybridity of Chicano and Latino life, and the tensions created by cultural flux, make apt material for the conventions of short fiction. It is no coincidence that some of the most influential works by Chicanos and Latinos are collections of short stories, such as experimental work by Tomás Rivera and the groundbreaking fiction of Sandra Cisneros. Rivera's and Cisneros's works are especially dependent on the accessibility and flexibility of the short-story genre, because both weave together a patchwork of narratives, a polymorphous collection of voices to articulate the lives of Latinos—an ethnic American group that is complex and varied. These and other writers have been able to express the complexities yet demonstrate the thematic concerns and stylistic sensibilities that make a particular work of short fiction distinctly Latino.

One of those distinctions is language. Many Chicanos and Latinos are fully bilingual or at least participate in more than one linguistic community. This Spanish-English bilingualism is directly addressed in many works of short fiction. While a few writers, such as Sabine Ulibarrí, were published in Spanish first, countless others demonstrate this bilingualism through the use of Spanish in the text via the insertion of "Spanglish," or anglicization of Spanish words, and frequent code-switching—that is, the act of alternating between or using the two languages at once, often in the same sentence or phrase. Although the English-language reader is usually able to fully comprehend these insertions through contextual clues or immediate translation, sometimes meaning is obscured for the readers who are not bilingual.

Customs and culture also play a large role in Latino short fiction. The inclusion of religious ritual, local legend, and popular folklore, much of which is unfamiliar to non-Latino or mainstream readers, finds its way into a number of works. For the Latino writer, the delineations between fact and fantasy, dream and reality, legend and "truth" can sometimes be seen as arbitrary divisions, leading the work of writers such as Rudolfo Anaya to be labeled "Magical Realism." Many regional writers include particular myths, stories, and Catholic practices in their stories, as most of Latin America is Roman Catholic. Cisneros's story "Little Miracles, Kept Promises," for example, consists of a series of written thanks and descriptions of offerings, or *retablos* to various saints and the Virgin Mary, a custom particular to many Mexican Americans. Such customs and cultural practices, however, usually take place against the backdrop of a larger society, the United States, and so the stories at once represent cultural differences while negotiating the merging of Anglo-American U.S. and Latino cultures.

This negotiation leads to a preoccupation with geography in the literature. Latinos can be border-dwellers and border-crossers by virtue of the fact that they frequently have more than one national or cultural allegiance. Among these affiliations, Latinos are variously tied to New York, the Southwest, Chicago, or Texas in the United States and countries as culturally distinct as Cuba, the Dominican Republic, Mexico, or the U.S. territory of Puerto Rico. Additionally, Latino writers in the United States often write as exiles or as part of a larger diaspora, thereby evoking problematic sentiments of home, loyalty, cultural merging, and assimilation. For example, the Cubans, Dominicans and Puerto Ricans (or Nuyoricans) who have established themselves in the Northeast commonly write about the conflict between being part of the island culture, the land of their birth or ancestors, and life on the mainland. Different latitudes foster different attitudes, and these writers often contrast the harsh life in urban cities with tropical island living. The Chicanos of the Southwest integrate the landscape and its history of Anglo domination into the prose where it figures as either plot or character. Latino writers, therefore, are often deeply connected to the land they inhabit—either by native legacy or the attachments fostered by recent immigration—but cultural affiliations disrupt conventional national affiliations as regional terms like "Tejano" (a Mexican American from Texas) or "Californio" suggest, and so the site of Chicano/Latino narrative is physically and psychically shifting.

This continual shifting creates a tension in much of Latino short fiction, a tension that expresses itself in the duality of many of the characters as they struggle to be both Latino and North American, as they try to be at home in their barrios and comfortable in the world at large, and as they attempt to resist the pressures of an English-speaking world where racism still exists and cultural difference is not necessarily seen as an asset. Thus, assimilation and resistance to cultural dominance, along with themes of departure and return (and the migrant nature of culture) all play into the short fiction produced by Latinos in the United States. Clearly these are problems or issues that individuals encounter alone, and Chicano and Latino literature certainly portrays the single subject finding his or her way in two worlds, but these questions are vexing for the community at large; Latino characters are nearly always departing from or moving toward a reconciliation with a broader community. Indeed, perhaps the most notable and compelling feature of Chicano and Latino short fiction is the indelible sense of responsibility characters are shown to have for their respective communities.

Early Influences

While short fiction is a relatively recent phenomenon in Latino literature, it is useful to discuss the trajectory of the literature in general, before the appearance of the short story, in order to review the thematic concerns of Latino fiction and see how it is entwined with political history.

Latino literature in the United States has a long history that is distinct from the Anglo-American tradition. In the early history of this country, Latino literature was written in Spanish and looked to Spanish-language traditions for literary inspiration. The literature of the sixteenth, seventeenth, and much of the eighteenth centuries, for example, mainly consisted of writings by the Spanish who settled in the New World and were chronicles of travels, memoirs, and letters, with some poetry and drama, as was typical of this time. Such works are now viewed as "American" works and are included in anthologies of U.S. literature, but set in context they stand out as antecedents to today's Latino fiction. A New World tradition of recounting and recording oral legends and myths, for example, combined with Spanish balladry prefigured much of the storytelling in forms such as the Mexican *corrido* that was to come.

It is during the nineteenth and early twentieth centuries that the territory now known as the United States began to take shape in what had been Hispanic territories. In 1821, Florida was ceded to the United States, and in 1848, with the Treaty of Guadalupe Hidalgo, Mexico lost about a third of its territory including Alta California, Arizona, New Mexico, and Texas. Despite a great influx of Anglos to the region, Spanish remained the dominant language of the Southwest as the Mexican population struggled to remain in control of their property and culture. After the Spanish-American War of 1898, Cuba and Puerto Rico came under U.S. control, precipitating one of the first waves of Caribbean immigration into the Northeast and the South. Additionally, a wave of Mexican immigrants came into the country, concentrating in the Southwest after the Mexican Revolution of 1910—some to escape the war, others in search of economic opportunities in the western United States.

During these turbulent decades the Latino literary world expanded tremendously and began to give voice to the concerns that are still being addressed in short fiction today. Fiction, however, was the slowest literary form to develop during this period, after memoirs, histories, chronicles, ballads, and poetry. According to Chicano literary scholar Raymund Paredes

> ... [The Treaty of] Guadalupe Hidalgo had guaranteed Mexican-Americans frill rights as citizens but, in fact, they were frequently stripped of their property and subjected to severe discrimination. The Mexican-Americans expressed their resentment of this treatment in the large number of *corridos* that sprang from this region.

The *corrido*, a border-based ballad form, became the preeminent narrative genre in the late nineteenth through mid-twentieth centuries along the border and was used to describe the sequence of domination and resistance between Mexicans and Anglos in the Southwest. Likewise, the Chicano fiction produced during this time took as its subject the land, its people, and its history. In California, Adolfo Carrillo published short stories and legends about the California missions and the gold rush. Eusebio Chacón, of New Mexico, published romantic novellas before the turn of the century. Urbano Chacón and his son, Felipe Chacón, were newspaper editors in New Mexico. Felipe published a number of short stories in his newspaper and in books; however, this work was in Spanish as were many of the literary contributions around the turn of the century.

In fact, during this time, numerous Spanish-language newspapers were circulating, a large number of which carried poetry, stories, ballads, and serialized novels. *El Misisipi*, based in New Orleans, was probably the first Spanish-language newspaper in the United States. Other notable dailies and weeklies included *La Gaceta* of Santa Barbara, the literary magazine *Aurora*, and *La Prensa*, a newspaper which created its own weekly literary supplement. While much literary activity was centered on the Southwest and the former Mexican territories, in the Northeast, primarily New York, the *cronistas*, or newspaper columnists from

Spanish-speaking communities, sought to nurture the cultural life of their groups of origin, most of which hailed from the Caribbean. Though there is little evidence that short fiction was produced by that community during the early part of the century, the seeds were sown for literary artistry in these newspapers.

The Advent of Latino Short Fiction
There are several authors from the first half of the twentieth century who have presaged the thematic concerns of Latino authors to follow and have received notice for their fiction. Josefina Niggli, who was born and lived in Mexico (though not to Mexican parents) is now generally considered one of the precursors of Chicano writers. Her best-selling story series of 1945, *Mexican Village*, charmingly and richly describes the Mexican town of Hidalgo and its people, yet at its center lies the issue of race: The reappearing protagonist of the stories is a half-Anglo, half-Mexican man who is rejected by his white father.

Mario Suárez is one of the first writers to have used the term "Chicano" in print. His stories, many of which were published around mid-century, take Arizona as their scene; he describes the barrio in Tucson, replete with details about regional life, such as cultural customs that demonstrate the bridge between the ways of old Mexico and the U.S. Southwest. Though he did not publish abundantly, his realism and sympathetic portrayals of Chicanos have earned him respect as an early Chicano fiction writer.

A Franciscan priest born Manuel Chávez, Fray Angélico Chávez was a prolific writer who wrote historical narratives, as well as tracts on history and religion. The three stories that form *New Mexico Triptych* from 1940, combined with his other fictional works, have been compiled in *The Short Stories of Fray Angélico Chávez* (1987). Chávez draws inspiration from traditional *hispano*, or Southwest Mexican and Mexican American, Spanish-language stories. These stories are characterized by the use of provincial characters and situations, archetypal and religious narrative elements, and allegorical structures. The stories, considered by many to be quaint and charming renderings of the

Hispanos, or Spanish-speakers of New Mexico, are the subject of much critical attention. While drawing upon the religious customs and folklore of the region, Chávez takes on the social reality of the long process of transition from Mexican cultural norms in the Southwest and the inevitable cultural clashes that arose, illuminating the condescension of the Anglo-American toward the Mexican American. As the collection's editor, Genaro Padilla has put it, the stories present a "whimsical, romantic and mystic surface" to life in New Mexico, which is "quietly undermined by social criticism."

Américo Paredes, too, was writing about the American experience from a Mexican American perspective in the 1920's through the 1950's. Paredes, who is best known for his ethnographic work on Mexican and Mexican American folklore, nonetheless published a number of short stories distinctive for their spare, realistic, and dialogic prose and contemporary contexts. Collected in *The Hammon and the Beans, and Other Stories* (1994), these stories examine Chicano life from many social perspectives and take the reader from South Texas to Japan, from the Depression through World War II. The wide range of subjects and narrative points of view represent Paredes's view that the Chicano, no local or accidental cultural phenomenon, could be understood only in his or her relation to the United States and the world at large. According to literary critic Ramón Saldívar, *The Hammon and the Beans, and Other Stories,* along with Paredes's scholarly work, constitutes "a figural discourse of transnational epic proportions appropriate to the construction of a new narrative of a modern American social and cultural history."

The title piece of Paredes's collection, "The Hammon and the Beans," is set in the 1920's, takes place in a small town with a military base, and portrays the interweaving of the lives of sanctioned citizens, the military, with those marginalized on the border. In the story, a small Mexican-populated Texas town butts up against a U.S. military base. Focusing on the children of the town, the story shows the process by which the quotidian culture of Anglo-Americans is passed along to those on the margins. One little girl spies on the soldiers while they eat and steals their scraps for her family. Her playmates goad her into performing the banalities of the army mess hall with mock orations, at once for their own amusement and to master the discourse and interests of the dominant culture. The children realize they must learn English to survive in America but can do so only through subversion. In a telling episode, the young girl stands before her peers and mimics—with notable linguistic revision—the gruntings of hungry soldiers whom she has spied in the base mess hall: "Give me the *hammon* and the beans! give me the *hammon* and the beans!" The story ends with the narrator, now a young adult standing in food lines during the depression, thinking about the young girl and the (in)efficacy of her demand for food, which he now reads as a call for justice. The story is remarkable and characteristic of the collection as a whole in the way it represents the tangle of official vehicles of oppression— the military on the border—with quotidian lives, the lives of the hungry border-dwellers.

The short fiction of Paredes, along with that of Chávez, is preoccupied with life in the borderlands of the American Southwest during these decades, though in stylistically very different ways. However different the stories may read, they demonstrate that these concerns—those of geography, the concept of home, and social justice—are relevant to the Chicano/Latino community both then and now.

Contemporary Works and Authors

Contemporary Latino literature gains its unique voice from the civil rights struggles in the 1960's in general and the academic protests by Chicanos and Latinos in the late 1960's and early 1970's in particular. The Chicano movement, or El Movemiento as it was called in local circles, was a grassroots protest movement based in Texas and parts of the Southwest which called for equality and integration in schools, a fair language program that respected the primacy of Spanish in the homes of Chicano and Latino students, and a more balanced view of the history of the region. The movement made strong political gains for Chicanos and Latinos, and it also sparked a social and cultural awakening, providing the inspiration and the symbolism for much of the literature that would follow. The Chicano movement highlighted the rights of Chicanos and Latinos to their language, their cultural past, and their (symbolic) sovereignty over their land. These themes show up in the efflorescence of literature and the deep commitment to artistic production and expression that followed. Chicano/Latino writers were less concerned during this time with the literary experimentation that was taking place among mainstream writers of the period and more concerned with thematic problems of identity, racial discrimination, immigration, and socioeconomic repression.

Tomás Rivera's . . . *y no se lo tragó la tierra* (1971; . . . *and the earth did not part*) and *The Harvest: Short Stories* (1989) find a home in these thematic concerns. Considered a classic of Chicano fiction, . . . *and the earth did not part* was published initially in Spanish and then as a bilingual work, with side-by-side English and Spanish versions of the text. This book consists of fourteen stories, twelve of which correspond to the months of the year, divided by thirteen vignettes. The stories piece together the life of a nameless boy over that year, a working-class character who embodies the collective voice of migrant workers—a group whose stories had rarely graced the pages of literature. A prayer for a son in Vietnam, a boy suffering from thirst in the fields, and the ostracization of migrant Mexican schoolchildren in the classroom are the focuses of some of the pieces. The short, fragmentary pieces that make up the whole, combined with the bilingual presentation of the text, echo the fragmentation of identity of people caught between two cultures. The work is considered to be a tremendous influence on Chicano/Latino writers who followed him, such as Sandra Cisneros.

The characters in Rivera's collection *The Harvest*, too, lead lives that mirror the experimental, minimalist prose. Rivera's stories, like his subjects' lives, are nonlinear, as characters migrate according to the season and live at the mercy of the growers who employ them. The characters are divested of conventional forms of agency, and so it is not their actions that determine the plot of the stories but the sudden and fatalistic whims of nature and economics. Rivera expresses the humanity of his subjects through their enduring commitment to one another and through their attempts to make meaning of their landscape and their lives. Again, and as will be seen with Cisneros, it is crucial to add that meaning itself is not achieved by any given story—Rivera's tales are not fables or allegories, and there are not always realizations for the reader—but the representation of a community attempting to understand their own lives is itself a meaningful act and the effect of much Chicano/ Latino short fiction.

Another deeply influential author is Rudolfo A. Anaya, whose fiction has won numerous awards and much acclaim. In *The Silence of the Llano* (1982), Anaya takes as his subject the people of New Mexico and their lives in the rural areas of the state. Called a "Magical Realist," Anaya skillfully interweaves local belief and custom into his narratives, creating works that are steeped in the spiritual experiences that comprise the everyday lives of Chicanos and Mexicanos of that area. Sabine Reyes Ulibarrí also a New Mexican, has published short-story collections in both Spanish and English. *Tierra Amarilla: Cuentos de Nuevo Mexico* (1964; *Tierra Amarilla: Stories of New Mexico*, 1971) and *Mi abuela fumaba puros y otros cuentos de Tierra Amarilla/ My Grandma Smoked Cigars, and Other Stories of Tierra Amarilla* (1977) were published with parallel texts in English and Spanish. Like the works of Anaya, Ulibarrí's stories are inspired by the landscape and people of New Mexico and draw upon local lore and oral tradition to portray the *hispano* communities there. Depicting a people who are deeply Catholic, Ulibarrí demonstrates the effect of lore on their lives, with stories such as "Mi caballo mago" about a magical stallion which recounts a version of La Llorona, the Mexican tale of the legendary weeping woman who still travels the earth crying for her drowned children.

Though the authors mentioned above have received significant notice in journals and anthologies, there are still more Chicano writers whose work is less well known but also deeply tied to regional concerns, describing life on the border and in the barrios, respectively. Genaro González has published stories in a number of literary magazines. His collection *Only Sons* (1991) deals with living on the border in Texas and is concerned with the effect this political geography has on the people who inhabit this area. Nash Candelaria, Dagoberto Gilb, and Alberto Ríos have all published stories both in journals and in collections and have received critical attention for their work. Max Martínez's stories in *The Adventures of the Chicano Kid, and Other Stories* (1982) and *A Red Bikini Dream* (1990) depict the varied lives of Chicanos, from the poor of the barrio to upper-middle-class educated Chicanos, frequently with humor.

Estela Portillo Trambley, from Texas, was the first Chicana to publish a book of short stories with *Rain of Scorpions and Other Writings* in 1975. Embodying feminist ideals of equality, women are the center of the narratives here, as Trambley decries the inequality and unjust treatment of women and celebrates their unique biology. In her fiction, Trambley proffers the belief that, because of the biological imperative of giving birth, women are by nature nurturing and sensitive to other beings. Common as they were in early 1970's mainstream feminist writing, these ideas also proliferated in early Chicana writing. Just as anti-essentialist feminist thought rebuffed the conundrum of biological essentialism, so too did early Chicana feminist fiction give way to a more sophisticated literary aesthetic, at once aware of the imperative to liberate Chicanas from the patriarchal representations of their bodies while able to represent the diversity among Chicanas' lives.

In the 1980's and 1990's there began a renaissance of fiction by Chicana/Latina women in the United States. This has been an important cultural intervention into what has been a largely male-dominated ethnic literary movement. Many of these authors have taken on disrupting stereotypical constructions of gender through ethnic identification, satirizing and criticizing the portrayals of women as either wife/mother or sexually promiscuous vamp and interwoven the issues of immigration, work, love, identity, and self-realization. Interest in the writing of women such as Alicia Gaspar de Alba, Judith Ortiz Cofer, and Roberta Fernández precipitated much of the explosion in Latina fiction.

Probably the most popular and famous writer of this renaissance is Sandra Cisneros, author of *The House on Mango Street* (1984) and *Woman Hollering Creek, and Other Stories* (1991). *The*

House on Mango Street is a series of forty-four vignettes centered on a single protagonist, reminiscent of Rivera's . . . *and the earth did not part.* Considered a feminist *Bildungsroman,* Cisneros's work has enjoyed a popularity unprecedented in Latino fiction and is now widely used in high school and college literature classes. It is the collection *Woman Hollering Creek, and Other Stories,* however, that solidifies Cisneros as a powerful writer of short fiction. The stories of this collection take place in Chicago (the city of Cisneros's birth, and home to a both a large Mexican American and Puerto Rican community), Mexico, and the American Southwest. Exemplifying the best of personal and political consciousness, Cisneros draws heavily on Mexican and Mexican American history and lore in many of these stories, such as "Eyes of Zapata," a tale told from the vantage point of Mexican revolutionary Emiliano Zapata's lover. The Virgin of Guadalupe, a Mexican icon who functions as symbol of inspirational womanhood, figures in a number of stories with settings on both sides of the border.

Writing almost entirely from a first-person point of view, Cisneros shows her mostly female protagonists struggling with their Latina identity and the constraints and strengths that those identities confer upon the characters. These characters are varied in their life experiences and roles. Some are mothers and wives; others are single females trying to find a place for themselves in a society which has presented them with few non-traditional options. Cisneros tackles issues as varied as spousal abuse ("Woman Hollering Creek"), acquired immunodeficiency syndrome ("Remember the Alamo"), and intracommunity racism ("Never Marry a Mexican"). The challenges that the protagonists take on—and that Cisneros takes on as a writer—exemplify the complexities of life as a Latina.

Cisneros has been a pioneer in the representation of the linguistic hybridity of border-based Chicanos and all Latinos. In her fiction there is frequently a strong emphasis on the verbal, expressed through long passages of dialogue, much of which is rapid and lively, and through the extensive use of interior monologues. The verbal quality is enhanced by continual infusions of Spanglish and slang terms and almost constant cross-pollination, evident even in the titles of the stories, such as "Bien Pretty" or "My Tocaya." "The Marlboro Man" or "La Fabulosa," for example, consist of conversations between unnamed friends who create, through their dialogue, modern myths about people of their community, creating a contemporary version of traditional orality and popular legend that characterizes speech and storytelling in Latino communities.

Sandra Cisneros's narrative is in fact, often polyvocal, with the voice of a single protagonist displaced in favor of a community of (at times conflicting) voices. In "Little Miracles, Kept Promises," recitations of prayers and miracles formulate multiple narratives within a single tale. In the story "Woman Hollering Creek" the narrative voice shifts several times from the singular to the plural, from the protagonist to community members—at times echoing the shift in locality, as characters cross from the Mexican side of the border to the U.S. side and back again. These narrative voices combine not so much to plot the story as to represent the impact the main event of the story—already passed—has had on a neighborhood. Though it is not always clear *what* has happened, Cisneros shows *who* it has happened to and so gives expression to an otherwise underrepresented community of border-dwellers.

Writing in an accessible, lively style, Denise Chávez has authored the popular collection *The Last of the Menu Girls* (1986), a series of stories and vignettes narrated by a central character, Rocio Esquibel, who distributes menus to patients in a hospital. These highly verbal stories, along with those of Cisneros, are representative of some of the best of Latina fiction. The stories are arranged not chronologically but thematically, dealing with such issues as the search for strong female role models, the value of women's work and daily tasks, and the role of memory, time, and communal and familial ties in the search for identity. Not coincidentally, the protagonist, Rocio, decides to become a writer and to chronicle the lives of friends and family in her community. Like several of the female protagonists of Cisneros's stories, Rocio finds strength and autonomy through artistic expression. Like the work of Cisneros, Chávez's work has received much positive criticism: Selections from *The*

Last of the Menu Girls have found their way into a number of anthologies of both Latino and mainstream American literature.

Helena María Viramontes is another major Chicana author who grapples with issues of ethnic identity and infuses her stories with feminist sensibilities, as in her collection *The Moths, and Other Stories* (1985), her best-known work. The title story "The Moths" has been frequently anthologized in recent years, and the tragic story "The Cariboo Café" in particular has received considerable critical attention. In "The Cariboo Café" Viramontes narrates the experience of recent Mexican and Central American immigrants living in Los Angeles, weaving the lives of usually invisible characters into the fabric of the city as a whole. "The Cariboo Café," parsed in separate, disjointed sections, follows a series of characters whose lives become tragically tangled. In the first section Sonya (about six years old) and her baby brother Macky are inadvertently locked out of their apartment, somewhere north of the Mexican border. The parents, illegal immigrants, are both at work and have warned the children to never venture far from the apartment, never trust the "polie" for they are *la migra* (immigration) officials in disguise, and never talk to strangers. Section 1 ends with the children lost, wandering in a warehouse district, and approaching a strange lady who seems to offer help. Section 2 introduces the owner and operator of the Cariboo Café, a man down on his luck, unable to afford to hire any help, not even a dishwasher. Coping poorly with the recent breakup of his family, the café owner finds himself increasingly the peer of the junkies, drunks, and homeless who loiter in his cafe. Among the other liminal figures who enter are a strange woman and two children, clearly not her own. Watching the nightly news, the café owner learns that the children have been reported missing, possibly kidnapped, but upholding his own rule to never talk to the "polie," he declines to inform them of what he knows. In the final section, the putative kidnapper, a washerwoman by trade, narrates her own story in a hazy jumble of memory and motive. A native of Central America, the woman suffers the loss of her own child, probably a victim of the U.S.-sponsored Contra rebellion in the 1980's. Still suffering the trauma of loss, still in a haze of grief, the woman encounters the wandering Sonya and Macky and perceives the boy as her own lost son, attempting to bridge her trauma by taking him in. In her final and fatal confrontation with the police, she imagines she is back in Central America, fighting guerrilla forces.

Though "The Cariboo Café" ends with a determinedly heroic act, other stories in the collection are more ambivalently rendered, as Viramontes avoids the easy political dichotomies and portrays the complexity of Latino life. Her main characters are mostly women, and a common theme in her fiction is the struggle for women to recognize the source and means of their oppression, both by the majority culture and the patriarchal strictures of Mexican American culture. Plots turn on transitional moments for the women, as they build bridges across generations to other women ("The Moths") or come to recognize their loneliness ("The Neighbors"). A powerful theme in several stories is the Latina's developing relationship with her own sexuality, fraught by her family's prohibitions—for whom a woman's sexuality is a source of honor to be guarded—or by religious sanction. The ending passage of the story "Birthday," for example, narrates Alice's terrible confusion as she prepares to have an abortion. Here, Viramontes's prose style marks both the determined resolve of Alice's decision (a painful coming into womanhood) and the internal battle she still wages with her cultural upbringing:

> Now the doctor will insert . . . *the waves rock me into*
> *an anxious sleep. And i love. NO! I don't love you, not you,*
> *God, knotted ball. I hate you,* Alice. . . . Relax Alice,
> and try not to move again *reaching up to the vastness. calm. i*
> *relax under the fluids that thicken like jelly.* i am still;
> my body is transparent and light, and ounceless.

The oscillation between love and hate, faith and its rejection, occur simultaneously with the abortion, which is itself an ultimate action. Her decision renders her empty, or "ounceless," but she endures nonetheless; "i am still."

Puerto Rican, Cuban, and Dominican American Writers

For much of the Caribbean American community, concerns about space and place are every bit as important as they are for Chicano writers. With the movements to the mainland from Cuba and Puerto Rico, each wave of immigrants has created a new generation of writers.

Pedro Juan Soto and José Luis González, two Puerto Rican writers, were part of the Generation of 1940, who wrote about life in New York at mid-century. Though he later returned to the island, Soto took as his subject the immigrant experience and barrio life. In *Spiks* (English translation, 1973), his collection of short stories published in 1956, Soto examined life on the streets. A heightened awareness of race, as indicated in the collection's title—"spik" being a derogatory term for Puerto Ricans—affects his acute portrayal of the difficulty of life in New York for the Puerto Rican community. *Spiks* is also noteworthy for its realism, extensive use of street slang, and codeswitching—all fairly new techniques at the time. González, too, was one of the first writers to discuss the exile of Puerto Ricans in the United States and the racial tensions and economic difficulties of the community in numerous short stories. These writers and others of the 1940's and 1950's influenced subsequent Puerto Rican and other Latino writers of the Northeast.

Just as the civil and cultural rights movements of the 1960's influenced Chicano literature, so too did the heightened awareness of cultural roots and political struggle affect Puerto Ricans on the mainland. This awareness manifested itself in the literary production of the "Nuyoricans," a term coined to describe the hybridity formed when island culture was imported to urban life. Early Nuyorican fiction prominently represented mostly male protagonists coming of age on the streets of New York. Consistently, the tension between life on the (Anglo-American) mainland and the persistence of native language, ethics, and social mores gave rise to a new ethnic sensibility. No longer Puerto Rican only, the Nuyorican writer reconceptualized identity and social landscape, writing into existence not only a new ethnicity but also a new social construction of New

York City. While the difficulty of life in the United States and the racism of Anglo-American society were the focus of much fiction coming out of this period, it was accompanied by an idealized version of life on the island. A greater embrace of cultural difference began, a difference expressed in the writing through the extensive use of Spanish, frequent code-switching, and insertion of customs, practices, and terminologies particular to Puerto Ricans.

One such writer is Piri Thomas, whose autobiography *Down These Mean Streets* (1967) became widely popular; the tensions that arose for him, being a dark-skinned Puerto Rican in America, familiar with the ways of the streets, reveal themselves in his fiction and memoir alike. Yet his collection of short fiction, *Stories from El Barrio* (1978), does not dwell entirely upon the negative aspects of life in the barrio but affirms values such as male friendship and personal strength.

Ed Vega (Edgardo Vega Yunqué), too, writes short stories that have their setting in the barrio. *Mendoza's Dreams* (1987) is a collection of stories linked through a narrator named Alberto Mendoza. Rather than a chronicle of difficulty and urban strife, Vega infuses these stories with humor. In this earlier work his characters are not suffering migrants but complexly rendered individuals who encounter success in unlikely but very American ways. His *Casualty Report* (1991), however, departs from the earlier works and focuses on the destruction wrought by violence and drugs in the Puerto Rican barrios.

Probably the most prolific Puerto Rican writer, Nicholasa Mohr, too, has been obsessed with the struggle of life between two cultures. Much of her writing has been for a young adult audience, including her *El Bronx Remembered* (1975), a novella with short stories, which was a finalist for the National Book Award. In this collection the stories span the years between 1946 and 1956, taking New York as the backdrop for Puerto Rican youth for whom the island life is distant but far from removed. Her *Rituals of Survival: A Woman's Portfolio* (1985) was her first work for adults, and in 1997 she published *A Matter of Pride, and Other Stories*. Both these collections center on Puerto Rican women in New York struggling to cope with Latino machismo and break out of the barrio, and they highlight the poignancy of returning to the neighborhood of one's birth. Traditions and beliefs from the Caribbean still persist in these neighborhoods, despite the frequently hostile influence of "American" New York, a theme Mohr carries through all her works. In the story "Aunt Rosana's Rocker," for example, the female protagonist, Zoraida, is thought to be possessed, and a spiritualist is consulted and rituals performed to exorcize the invasive spirit.

Like Mohr, Judith Ortiz Cofer, in *An Island Like You* (1995), writes of young, contemporary protagonists who are Puerto Rican immigrants negotiating the space between the two cultures. As in the work of her fellow Puerto Rican writers, the language and cultural particulars of the community figure here. Considered the most mainstream of Puerto Rican writers, Cofer markets both her poetry and young adult works to a wide audience and makes her work accessible and friendly.

In 1992, the writer Abraham Rodriguez, Jr., published *The Boy Without a Flag*. These seven short stories center on Puerto Rican Americans—mainly adolescents—in the south Bronx and reflections of the alienation, rebellion, and submission experienced by that group in the United States. The title story is emblematic of the cultural collisions and confusion sometimes encountered when straddling a bifurcated identity. "The Boy Without a Flag" tells of a boy who refuses to salute the American flag in school, after being told by his father that the United States is the enemy of the Puerto Rican people. The boy is sent to the principal, and his father is called in. Instead of denouncing the United States to the principal, as the boy expects, the father apologizes to the principal. The scene of capitulation is nearly archetypal in immigrant and ethnic fiction, and the collection received positive critical attention.

Cuban exiles and Cuban Americans form another vibrant sector of Latino short fiction. Roberto Fernández, who came to the United States at eleven years of age, has written short-story collections in Spanish: *Cantos sin rumbos* (1975; directionless tales) and *El jardin de la luna* (1976; the garden of the moon). In the stories, Fernández writes humorously about the Cuban community in the United States and life in exile. Virgil Suárez, a Cuban American, writes about Cubans and their families who have left their island for life in the United States in *Welcome to the Oasis, and Other Stories* (1992).

Junot Díaz, a Dominican American writer, seems poised to move Latino short fiction into the sights of mainstream readers and garner wide attention for his work and the work of other Latinos. Díaz has published stories in *The New Yorker, Story,* and *The Best American Short Stories 1996,* as well as mainstream magazines. In 1996 Díaz published a collection of his stories titled *Drown,* which was widely praised and quickly became a bestseller. With stories that take place in both the Dominican Republic and the northeastern United States, Díaz takes his place in the tradition of Caribbean writers who tell of the contrast between island and mainland life and all its attendant struggles. Like other Latino writers before him, Díaz employs extensive dialogue, slang, anglicizations of English, and code-switching— yet manages a remarkably restrained style and lyricism that have won him much acclaim. *Drown* has been translated into Spanish as well, thereby widening his reading community and offering a literary link between mainland and Caribbean readers.

Díaz is indicative of a trend. Latino fiction in the United States continues to explode, both in terms of volume and sales and in terms of the numbers of upcoming young authors. Michele Serros's *How to Be a Chicana Role Model* (2000) received positive notices. Danny Romero, Veronica González, and Sergio Troncoso are but a few of today's major authors in Latino short fiction. There is increasing interest, too, in tracing the literary history of Latinos and creating a body of critical work to address the many issues embedded in the fiction. As Latino short fiction gains prominence, it also gains gravity, drawing the attention of mainstream readers and presses. Indeed, it may be said that, as Latino fiction has shaped the landscape of Latino culture at large, it has helped reconstruct (along with other ethnic literatures) the broader American culture, thereby fully claiming a place in the American literary canon.

— Adrienne Pilon and Dean Franco

Learn More

Augenbraum, Harold, and Margarite Fernández Olmos, eds. *The Latino Reader: An American Literary Tradition from 1542 to the Present.* New York: Houghton Mifflin, 1997. This collection provides historical background on writers and their sociopolitical context while featuring their works. A list of additional readings presents criticism and history for research on all periods.

Calderón, Hectór, and José David Saldívar, eds. *Criticism in the Borderlands: Studies in Chicano Literature, Culture and Ideology.* Durham, N.C.: Duke University Press, 1991. This collection brings together some of the most compelling and important criticism on Chicano literature today by major Chicano scholars from around the country.

Cortina, Rodolfo, ed. *Hispanic American Literature: An Anthology.* Chicago: NTC, 1998. A comprehensive collection of Hispanic and Latino prose and poetry spanning from the sixteenth century to the present.

Luis, William. *Dance Between Two Cultures: Latino Caribbean Literature Written in the United States.* Nashville, Tenn.: Vanderbilt University Press, 1997. An historical overview of Puerto Rican, Dominican and Cuban literature in the United States along with critical essays.

Milligan, Bryce, Mary Guerrero Milligan, and Angela de Hoyos, eds. *Daughters of the Fifth Sun.* New York: Putnam, 1995. A feminist introduction starts off this collection of contemporary Latina short fiction and poetry.

Santiago, Roberto, ed. *Boricuas: Influential Puerto Rican Writings—An Anthology.* New York: Ballantine, 1995. A good general reference on the subject, this text is comprehensive in its inclusion of a variety of genres.

Stavans, Ilan, ed. *New World: Young Latino Writers.* New York: Delta, 1997. Stavans has compiled twenty-three stories by some of the youngest and most exciting Latino writers working today.

Suárez, Virgil, and Delia Poey, eds. *Iguana Dreams: New Latino Fiction.* New York: Harper, 1992. The first anthology of contemporary Latino fiction, featuring twenty-nine different writers.

Latin American
Short Fiction

A s common and somewhat acceptable as the term "Latin
American literature" is as a functional label for literature
produced in the "Latin" countries of the Americas, most anthol-
ogists and scholars tend to take time to apologize for its usage
or, at least, to justify its usage in the face of some opposition. The
basic contention is valid: Latin America is not a distinctive geographical or geopolitical space. Nor is it a culturally homoge-
nous space. The term is a convenience, but it is a convenience
that is rooted in some basic facts of history. For the purposes of
this survey, the term encompasses those countries in the "New
World" formerly colonized by Portugal, Spain, and Italy. Included, therefore, are the countries that are located on the
South American continent and those countries in the area that
is now called Central America. Those islands in the Caribbean
that share a history of colonization with the South American
continent are also included. The functional languages of Latin
American literature are Spanish and Portuguese. Spanish domi-
nates. Without Brazil and its formidable tradition of literature,
Latin America would be exclusively a Spanish domain. Very little exists in Latin America that pertains to Italy, even though
Italians have had a significant presence in countries like Argentina and Bolivia, but then so have the English. English remains a
distinct foil to the march of Latin American literature and culture.

The history of Latin America is a history which could have
paralleled the history of North America and its increasingly homogenized single-nation identity. Like the American North, the
South has had a strong imaginative sense of its unity. This imaginative identity dominated much of the seventeenth and eighteenth centuries largely because of the liberation efforts of individuals like Simón Bolívar. Bolívar imagined and wrote about a
Latin American state that would share much of the sense of nationalism that would come to define the North. There is a rea-

son for this development. As with the British empire, the Spanish empire was quite clearly understood to be an extension of the Spanish nation-state. Brazil remained a peculiar and massive interruption of the dominance of Spanish culture in the Americas. That dominance extended well into the North American continent until a century ago and has slowly begun to crawl its way back into that continent now through immigration and a redefining of cultural and racial demographics.

The Spanish colonial government understood its empire as a single force and a single protectorate and thus sought to conceive of a culture that was distinctive and somewhat homogeneous. The variations emerged through the peculiar dialogues and clashes that took place between these Spanish societies and the native communities that existed in the regions before the arrival of the Spanish. The Inca in eastern South America, the Aztec in Central America, and the Maya in the rain forests of northeastern South America were large and dominant cultures before the arrival of the Spanish. Spanish colonialism forced these cultures to struggle for survival, but in their struggle they had a lasting effect on the culture of the region—the understanding of landscape and the shaping of the imagination.

Latin American literature and, in many ways, Latin American short fiction emerge out of the strange contradictions between nationalism and empire that characterize the experience of the region. The movement toward independence in Latin America, as in all other formerly colonized states, entailed a cultural quest for a distinctive cultural and national identity. This identity would be found in the history and native presence of these nations and in the agendas for self-actualization that would emerge during the period leading toward independence and the demise of the Spanish empire's rule. Latin American identity is peculiarly defined by the tension between the colonial force of Spanish dominance, the spirit of discovery and the quest to found a new society with new values and a new understanding of landscape and individuality, and the presence of non-European cultures in the region. In Brazil, this pattern is very much a part of what has given a distinction to its cultural identity and to its literature. Brazil's distinction lies in the dialogue that the society has had with its racial complexity, particularly the presence of African slaves and freed people, especially from Nigeria, in the region. The religious and narrative experiences have given rise to a distinctive literary sensibility, which remains one of the more remarkable and fresh in the modern world.

Most scholars recognize in Latin American culture and literary practice the importance of history and the way that history has come to shape the way people see themselves. The question is, do Argentines see themselves as quite distinct from Colombians? Do Mexicans feel any affinity with Cubans? Do Peruvians believe that one can read their literature with the same lens that would be used to read Brazilian literature? Nationalism has made it possible to recognize very peculiar and specific trends in Latin American writing that are specific to different regions and countries. The history of modern Latin American writing, like the history of Caribbean writing or African writing, has been one of balancing the pressures of the publishing industry, which has a tendency to homogenize and lump all countries into a single, manageable unit, and the desire for a distinctive nationalism that would recognize that the histories of these various countries, while intersecting at certain points, remain quite distinct.

This survey presents more similarities and patterns of Latin American literature than differences. It acknowledges also that the writers being discussed are themselves related to one another as part of a fraternity (or sorority) of like-minded artists working in a distinctive milieu. During the middle of the nineteenth century, a large contingent of Latin American writers found one another while studying in Paris. At the Parisian cafés, the talk was of politics, revolution, and the unification of Latin America. They found that they shared a language and a history of trying to break the shackles of the culture that undergirded their language. In Paris, they knew they were not Spanish or European writers—not in any useful political or cultural sense. They knew they were shaping a literature that was going to be uniquely birthed from the bloodied soil of Latin America. The shaping of a Latin American literary sensibility would grow out of the fact of language. Language helps to shape audience, and audience leads to the natural assumption of a literature—a national literature. The audience in this sense is an English-speaking audience that does presume the Latin American culture as a collective other. They share a language and, in time, have come to share certain distinctive traits in literary practice.

The 1960's brought with it the work of Alejo Carpentier in Cuba, Gabriel García Márquez in Colombia, Jorge Luis Borges in Bolivia, and Mario Vargas Llosa in Peru and what has been termed "Magical Realism" or "marvelous realism." This sometimes uncertainly and variously defined literary style came to shape much of the literature produced in the larger world in the last thirty years of the twentieth century. It is a remarkable phenomenon, but those who have been drawn to it have understood it in rather homogenized terms. There have been other trends, even if less influential, over the years. There was a period of Latin American writing in the 1930's when realist novelists, influenced by the Russian masters, were producing works of naturalism and political commitment. Brazilian writers wrote about the horrors of life on sugar plantations, and those in the Spanish-speaking countries wrote of peasant life in the rural areas of these nations. These styles appeared in the many periodicals that would come to publish the work of the most important Latin American writers over the centuries.

In the late 1800's, Edgar Allan Poe supplied many Latin American writers with the grotesque sensibility that some have argued was the precursor of the magical side of Magical Realism. Latin writers encountered Poe's work while living in Paris. These writers were reading and translating the work of English and French writers and were bringing those sensibilities to bear on their own work. These patterns emerged in somewhat collective ways. Communication through periodicals, conferences, exile, and cross-country travel led to a situation in which these writers, while acknowledging their nationalist distinctions, also understood themselves to be part of a larger movement in literature. Philosophies therefore abound regarding the character of the Latin American aesthetic. The short story remains one of the most important forms of literary practice in Latin American literature because it has, whether by design or the accident of its length, been the laboratory of Latin American fictional writing. Any attempt to study the short story's peculiar history in Latin America amounts to a remarkable entry into the evolution of Latin American writing.

It would seem that a short story does, by its very nature, make certain aesthetic demands that have come to be accepted values or traits of the form. When does a short story become a novella, and when does a long short story become a novel? It is normally argued that the short story's popularity in Latin America emerges from the fact that the publishing industry there has been notoriously limited. The heart of fiction writing in the region has not been the novel-making of publishing houses (as has been the case in Britain and America, for instance) but has rested instead in the powerful and innovative works of periodicals and journals. These venues, the nature of their size, favored the short story. Others have argued that the short story is peculiarly popular and famous in Latin America because the aesthetics of the short story are closely tied to the narrative tradition of folklore and the oral tradition that have shaped the region over the years. Such scholars have linked the modern Latin American short story to the folktales of the Inca, Maya, Taino, and Aztec peoples; the oral epics of the Yoruba; and the detailed accounts of discovery and proselytizing that were written by conquerors and monks alike during the age of expansion. The idea is a compelling one but one that does not always explain some of the heavily Westernized qualities of the Latin American text. Others hold to the view that the short story developed well in Latin America because a few successful and sometimes exclusive short-story geniuses in the region (like Borges) made writing short stories a distinct cultural phenomenon. It forced all writers to take the perfection of the form seriously and to be venturesome in promoting it. Regardless of the reason, the short story is a major force in Latin American writing.

The short story is one way in which the literary developments of the region have been defined. There are hundreds of "groundbreaking" anthologies of the Latin American short story in translation emerging in the English-speaking parts of the world. These anthologies have also become one of the important vehicles by which the works of Latin American female writers are reaching the rest of the world. The short-story anthology is a convenient vehicle because it allows for the inclusion of many writers in a single volume and it serves as a splendid primer for university courses on Latin American writing.

This survey will examine some of the highlights of the development of Latin American writing and will draw attention to both the collective and shared sensibilities of the Latin American short story and the important nationalistic differences. It is more helpful, however, to examine these developments through the work of some of the most important writers of short fiction in the region.

The Colonial Period
Ascribing literary precedence to the colonial period in Latin American history is something that has been done increasingly by contemporary writers who have turned to the writings of that period for a tradition. They have, in effect, turned to the historical and bureaucratic documents of a massive and complex empire that established, in the middle of the sixteenth century, two major viceroyalties in Lima, Peru, and in Mexico City. These complex communities were shaped by the acts of the conquistadors, who marched through the continent transforming what had once been an empire of islands into a vast empire of lands and peoples, which stretched throughout the Americas, as far north as Texas and as far east as the Philippines. At first the island of Hispanola was the heart of the Spanish empire, but once Hernán Cortés had ransacked Mexico and had been followed first by an equally formidable army of monks and priests and later by a remarkably organized battalion of lawyers and bureaucrats, the Spanish empire was in full swing in the Americas.

For nearly two hundred years, the Spanish were the dominant force in the region. Havana remained an important Spanish American center and trade city, while Lima and Mexico City evolved as cultural hubs that in many ways challenged the ascendancy of Castile and Madrid. In these New World cities, there was a thriving artistic and literary community. The work produced by this community, however, was notably imitative of the work of the Golden Age in Spanish letters, and it produced a poet who is still recognized as one of the last of the great Golden Age poets, Sor Juana Inés de la Cruz. Modern Latin American writers have found greater affinity and relevance not in the literary output of the early colonials but in the historical documents of the great figures of that period.

Spain's government bureaucracies were, if nothing else, fascinated by the act of recording. Files upon files remain that detail the strange and vicious process of colonialization and the terrible anxiety and guilt that surrounded many of the actions of the colonizers in the region. The narratives of historians, governors, priests, and leaders of the evolving empire remain some of the most fascinating accounts of an emerging culture, an emerging identity that can now be regarded as distinctly Latin American.

Christopher Columbus himself began a trend in writing about the Indies that regards the apprehension of the new space as an act of "discovering" the other or coming to grips with the other. This otherness would come to influence the works of such Western artists as William Shakespeare, who in his play *The Tempest* (pr. 1611) echoed the fantastical narratives of the colonizing world in his construction of a play. The play is as much rooted in magic and the supernatural as it is in the celebration of colonial authority and the patriarchy of the colonialist agenda. Columbus told his tale and sought to reconstruct his tales of mystery and discovery. These tales, positioning the colonial space as a world of impossible and different happenings, can easily be seen as one of the important precursors to the Latin American text.

The political agenda of Columbus remained relevant to many who would follow him: a strong need to convince the rest of the world that a new space, a new sensibility, and a new world of powerful images and wealth had been found. It is not hard to see in much of the way that Latin American literature is apprehended today something of this quest. It is also not hard to see the inclination toward the magical as part of the larger project to create a sense of otherness, a sense of cultural removal in the work of contemporary writers.

Some of the important writers of histories and other fascinating narratives include seeming admonitions to pure and chaste life in bawdy stories that barely mask the relish that writers like Juan Rodríguez Freyle took in outlining some of the lewd acts of sinners. These writers remain the singular conduit by which the history of the Inca, Taino, Maya, and Aztec people of that continent have passed to the modern reader. Looming above all others is Bartolomé de Las Casas, who can be credited in many ways with defining the racial shape of the region in his many efforts to tackle the troubling question of the fate of the native peoples of the region. Las Casas's writings are peppered with detailed emblematic accounts of atrocities against native peoples. His efforts were to convince the Spanish crown of the need to treat the native peoples as humans, as worthy of the efforts of evangelism by the Catholic Church. Along with him were writers like Gonzalo Fernández de Oviedo, Francisco López de Gómara, and Bernal Díaz del Castillo.

There is no way to describe the works of these writers as short stories or even fictional narratives, but contemporary writers have shown again and again that there are, buried in these narratives, a series of shorter exemplary stories that have led to a tradition of aesthetics and narrative consistency in the work of the writers who came after them. The themes with which these writers grappled, the politics that shaped their existence, and the terrible conditions they witnessed, even as they enjoyed the excitement of establishing a whole new world, are elements that have come to shape the character of Latin American fiction in the last several hundred years.

It would therefore be a mistake to presume that the Latin American short story began in the nineteenth century. Indeed the Latin American tale, understood as emerging out of a larger tradition that was attempting to give names to a new space, began much earlier as part of the conflicted truth of the colonial agenda itself. Modern writers remain inscribed in the truth of this history and have, for years, been involved in restoring to the Latin American imagination the fact of these histories. In other words, it is impossible to read Carlos Fuentes, Gabriel García Márquez, or Alejo Carpentier without reference to the writings of those figures of Latin American history listed above.

There exist several native narratives collected by priests and government officials that now form a part of the larger fabric of the Latin American text. No one can claim purity in these narratives, which were collected by colonizers and used for their own agendas, but many of these stories have somehow tallied with the oral narratives that have been passed down from generation to generation in the remote parts of Latin America.

Nationalism and the Emergence of the Short Story

The nineteenth century saw the continent-wide press toward nationalism. In many ways this pattern would not take root in Brazil in the same way because Brazil's position as the seat of the Portuguese empire was largely unassailable from the onset. In fact, much of the literature that has emerged in Brazil, while being rooted in the landscape and culture of the region, has so shaped and defined Portuguese letters that there is far less of a sense of inferiority and acquiescence to the metropolis or the mother country than has occurred in the literatures from the former English colonies and the Spanish colonial countries. The emergence of nationalism in the nineteenth century, however, played a major part in the shaping of a literary aesthetic. This aesthetic, influenced by the push for nationalism in such places as the United States, Haiti, and the march for revolution in France, generated, at first, works that sought to locate a literary tradition in the region. This attempt was not unlike the nineteenth century preoccupation with origins that characterized literary practice in Europe. In England, there was the championing of the Anglo-Saxon mythic narrative *Beowulf* (c. 1000), while in Germany numerous renderings of *Nibelungenlied* (c. 1200; *The Nibelungenlied*, 1848) served as foundation blocks for a nationalist aesthetic. In Chile, Diego Barros Arana produced a seminal edition of the epic poem by Fernando Álvarez de Toledo, *Purén indómito* (1862), which would compete with the Argentine Juan María Gutiérrez's 1848 edition of Pedro de Oña's epic *Arauco domado* (*Arauco Tamed*, 1948), which appeared in 1596.

It was also during this period that the first distinctive collections of short stories began to appear in Latin America. While some critics remain adamant that the *cuadros de costumbres* were in fact not quite short stories but narratives, which functioned as anecdotal tales with little of the structural unities normally associated with the short story as it emerged in the latter part of the nineteenth century. These narratives undeniably influenced the short-story movement that assumed full force at the beginning of the twentieth century.

The earlier part of the nineteenth century saw many examples of the long narrative. The novel was thriving, influenced largely by the massive efforts of writers like Charles Dickens, Nathaniel Hawthorne, Herman Melville, and other writers from outside the Latin American tradition. Significant epic novels would emerge as part of the articulation of nationalism. Postcolonial critic Homi Bhaba asserted that the novel is inextricably linked to the notion of nationalism. His belief was borne out in the literature produced in the early part of the century. Indeed this idea is the foundation of the work by Doris Sommer, *Foundational Fictions: The National Romances of Latin America* (1991), which argues convincingly that the shaping of the nationalism of the region was tied to the fiction generated during that time.

The *cuadros de costumbres* emerged out of a nineteenth century Latin American preoccupation with looking closely at the realities of the continent and the various societies that were emerging out of the colonial backdrop. Politics, sociological conditions, and a fascination with the flora and fauna of the region led to works that offered vignettes and narratives depicting the life of natives, Africans, and other peasant classes. The term *cuadros de costumbres* was coined in Colombia, where writers would submit these somewhat static and detailed accounts of Latin American culture to a select group of periodicals devoted to such narratives. *El Mosaico* (1858-1872) published the works of such writers as José Caicedo Rojas, Juan de Dios Restrepo, and José María Vergara y Vergara. The fascination with bizarre details and the focus on local experience would come to shape the work of writers that would follow them. Most important, however, they established in the imagination of Latin American readers and writers a language that was located in the region and that was involved with the casting of a reality that was distinctive and self-reflexive.

The true emergence of the modern short story—a genre in its own right—would not take place in Latin American letters until the latter half of the nineteenth century. At that time, the shared sense of a Latin American identity was taking shape. Periodicals throughout the region were publishing the writing of authors from all across the continent, and there was a growing sense that a distinctive sensibility was emerging. The next one hundred and thirty years would see the emergence of some of the most important and gifted writers of the twentieth century. These writers evolved a nationalist agenda in their work—an agenda that would secure the nationalist identities of the various nations. They shaped an aesthetic that could be theorized as Latin American—an aesthetic emerging from a shared history, a shared political evolution, and a shared sense of literary antecedent.

Authors of what can be best termed *cuadros de costumbres,* such as Argentina's Esteban Echeverría, paved the way for writers such as Domingo Faustino Sarmiento, who has been described by Roberto González Echevarría as "one of the most prominent figures in nineteenth century Latin American literature, politics, social thought and education" largely on the strength of his sometimes-infamous *Civilización y barbarie: Vida de Juan Facundo Quiroga, y aspecto físico, costumbres, y hábitos de la República Argentina* (commonly known as *Facundo;* 1845; *Life in the Argentine Republic in the Days of the Tyrants: Or, Civilization and Barbarism,* 1868), and the early feminist Juana Manuela Gorriti. Other notable nineteenth century authors include Ricardo Palma of Peru, and a writer who is quite decidedly one of the greatest writers of the last two hundred years, the mulatto Joaquim Maria Machado de Assis of Brazil. Machado published nine novels and more than two hundred short stories in his lifetime.

The Modern Short Story

There are several ways to talk about the Latin American short story. Some scholars have, in an attempt to underplay the regional distinctions of the genre, focused on a select number of stellar writers who have formed an impressive pantheon of Latin American giants stretching across the "cone" of South America and into the islands of the Caribbean archipelago. These writers all helped to shape a Latin American aesthetic that would give rise to even more cosmopolitan writers of the contemporary period. While movements are acknowledged, they are not defined by nationality but by literary trends and concerns. Others have sought more regional and nationalistic readings of the literature of the region. The distinctions that separate the Brazilian and Cuban literary traditions from those of the larger nation-states on the mainland of South America, for instance, are often cited as the basis for this approach. A number of short-story anthologies argue the case for a well-defined tradition by nationality, which must be identified, understood, and appreciated for any genuine understanding of the work of the region. These two approaches to the Latin American short story, however, cannot be seen as exclusive. Indeed, what is worth noting here is that the Latin American short story, like all of Latin American letters has, in the last century, been forced to define its relevance and strength in a milieu that lends itself to easy generalizations and the regionalism of the publishing world. In other words, for the last hundred years, Latin American literature has been perceived as a "new thing," a fantastic and unknown thing to be discovered. While literature from the region has never been obscure and inaccessible, it has been distant enough to make the discovery of a new voice an occasion for the celebration of otherness.

Many of the major writers of the region have, at some point in their careers, lived in extended exile from their home countries either in Latin American or Europe. This fact encourages a survey of the literature of the region through examination of the writers who have come to have an impact on the international stage. There are a number of indisputable giants of Latin American writing, figures who have been seen as representatives of the region and who have unquestionably influenced writers in the twentieth century. These stalwart figures have shaped the way in which the short story has been written in Latin America and around the world. They are influential writers, major figures of the century, and writers who should be studied carefully by anyone interested in examining Latin American literature. These writers, tellingly, have developed international reputations, but their lasting legacy is "local"—it rests in their success at establishing a tradition in Latin American writing.

Of this group of writers, Rubén Darío of Nicaragua is the least likely to be considered a master of the short story. He was better known as a poet. Darío is arguably the most important Spanish poet in centuries. His fresh modernism was, at its core, a rejection of the old literary traditions of Spain and an embrace of anything outside that sensibility. In a jazzlike openness to all other forms, Darío, on the strength of his first major success, *Azul* (1888), saw develop around him a movement that would be called *Modernismo*—a movement which would change the direction of Latin American writing. Dario's contributions were largely in poetry but he also wrote a series of very short, poetic narratives, which would influence the works of numerous short-story writers to come.

If Darío was a central influence, the person who would take Darío's ideas and transform them into the short-story genre, bringing to the form a perfection rarely surpassed since, was Horacio Quiroga, often labeled the father of the Latin American short story. His dispassionate rendering of narratives set in the jungles of Uruguay and his exploration of themes of violence and human abjection shaped an aesthetic which would come to be called Borges-like in the latter part of the twentieth century. Jorge Luis Borges, along with Gabriel García Márquez and Julio Cortázar, admitted an indebtedness to this writer of sublime tragedies.

During the early twentieth century, several important fiction writers emerged, many of them specializing in the short story. Their importance as writers rested largely on their international reputations. These writers included the Argentine Ricardo Güiraldes, author of *Cuentos de muerte y de sangre* (1915); Rómulo Gallegos of Venezuela, who, apart from writing one of the most important and definitive novels of Latin American letters, *Doña Bárbara* (1929; English translation, 1984), also published several short stories in the realist vein; and Luisa Mercedes Levinson, an Argentine who lived much of her life outside Argentina and who produced a small but significant body of stories and novels, which are notable for their striking comingling of the erotic and the violent.

It would be Jorge Luis Borges, however, her blind countryman and one of the first writers to declare exclusive loyalty to the short story (having found the novel to be far too long and flawed in its very essence), who has come to define the Latin American short story. Borges, in many ways, seems an unlikely spokesperson for a nationalist literary tradition since very little of his work is set in Latin America. Indeed, Borges was notorious for locating his narratives outside the region. Furthermore, Borges spent much of his writing life living outside Latin America. His literary style, rather than adhering to the stereotype established by other writers who focused so fully and passionately on the landscape and culture of the region, turned toward a more ironic and dispassionate tone. His devotion to German and English writers, whom he read in their original languages, is unquestionable, but he opened the Latin American text, allowing it to become more international in its vision. Borges also forced the artists of the region to seriously examine what an aesthetic truly is. Is an aesthetic defined by subject matter, by the use of local fauna and flora, or is an aesthetic related to literary style, having its shape and structure defined by a coherent and traceable tradition? Borges's narratives introduced certain critical features to the Latin American text. His *Ficciones, 1935-1944* (1944; English translation, 1962) can be called only seminal; it established his penchant for the use of fictionalized historical details, his fascination with the idea of the short story as a metaphysical essay—a polemical construct which never loses sight of the need for drama, tension, and conflict. Sentimentality was eschewed at all costs by Borges, and his work sought to stretch the narrative possibilities of the genre.

If Borges introduced the practice of irony and a dispassionate sensibility to the Latin American oeuvre, his Cuban contemporary Alejo Carpentier introduced a devotion to history that remains unchallenged. Carpentier's fiction is always fascinated by time, is always rooted in a strong sense of historical space, and always adheres to the notion that Latin American culture is shaped by a distinctive history that can be excavated for narrative possibilities. His ability to bring together a strong sense of history and a fascination with the magic of human experience and narrative is one of the reasons he is sometimes regarded as the first genuine practitioner of the Magical Realist approach to fiction. In his short-story collection *Guerra del tiempo* (1958; *War of Time*, 1970), Carpentier explores various narrative modes and thematic complexities, which have been extremely influential in modern Latin American fiction.

Miguel Ángel Asturias, the Guatemalan winner of the Nobel Prize in Literature, may have been pivotal in alerting the Latin American literary world to the rich possibilities located in the native languages and cultures of the region. His short fictions, for years, seemed devoted to exploring the folk traditions of the Mayan tradition to which he belonged. Much of his early work involved the translation of these Mayan narratives into Spanish and the use of these tales to shape his novels and short stories. The incredible, mythic quality of these stories would serve as ample fodder for the "magical" side of the Magical Realist construct in Latin American writing.

The 1960's saw a seemingly sudden explosion of Latin American writing on the world stage and, in the process, led to the emergence of several figures who are now considered to be the stalwart figures of the modern Latin American short story. In 1960, Julio Cortázar published *Rayuela* (1963; *Hopscotch*, 1966) and in the process ushered in the careers of Carlos Fuentes, Gabriel García Márquez, and Mario Vargas Llosa. Cortázar's short-story collections, which include the formidable *Bestiario* (1951) and the well-known *Todos los fuegos el fuego* (1966; *All Fires the Fire, and Other Stories*, 1973), reflect his fascination with the extraordinary and the bizarre, a surrealist sensibility he honed while living in Paris.

Carlos Fuentes, a Mexican with a most cosmopolitan background, has published some of the more important novels in Latin American letters. Like Carpentier in Cuba, Fuentes embarked on a journey to reconcile Mexico's violent and dichotomous past through sometimes conflicted but always probing narrative fiction. Fuentes's interest has always been to demonstrate that it is impossible to understand the Latin American sensibility without understanding both the native (in his case, the Aztec) and the colonial (Spanish) past and how these two pasts have intersected, clashed, and merged.

Gabriel García Márquez sets most of his narratives in his native Colombia. His fiction is fluent and remarkable for its capacity to balance his commitment to the exploration of political ideas and the study of human nature and human action. He remains, along with Borges, one of the best-known writers from Latin America, and he has always been a champion of writing from that region. While his output has been primarily in the form of the novel, he has published a number of remarkable short stories including the much-anthologized "A Very Old Man with Wings" and "Balthazar's Marvelous Afternoon," which reveal his interest in the surreal and supernatural and the uncannily deft way he excavates the foibles of the human condition. By locating the bulk of his narratives in his own region and by borrowing from such American writers as William Faulkner, García Márquez has effectively established one of the critical characteristics of the modern Latin American writer: an international bent that remains rooted in an understanding of the local. It is a balance that is not always achieved but one that many writers seek to accomplish.

Mario Vargas Llosa, like Márquez, has not published as widely as others in the area of the short story; however, like Márquez, Vargas Llosa has brought fame and some popularity to the Latin American literary world through the publication of several very important novels. Vargas Llosa, who was born in Peru, and who honed his craft in the region, published one collection of short stories, *Los jefes* (1959; *The Cubs, and Other Stories*, 1979), which reflects some of the themes that would mark his work. Vargas Llosa's narratives are consistently preoccupied with guilt and regret—guilt shaped by the arrival of maturity and the capacity of an individual to view his or her sordid past with the hindsight of enlightenment. The horrors and failures of the past lead to intense guilt such that the narratives themselves tend to be extended acts of penance and expiation. It should not be lost on readers that this attempt to reconcile a past full of secrets and errors is quite emblematic of the Latin American text.

Beyond this grouping of important figures there are numerous other Latin American writers who have contributed significantly to the shaping of the Latin American short story. Each year new anthologies appear with translations of a "new wave" of narratives from Latin America. A significant development has been the appearance of many specialist anthologies, which have focused on the sometimes-ignored work of women writers from the region. These anthologies demonstrate that Latin American women have been writing stories for at least two centuries, and their work has proved as equally compelling and fascinating as the work of their male counterparts. At the same time, anthologies that focus on the work from specific countries continue to appear. Most of these anthologies attempt to justify the act of speaking about a national literature, but for the most part the act of collecting work from a given country is prompted by the pragmatics of publishing and the logistical nightmare that could come from other, more regional, anthologies.

Increasingly, the Latin American short story is expanding to include works by writers who were born and reared in the United States, some of whom are writing in English and others in Spanish. If nothing else, such developments show that Latin American writing is introducing more and more complex ways to view itself and is becoming a significant force in the evolution of the short-story genre. With the growth of a Latino population in North America, mass interest in Latin American authors has led to the emergence of many writers who have developed an international standing. These writers form the core of a new generation that has carried the Latin American short story into the twenty-first century.

— *Kwame Dawes*

Learn More

Arnold, A. James, Julio Rodríguez-Luis, and J. Michael Dash, eds. *A History of Literature in the Caribbean*. Philadelphia: J. Benjamins, 1994. A historical and critical look at literature from the Caribbean. Includes bibliographical references and an index.

Balderston, Daniel, ed. *The Latin American Short Story: An Annotated Guide to Anthologies and Criticism*. Westport, Conn.: Greenwood Press, 1992. Organizes the enormous body of short-story anthologies from the nineteen countries of Spanish America and Brazil for systematic study. The main section comprises annotated listings of 1,302 short-story anthologies. A second section comprises annotated bibliographies of criticism of the short story. Includes bibliographical references and an index.

Bloom, Harold, ed. *Caribbean Women Writers*. Philadelphia: Chelsea House, 1997. A thorough examination of contemporary, female Caribbean writers of English, including Jean Rhys, Jamaica Kincaid, Beryl Gilroy, and Edwidge Danticat. Includes bibliographical references and an index.

Brown, Stewart, ed. *Caribbean New Wave: Contemporary Short Stories*. Portsmouth, N.H.: Heinemann, 1990. This anthology collection covers Caribbean short stories written in English and discusses Caribbean social life and customs.

Echevarría, Roberto González, and Enrique Pupo-Walker, eds. *The Cambridge History of Latin American Literature*. 3 vols. New York: Cambridge University Press, 1996. Volume 1 covers the period from discovery to modernism, volume 2 covers the twentieth century, and volume 3 covers Brazilian literature. Includes bibliographical references and an index.

Erro-Peralta, Nora, and Caridad Silva-Núñez, eds. *Beyond the Border: A New Age in Latin American Women's Fiction*. Pittsburgh, Pa.: Cleis Press, 1991. Covers works by Latin American female writers. Includes bibliographical references.

Foster, David William, ed. *Handbook of Latin American Literature*. 2d ed. New York: Garland Publishing, 1992. Offers separate essays on all Latin American countries, including French and Creole Haiti and Portuguese Brazil, written by scholars who focus on dominant issues and major movements, figures, and works, with emphasis on sociocultural and interpretive assessments. Includes bibliographical references and an index.

Markham, E. A., ed. *The Penguin Book of Caribbean Short Stories.* New York: Penguin Books, 1996. Covers Caribbean social life and customs and examines selected short stories. Includes bibliographical references.

Moss, Joyce, and Lorraine Valestuk. *Latin American Literature and Its Times: Profiles of Notable Literary Works and the Historical Events That Influenced Them.* Detroit: Gale Group, 1999. The fifty works included in this volume span a variety of genres and countries (including the United States) as well as historical periods. Includes bibliographical references and an index.

Partnoy, Alicia, ed. *You Can't Drown the Fire: Latin American Women Writing in Exile.* Pittsburgh, Pa.: Cleis Press, 1988. Covers twentieth century female writers whose works have been translated into English. Includes bibliographical references.

Smith, Verity, ed. *Encyclopedia of Latin American Literature.* Chicago: Fitzroy Dearborn, 1997. Contains entries on writers, works, and topics relating to the literature of Latin America, including survey articles on all the continent's individual countries. Includes bibliographical references and an index.

Wickham, John, and Stewart Brown, eds. *The Oxford Book of Caribbean Short Stories.* New York: Oxford University Press, 1999. A pan-Caribbean collection, ranging beyond the Anglophone territories to include stories originally published in Spanish, French, and Dutch. Includes bibliographical references.

APPENDICES

More Latino Writers

The following list of 401 additional Latino writers is arranged by region: Caribbean, Central America, North America, and South America. Within regions, names appear by ethnicity or nationality, then alphabetically by surname. Each author is identified by the genre or discipline (essayist, novelist, dramatist, journalist, poet, anthropologist, etc.) that constitutes his or her main area of literary production. Selected titles follow each author's name (English titles are listed for those works in English translation), or in Spanish or Portuguese where no English translation exists; these books represent the authors' best-known works and are recommended for those wishing to become familiar with the author's work.

Caribbean

Cuba

Arrufat, Antón (poet and playwright, b. 1935)
  En claro
  Todos los domingos
Augier, Ángel (poet, b. 1910)
  Todo el mar en la ola
  Isla en el tacto
Ballagas, Emilio (poet, 1908-1954)
  Sabor eterno
  Elegía sin nombre y otros poemas
Cabrera, Lydia (folklorist, 1900-1991)
  Supersticiones y buenos consejos
  Afro-Cuban Tales
Casaus, Victor (essayist, b. 1944)
  Girón en la memoria
  Ojos sobre el pañuelo, Los
Díaz, Jesús (novelist, b. 1941)
  Canto de amor y de guerra
  Años duros, Los

Díaz Martínez, Manuel (poet, b. 1936)
  Poesía inconclusa
  Mientras traza su curva el pez de fuego
  Carro de los mortales, El
Eguren, Gustavo (novelist, b. 1925)
  Pingüinos, Los
  Alguien llama a la puerta
  Algo para la palidez y una ventana sobre el regreso
Fernández Retamar, Roberto (poet and essayist, b. 1930)
  Caliban and Other Essays
  Aquí
  Algo semejante a los monstruos antediluvianos
Fornet, Ambrosio (essayist, b. 1932)
  Paso del diluvio, Un
  En tres y dos
  Cuentos de la revolución cubana
Gómez de Avellaneda y Arteaga, Gertrudis (novelist, 1814-1873)
  Diario de amor
  Cuahtemoc, the Last Aztec Emperor
Labrador Ruiz, Enrique (novelist, 1902-1991)
  Trailer de sueños
  Cartas a la carte
  Anteo
Loynaz, Dulce María (novelist, 1902-1997)
  Juegos de agua
  Carta de amor de Tut-ank-amen
Montero, Mayra (novelist, b. 1952)
  Red of His Shadow, The
  Last Night I Spent with You, The
  Deep Purple
Morejón, Nancy (poet, b. 1944)
  Where the Island Sleeps Like a Wing
  Richard trajó su flauta y otros poemas
  Mutismos
Novas Calvo, Lino (essayist, 1905-1983)
  Maneras de contar
  Cayo Canas

Ortiz, Fernando (essayist, 1881-1969)
  Etnía y sociedad
  Cuban Counterpoint, Tobacco and Sugar
Padilla, Heberto (novelist, 1932-2000)
  Sent Off the Field
  House of Stone, A
  Heroes Are Grazing in My Garden
Piglia, Ricardo (novelist, b. 1941)
  Respiración artificial
  Nombre falso
  Invasión
Piñera, Virgilio (novelist, 1912-1979)
  Cuentos fríos
  Aire frío
Pita Rodríguez, Felix (short-story writer, b. 1909)
  Vietnam o notas de un diario
  Carlos Enríquez
Sarusky, Jaime (novelist, b. 1931)
  Tiempo de los desconocidos
  Rebelión en la octava casa
Soler Puig, José (novelist, b. 1916)
  Pan dormido
  Macho y la guanaja
Triana, José (playwright, b. 1931)
  Modern Stage in Latin America
  Medea en el espejo
Villaverde, Cirilo (novelist, 1812-1894)
  Teresa
  General Lopez, the Cuban Patriot
Zamacois, Eduardo (novelist, 1878-1972)
  Opinión ajena, La
  Loca de amor

Dominican Republic

Cabral, Manuel del (poet, 1907-1999)
  Trópico negro
  Doce poemas negros

Cartagena Portalatín, Aida (poet, b. 1918)
Woman Alone, A
Voz, La
Tierra escrita, La
Henríquez Ureña, Pedro (essayist, 1884-1946)
Plenitud de América
Desde Washington
Incháustegui Cabral, Héctor (novelist, 1912-1979)
En soledad de amor herido
Casi de ayer
Mir, Pedro (poet, b. 1913)
Poesías casi completas
Buen viaje
Amen de mariposas

Trinidad and Tobago
Palacios, Lucila (novelist, b. 1902)
Teresa Carreño
Ayer violento

Central America

Costa Rica
Chase, Alfonso (poet, b. 1945)
Cuerpos
Árbol del tiempo, El
Fallas, Carlos Luis (novelist, 1909-1966)
Mi madrina
Marcos Ramírez
Mamita Yunai
García Monge, Joaquín (novelist, 1881-1958)
Hijas del campo
Abnegación
Herra, Rafael Ángel (novelist, b. 1943)
Hablemos de teatro
Cosas de este mundo, Las
Istarú, Ana (poet, b. 1960)
Baby Boom en el Paraiso

Naranjo, Carmen (novelist, b. 1928)
There Never Was a Once upon a Time
Camino al mediodía
Odio, Eunice (short-story writer, 1922-1974)
Territorio del alba y otros poemas
Elementos terrestres, Los
Oreamuno, Yolanda (novelist, 1916-1956)
Relatos escogidos
Lo largo del corto camino

El Salvador
Argueta, Manlio (novelist and poet, b. 1936)
En el costado de la luz
De aquí en adelante
Dalton, Roque (poet, 1935-1975)
Salvador at War
Militant Poetry
Escobar Galindo, David (poet, b. 1943)
Universo neutral
Grieta en el agua, Una
Fábulas
Lars, Claudía (poet, 1899-1974)
Tierra de infancia
Casa de vídrio
Lindo, Hugo (novelist, 1917-1985)
Ways of Rain
Libro de horas
Aquí se cuentan cuentos
Salarrué [Salvador Salazar Arrué] (novelist, 1899-1975)
Catleya luna
Cuentos de barro

Guatemala
Arévalo Martínez, Rafael (poet, 1884-1975)
Nights in the Nunciature Palace
Life, A
Arias, Arturo (novelist, b. 1950)
Norte, El
After the Bombs

Castañeda, Omar S. (novelist, b. 1954)
Naranjo the Muse
Imagining Isabel
Herrera, Flavio (novelist, 1895-1968)
Mujeres
Lente opaca
Bulbuxya
Monteforte Toledo, Mario (novelist, b. 1911)
Entre la piedra y la cruz
Casi todos los cuentos
Anaite
Solorzano, Carlos (playwright, b. 1922)
Zapato
Crossroads, and Other Plays

Honduras
Bähr, Eduardo (short-story writer, b. 1940)
Fotografía del peñasco
Cuento de la guerra, El
Carías, Marcos (novelist, 1905-1949)
Heredad, La
Guerra inútil, La
Díaz Lozano, Argentina (short-story writer, b. 1912)
Topacios
Peregrinaje
Monterroso, Augusto (short-story writer, b. 1921)
Short Shorts
Nim
Aff
Sosa, Roberto (poet, b. 1930)
Pobres, Los
Muros

Mexico
Alemán, Mateo (novelist, 1547-1614)
Rogue: Or the Life of Guzmán de Alfarache, The
Aridjis, Homero (poet, b. 1940)
Vivir para ver
1492

Agustín, José (novelist and playwright, b. 1944)
  Tumba, La
  De perfil
Avilés Fabila, René (short-story writer, b. 1940)
  Todo el amor
  Borges y yo
Azuela, Arturo (novelist, b. 1938)
  Shadows of Silence
  Mar de utopias, La
Boullosa, Carmen (novelist, b. 1954)
  Miracle Worker, The
  Leaving Tabasco
  They're Cows, We're Pigs
Campos, Julieta (novelist, b. 1932)
  Fear of Losing Eurydice, The
  Celina or the Cats
Carballido, Emilio (playwright, b. 1925)
  Rosalba and the Llaveros Family
  I Too Speak of the Rose
Cosío Villegas, Daniel (scholar, 1898-1976)
  Frente a la revolución mexicana
  Biografía intelectual
Costantini, Humberto (poet and playwright, 1924-1987)
  Long Night of Francisco Sanctis, The
  Gods, the Little Guys, and the Police, The
Díaz Mirón, Salvador (poet, 1858-1928)
  Poesías
  Lascas
Elizondo, Salvador (novelist, b. 1932)
  Retrato de Zoe y otras mentiras
  Chronicle of an Instant
Galindo, Sergio (novelist, 1926-1993)
  Precipice, The
  Mexican Masquerade
  Hombre de los hongos, El

Gardea, Jesús (novelist, b. 1939)
Tornavoz, El
Sonar la guerra
Canciónes para una sola cuerda
Garro, Elena (novelist, 1920-1998)
Reencuentro de personajes
Recollections of Things to Come
Huerta, Efraín (poet, 1914-1982)
Poemas de viaje
Amor, patria mía
Absoluto amor
Ibargüengoitia, Jorge (playwright, 1928-1983)
Llego Margo
Lightning of August
Dead Girls, The
Jamís, Fayad (poet, 1930-1988)
Fuente de la palabra
Abrí la verja de hierro
Leñero, Vicente (playwright, b. 1933)
Vivir del teatro
Asesinato, el doble crimen de los Flores Muñoz
Menéndez, Miguel Ángel (novelist, 1905-1982)
Unidad de América
Malintzin en un fuste, seis rostros y una sola máscara
Hollywood sin pijamas
Monsiváis, Carlos (essayist, b. 1938)
Nuevo catecismo para indios remisos
Mexican Postcards
Amor perdido
Montemayor, Carlos (novelist, b. 1947)
Veta de sangre
Abril y otras estaciónes, 1977-1989
Novo, Salvador (playwright, 1904-1974)
Return Ticket
Continente vacío

Owen, Gilberto (poet, 1905-1952)
  Libro de Ruth
  Infierno perdido
  Desvelo
Paso, Fernando del (novelist, b. 1935)
  Palinuro of Mexico
  José Trigo
Pitol, Sergio (novelist, b. 1941)
  Centro de la noche
  Camino de las cosas
Puga, María Luisa (novelist, b. 1944)
  Forma del silencio
  Accidentes
Sabines, Jaime (poet, 1926-1999)
  Twin Peaks
  Algo sobre la muerte del mayor Sabines
Solares, Ignacio (novelist, b. 1945)
  Puerta del cielo
  Hombre habitado
Taibo, Paco Ignacio (novelist, b. 1949)
  Return to the Same City
  Easy Thing, An
Vasconcelos, José (philosopher, 1882-1959)
  Mexican Ulysses, A
  Cosmic Race, The
  Bolivarismo y monroísmo
  Aspects of Mexican Civilization
Vicens, Joséfina (novelist, 1911-1988)
  False Years, The
  Empty Book, The
Villaurrutia, Xavier (playwright, 1903-1950)
  Textos y pretextos
  Pobre Barba Azul, El
Zea, Leopoldo (essayist, b. 1912)
  Pensamiento latinoamericano, El
  Mexican Consciousness and Its Role in the West

Zepeda, Eraclio (short-story writer, b. 1937)
Colibrí
Asela

Nicaragua
Belli, Giaconda (poet, b. 1948)
Mujer habitada, La
Amor insurrecto
Coronel Urtecho, José (short-story writer, 1906-1994)
Rápido tránsito (al ritmo de Norteamérica)
Diez cartas al Pater
Cuadra, Pablo António (poet, 1912-2002)
Zoo
Songs of Cifar and the Sweet Sea
Jaguar Myth and Other Poems
Martínez Rivas, Carlos (poet, b. 1924)
Paraíso recobrado
Insurrección solitaria
Murillo, Rosario (poet, b. 1951)
Angel in the Deluge
Ramírez, Sergio (novelist, b. 1942)
Tiempo de fulgor
Hatful of Tigers: Reflections on Art, Culture, and Politics

Panama
Alvarado de Ricord, Elsie (poet, b. 1928)
Holocausto de rosa
Entre materia y sueño
Beleño C., Joaquín (novelist, b. 1922)
Luna verde
Gamboa Road Gang
Estrella de Panamá
Guardia, Gloria (essayist, b. 1940)
Tiniebla blanca
Búsqueda del rostro, La
Jaramillo Levi, Enrique (poet, b. 1944)
When New Flowers Bloomed
Cajas de resonancia

Jurado, Ramón H. (novelist, 1922-1978)
  San Cristóbal
  Desertores
Miró, Ricardo (poet, 1883-1940)
  Leyenda del Pacífico
  Caminos silenciosos
Peralta, Bertalicia (short-story writer, b. 1939)
  Encore
  Atrincherado amor
Pitty, Dimas Lidio (novelist, b. 1941)
  Vida es una vida, Una
  Cantos para la paz
Sierra, Stella (poet, b. 1917)
  Palabras sobre poesía
  Agua dulce
Sinán, Rogelio (novelist, 1902-1994)
  Plenilunio
  Chiquilinga
Solarte, Tristán (novelist, b. 1924)
  In the Time of the Tyrants
  Ahogado

North America

Chilean American
Agosín, Marjorie (poet and novelist, b. 1955)
  Angel of Memory, The
  Alfareras, Las
Alegría, Fernando (novelist, b. 1918)
  Chilean Spring, The
  Allende

Colombian American
Angel, George (novelist, b. 1964)
  Fifth Season, The
Sanchez-Scott, Milcha (playwright, b. 1953)
  Stone Wedding
  Dorado, El

Costa Rican American
Bruce-Novoa, Juan D. (scholar and novelist, b. 1944)
Only the Good Times
Missions in Conflict: Essays on U.S.-Mexican Relations and
Chicano Culture

Cuban American
Ada, Alma Flor (children's books author, b. 1938)
Vuelo del quetzal
Comó nació el arco iris
Adams, Léonie (poet, 1899-1988)
Those Not Elect
This Measure
High Falcon and Other Poems
Bernardo, Anilú (novelist, playwright)
Loves Me, Loves Me Not
Fitting In
Bevin, Teresa (novelist, b. 1949)
Dreams and Other Ailments
Havana Split
Campo, Rafael (poet and physician, b. 1964)
What the Body Told
Other Man Was Me, The
Desire to Heal, The
Cruz, Nilo (playwright, b. 1961)
Two Sisters and a Piano
Night Train to Bolina
Anna in the Tropics
Deedy, Carmen Agra (children's author, b. 1960)
Secret of Old Zeb, The
Agatha's Feather Bed
Engle, Margarita (novelist, b. 1951)
Skywriting
Singing to Cuba
González, Lucía (children's author, b. 1957)
Señor Cat's Romance
Bossy Gallito, The

La Rosa, Pablo (novelist, b. 1944)
Forbidden Fruit and Other Stories
Santeiro, Luis (playwright, b. 1948)
Our Lady of the Tortilla
Barrio Babies

Dominican American
Díaz, Junot (novelist, b. 1968)
Negocios
Drown

Mexican American
Acosta, Oscar Zeta (novelist, 1936-1974)
Revolt of the Cockroach People, The
Autobiography of a Brown Buffalo, The
Acosta, Teresa Palomo (poet, b. 1949)
Passing Time
Nile and Other Poems
Alarcón, Francisco X. (poet, b. 1954)
Snake Poems: An Aztec Invocation
Laughing Tomatoes and Other Spring Poems
Body in Flames
Alcalá, Kathleen (novelist and poet, b. 1954)
Return
Flower in the Skull, The
Allyn, Douglas (novelist, b. 1942)
Cheerio Killings, The
Burning of Rachel Hayes, The
Alurista (poet, b. 1947)
Nationchild Plumaroja
Floricanto en Aztlán
Anzaldúa, Gloria (scholar, 1942-2004)
Making Face, Making Soul
Prieta, La
This Bridge We Call Home: Radical Visions for Transformation
Apodaca, Rudy Samuel (novelist, b. 1939)
Waxen Image, The

Arias, Ron (novelist, b. 1941)
Road to Tamazunchale, The
Interview, The
Bertrand, Diane Gonzales (novelist, b. 1956)
Trino's Time
Trino's Choice
Sweet Fifteen
Blake, James Carlos (novelist, b. 1950)
Pistoleer, The
Life and Times of John Wesley Hardin as Written by Himself, The
Borderlands
Burciaga, José António (poet, 1940-1996)
Undocumented Love
Spilling the Beans
Drink Cultura
Candelaria, Cordelia Chávez (poet, b. 1943)
Cave Springs
Chicano Poetry
Candelaria, Nash (novelist, b. 1928)
Not by the Sword
Memories of Alhambra
Inheritance of Strangers
Cano, Daniel (novelist, b. 1947)
Shifting Loyalties
Pepe Ríos
Cantú, Norma Elia (scholar, b. 1947)
Chicana Traditions
Canícula
Castellanos, Rosario (novelist and poet, 1925-1974)
Oficio de tinieblas
Ciudad real
Catacalos, Rosemary (poet, b. 1944)
As Long as It Takes
Again for the First Time
Chávez, Manuel A. (poet, 1910-1996)
Anáhuac, poema épico
Petróleo; tragedia

Collignon, Rick (novelist, b. 1948)
Santo in the Image of Cristóbal García, A
Perdido
Journal of António Montoya, The
Alarcón, Daniel (short-story writer, b. 1977)
War by Candlelight
Deck, Allen Figueroa (scholar, b. 1945)
Second Wave, The
Frontiers of Hispanic Theology in the United States
Delgado, Abelardo Barrientos (novelist and poet, 1930-2004)
Llorona, La
Letters to Louise
Delgado, M. E. (novelist)
First Sandcastle, The
Díaz, Tony (novelist, b. 1968)
Latino Heretics
Aztec Love God, The
Gallardo, Edward (playwright, b. 1949)
Women Without Men
In Another Part of the City
Bernie
Gaspar de Alba, Alicía (poet, b. 1958)
Mystery of Survival and Other Stories, The
Beggar on the Córdoba Bridge
Gilb, Dagoberto (novelist, b. 1950)
Winners on the Pass Line
Magic of Blood, The
Last Known Residence of Mickey Acuña, The
González, Genaro (novelist, b. 1949)
Rainbow's End
Only Sons
Gonzalez, Ray (essayist, b. 1952)
Without Discovery: A Native Response to Columbus
Muy Macho: Latino Men Confront Their Manhood
After Aztlán: Latino Poets of the Nineties
Guillermoprieto, Alma (journalist, b. 1949)
Samba
Heart That Bleeds, The

Herrera, Juan Felipe (poet, b. 1948)
  Night Train to Tuxtla
  Night in Tunisia
  Border-Crosser with a Lamborghini Dream
Herrera-Sobek, María (scholar, b. 1943)
  Three Times a Woman
  Bracero Experience, The
Islas, Arturo (novelist, 1938-1991)
  Rain God, The
  Migrant Souls
Jaramillo, Cleofas M. (novelist, 1878-1956)
  Shadows of the Past
  Romance of a Little Village Girl
Lizárraga, Sylvia S. (scholar and poet, b. 1925)
  Poetry in Chains
  Lo mejor, A
López, Diana (Isabella Rios) (novelist, b. 1948)
  Victuum
  Dance with the Eucalyptus, A
Martin, Patricia Preciado (novelist, b. 1939)
  Milagro and Other Stories, El
  Legend of the Bellringer of San Agustín, The
  Days of Plenty, Days of Want
Mora, Pat (children's author, b. 1942)
  This Big Sky
  Agua, Agua, Agua
Moraga, Cherríe (poet and playwright, b. 1952)
  Last Generation, The
  Heroes and Saints
Murray, Yxta Maya (novelist, b. 1968)
  What It Takes to Get to Vegas
  Locas
  Conquest, The
Paisley, Tom (screenwriter and novelist, b. 1932)
  Tune in Yesterday
  New Americans, The

Paredes, Américo (folklorist, 1915-1999)
Texas-Mexican Canciónero, A
Folktales of Mexico
Quintana, Leroy V. (poet, b. 1944)
Sangre
History of Home, The
Revueltas, José (novelist, 1914-1976)
Israel
Human Mourning
Rodriguez, Luis J. (poet, b. 1954)
Trochemoche
Concrete River, The
Romero, Danny (poet, short-story writer, and novelist, b. 1959)
Calle 10
Land of a Thousand Barrios
Romero, Orlando (novelist, b. 1945)
Nambe—Year One
Day of the Wind, The
Salinas, Luis Omar (poet, b. 1937)
Prelude to Darkness
Afternoon of the Unreal
Sánchez, Ricardo (poet, 1941-1995)
Loves of Ricardo, The
Eagle-Visioned/Feathered Adobes
Serros, Michele M. (novelist, b. 1967)
How to Be a Chicana Role Model
Chicana Falsa and Other Stories of Death, Identity and Oxnard
Sierra, Ruben (playwright, 1946-1998)
Millionaire y el Pobrecito, The
Conquering Father, The
Silva, Beverly (poet, b. 1930)
Second St. Poems, The
Cat and Other Stories, The
Stavans, Ilan (scholar and novelist, b. 1961)
Talia in Heaven
One-Handed Pianist and Other Stories, The

Tafolla, Carmen (poet, b. 1951)
To Split a Human
Curandera
Trambley, Estela Portillo (playwright, b. 1936)
Sor Juana and Other Plays
Day of the Swallows, The
Troncoso, Sergio (novelist and short-story writer, b. 1961)
Last Tortilla and Other Stories, The
Nature of Truth, The
Ulibarri, Sabine Reyes (short-story writer, 1919-2003)
My Grandma Smoked Cigars and Other Stories of Tierra Amarilla
Alma de la raza, El
Vallejo, Armando (poet, b. 1949)
Luna llena
Copper Thunderbird
Véa, Alfredo (novelist, b. 1952)
Maravilla, La
Gods Go Begging
Velásquez, Gloria (novelist, b. 1949)
Maya's Divided World
Ankiza
Vigil-Piñón, Evangelina (poet, b. 1949)
Woman of Her Word
Thirty an' Seen a Lot
Computer Is Down, The
Zamora, Bernice (poet, b. 1938)
Restless Serpents
Releasing Serpents

Peruvian American
Arana, Marie (editor, b. 1949)
American Chica: Two World, One Childhood
De La Torre, Lillian (novelist and playwright, 1902-1993)
New 60-Minute Chef, The
Actress, The

Puerto Rico

Agüeros, Jack (poet, b. 1934)
 Lord, Is This a Psalm?
 Dominoes and Other Stories from the Puerto Rican
Algarín, Miguel (poet, b. 1941)
 Nuyorican Poetry
 Body Bee Calling from the 21st Century
Ambert, Alba N. (poet, b. 1946)
 Perfect Silence, A
 Eighth Continent and Other Stories, The
Belaval, Emilio S. (playwright, 1903-1972)
 Cuentos para fomentar el turismo
 Cuentos de la universidad, Los
Belpré, Pura (folklorist, 1899-1982)
 Tiger and the Rabbit and Other Tales, The
 Once in Puerto Rico
Benitez, Sandra (novelist, b. 1941)
 Place Where the Sea Remembers, A
 Bitter Grounds
Carrero, Jaime (playwright and novelist, b. 1931)
 FM Safe, The
 Double
Corretjer, Juan António (poet, 1908-1985)
 Pausa para el amor
 Líder de la desesperación, El
 Aguinaldo escarlata, 1974
Díaz Alfaro, Abelardo Milton (short-story writer, 1916-1999)
 Terrazo
 Cuentos puertorriqueños de hoy
Díaz Valcarcel, Emilio (novelist, b. 1929)
 Hot Soles in Harlem
 Black Sun
García Ramis, Magali (novelist, b. 1946)
 Happy Days, Uncle Sergio
 Familia de todos nosotros, La
 Ciudad que me habita, La

González, José Luis (novelist, b. 1926)
Veinte cuentos y Paisa
Galería y otros cuentos, La
En Nueva York y otras desgracias
Laguerre, Enrique A. (novelist, b. 1906)
Labyrinth, The
Benevolent Masters
Marqués, René (playwright, 1919-1979)
En una ciudad llamada San Juan
Carnaval afuera
Apartamiento
Ramos, José António (novelist, b. 1948)
Hilando mortajas
En casa de Guillermo Tell
Rivera, José (playwright, b. 1955)
References to Salvador Dalí Make Me Hot
House of Ramón Iglesia, The
Rodríguez Juliá, Edgardo (novelist, b. 1946)
Tribulaciónes de Jonás, Las
Cartagena
Soto, Pedro Juan (novelist, b. 1928)
Usmail
Spiks
Hot Land, Cold Season
Vega, Ana Lydia (short-story writer, b. 1946)
Vírgenes y martires
Cuentos calientes
Vega, José Luis (poet, b. 1948)
Signos vitales
Reunión de espejos
Vega Yunqué, Edgardo (short-story writer, b. 1936)
Casualty Report
Mendoza's Dreams
Zavala, Iris Milagros (novelist and scholar, b. 1936)
Colonialism and Culture
Chiliagony

Salvadoran American
Bencastro, Mario (novelist and dramatist, b. 1949)
Odyssey to the North
Disparo en la catedral
Martínez, Demetria (poet and novelist, b. 1960)
Devil's Workshop, The
Mother Tongue

South America

Argentina
Alberto, Manguel (scriptwriter, b. 1948)
Man Who Liked Dickens, The
Gates of Paradise, The
Black Water
Andahazi, Federico (novelist, b. 1963)
Merciful Women, The
Anatomist, The
Cambacérès, Eugenio (novelist, 1843-1890)
Sin rumbo
En la sangre
Conti, Haroldo (novelist, 1925-1976)
Sudeste
Examinado
Causa, La
Davalos, Juan Carlos (short-story writer, 1887-1959)
Viento blanco, El
De mi vida y de mi tierra
Denevi, Marco (novelist, b. 1922)
Rosaura a las diez
Life en español
Di Benedetto, António (novelist, b. 1922)
Zama
Silenciero, El
Pentagono, El
Echeverría, Esteban (poet, 1805-1851)
Matadero, El
Dogma socialista

Fernández, Macedonio (short-story writer, 1874-1952)
Selección
Papeles de MF
Adriana Buenos Aires
Fernández Moreno, Baldomero (poet, 1886-1950)
Campo argentino
Aldea española
Aire confidencial
Gallardo, Sara (novelist, 1931-1988)
Siete puertas, Las
Enero
Gálvez, Manuel (essayist, 1882-1962)
Vida multiple, La
Holy Wednesday
Diario de Gabriel Quiroga, El
Gelman, Juan (poet, b. 1930)
Hacía el sur
Gotán
Fábulas
Carta a mi madre
Giardinelli, Mempo (novelist and short-story writer, b. 1947)
Cuestiones interiores
Sultry Moon
Girri, Alberto (poet, b. 1919)
Trece poemas
Envios
Casa de la mente
Guido, Beatriz (novelist, 1925-1988)
House of the Angel, The
End of a Day
Gumucio Dagron, Alfonso (poet, b. 1950)
Razones téchnicas
Radios mineras de Bolivia, Las
Bolivie
Hernández, Felisberto (short-story writer, 1902-1964)
Por los tiempos de Clemente Colling
Fray
Cara de Ana, La

Juarroz, Roberto (poet, 1925-1995)
Novena poesía vertical
Octava poesía vertical
Jurado, Alicia (essayist, b. 1922)
Rostros del engaño
En soledad vivía
Kordon, Bernardo (novelist, b. 1915)
Taxi amarillo y negro en Pakistán, Un
Bairestop
Alias gardelito
Larreta, Enrique Rodríguez (novelist, 1875-1961)
Santa María del Buen Aire
La que buscaba don Juan, Artemis
Historiales
Levinson, Luisa Mercedes (novelist, 1914-1988)
Sombra de buho
Mitos y realidades de Buenos Aires
Concierto en mi
Lugones, Leopoldo (poet, 1874-1938)
Payador, El
Horas doradas, Las
Historia de Sarmiento
Crepusculos del jardín, Los
Lynch, Marta (novelist, 1929-1985)
Vencedor, Al
Señora Ordóñez, La
Años de fuego, Los
Marechal, Leopoldo (playwright, 1900-1970)
Viaje de la primavera, El
Antígona Vélez
Adán Buenosayres
Mármol, José (essayist, 1817-1871)
Cruzado
Cantos del peregrino
Amalia

Martínez Estrada, Ezequiel (novelist, 1895-1964)
Verdadero cuento del Tío Sam, El
Tres cuentos sin amor
Nefelibal
Moyano, Daniel (novelist, b. 1928)
Flight of the Tiger, The
Devil's Trill, The
Mujica Láinez, Manuel (novelist, 1910-1984)
Wandering Unicorn, The
Canto a Buenos Aires
Murena, Héctor A.(essayist, 1923-1975)
Pecado original de América, El
Laws of the Night, The
Nalé Roxlo, Conrado (children's author, 1898-1971)
Cola de la sirena, La
Amado Vilar
Ocampo, Silvina (short-story writer, 1906-1993)
Que aman, odian, Los
Leopoldina's Dream
Amarillo celeste
Ocampo, Victoria (essayist, 1890-1979)
Sur y cia
Soledad sonora
Orozco, Olga (poet, 1920-1999)
Paginas de Olga Orozco
Muertes, Las
Cantos a Berenice
Pizarnik, Alejandra (poet, 1936-1972)
Trabajos y las noches, Los
Canto de extramuros
Árbol de Diana
Posse, Abel (novelist, b. 1934)
Dogs of Paradise, The
Daimón
Rojas, Manuel (novelist, 1896-1973)
Hombre de la rosa
Born Guilty

Saer, Juan José (novelist, b. 1937)
Witness, The
Palo y hueso
Sarmiento, Domingo Faustino (essayist, 1811-1888)
Travels
Facundo: Life in the Argentine Republic in the Days of the Tyrants
Soriano, Osvaldo (novelist, b. 1943)
Winter Quarters
Shadows
Funny Dirty Little War
Traba, Marta (novelist, 1930-1983)
Zona del silencio, La
Mothers and Shadows
Above and Beyond
Verbitsky, Bernardo (novelist, 1907-1979)
Vacaciónes
Hermana y sombra
Viñas, David (novelist, b. 1929)
Lisandro
Dar la cara
Walsh, María Elena (children's author, b. 1930)
Zoo loco
Ángelito

Bolivia
Cerruto, Oscar (poet, 1912-1981)
Muerte mágica, La
Estrella segregada
Céspedes, Augusto (novelist, b. 1904)
Sangre de mestizos
Palestra
Lara, Jesús (novelist, 1898-1980)
Surumi
Paucarware
Flor de loto
Prada Oropez, Renato (novelist, b. 1937)
Ofrenda
Borde del silencio, Al

Teixidó, Raúl (novelist, b. 1943)
Habitantes del alba, Los
Aportes
Vargas, Manuel (novelist, b. 1952)
Signos de la lluvia, Los
Cuentos tristes
Vega, Julio de la (novelist, b. 1924)
Temporada de liquenes
Matias

Brazil
Alencar, José Martiniano de (novelist, 1829-1877)
Iracema, the Honey-Lips: A Legend of Brazil
Guaraní Indian, The
Almeida, José Américo de (novelist, 1887-1980)
Trash
Bagaceira, A
Alves, António de Castro (poet, 1847-1871)
Poemas revoluciónarios
Floating Foam
Andrade, Oswald de (novelist and poet, 1890-1954)
Seraphim Grosse Pointe
Sentimental Memoirs of John Seaborne
Azevedo, Aluísio (novelist, 1857-1913)
Mulatto, O
Man, The
Esqueleto, O
Coelho, Paulo (novelist, b. 1947)
By the River Piedra I Sat Down and Wept
Brida
Alchemist, The
Días, Antônio Gonçalves (poet, 1823-1864)
Leonor de Mendonca
Cantos
Dourado, Autran (novelist, b. 1926)
Pattern for a Tapestry
Hidden Life, A
Bells of Agony, The

Filho, Adonias (novelist, 1915-1990)
Memories of Lazarus
Live Body
Fortress, The
Fonseca, Rubem (novelist, b. 1925)
Stuff of a Dream
Large Intestine
High Art
Avenger
Freire, Paulo (essayist, 1921-1997)
Pedagogy of the Oppressed
Letters to Cristina
Education for Critical Consciousness
Freyre, Gilberto (sociologist, 1900-1987)
Order and Progress
Mansions and the Shanties, The
Making of Modern Brazil, The
Lima Barreto, Afonso Henrique de (novelist, 1881-1922)
Clara dos Anjos
Bagatelas
Melo Neto, João Cabral de (poet, 1920-1999)
Rebounding Stone
Auto do frade
Moraes, Vinícius de (poet, 1913-1980)
Girl from Ipanema
Cinco elegías
Black Orpheus
Piñon, Nélida (novelist, b. 1936)
Republic of Dreams, The
Caetana's Sweet Song
Ribeiro, João Ubaldo (novelist, b. 1941)
Lizard's Smile, The
It Was a Different Day When They Killed the Pig
Romero, Silvio (scholar, 1851-1914)
História da literatura brasileira
Cantos populares do Brasil

Santos, Nelson Pereira dos (screenwriter, b. 1928)
Vidas secas
Fome de amor
Soares, Jô (novelist, b. 1938)
Twelve Fingers
Samba for Sherlock, A
Sousândrade (poet, 1833-1902)
Novo Eden
Guesa errante
Telles, Lygia Fagundes (novelist, b. 1923)
Tigrela and Other Stories
Girl in the Photograph, The
Trevisan, Dalton (short-story writer, b. 1925)
Guerra conjugal, A
Ah, é?
Verissimo, Erico (novelist, 1905-1975)
Time and the Wind
Saga
Consider the Lilies of the Field

Chile
Alegría, Fernando (novelist and poet, b. 1918)
Paso de los gansos, El
Coral de guerra
Changing Centuries
Coloane, Francisco (novelist, b. 1910)
Stowaway, The
Cape Horn and Other Stories from the End of the World
Cabo de 1945
Díaz, Jorge (playwright, b. 1930)
Hombre llamado Isla, Un
Cepillo de dientes, El
Díaz Casanueva, Humberto (poet, b. 1907)
Pájaro Dungo, El
Hierro y el hilo, El

Droguett, Carlos (short-story writer, b. 1912)
Sesenta muertos en la escalera
Escrito en el aire
Despúes del diluvio
Edwards, Jorge (novelist, b. 1931)
Museo de cera, El
Máscaras, Las
Eltit, Diamela (novelist, b. 1949)
Sacred Cow
Por la patria
Fourth World, The
d'Halmar, Augusto (novelist, 1882-1950)
Rolling Across the Land
In the Provinces
Huidobro, Vicente (poet, 1893-1948)
Portrait of a Paladin
Poet Is a Little God, The
Mirror of a Mage
Cagliostro
Jodorowsky, Raquel (poet, b. 1937)
Ensentidinverso
Ciudad inclemente, La
Latorre, Maríano (novelist, 1886-1955)
Cuna de cóndores
Chilenos del mar
Lavín Cerda, Hernán (novelist, b. 1939)
¿Que es la creación?
Altura desprendida, La
Lillo, Baldomero (short-story writer, 1867-1923)
Sub Terra
Devil's Pit and Other Stories
Rokha, Pablo de (poet, 1894-1968)
Oda a Cuba
Fúsiles de sangre
Skármeta, Antonio (novelist, b. 1940)
Watch Where the Wolf Is Going
I Dreamt the Snow Was Burning
Burning Patience

Subercaseaux, Benjamín (novelist, 1902-1973)
Jemmy Button
Chile: A Geographic Extravaganza
Valle, Juvencio (poet, 1900-1999)
Nimbo de Piedra
Libro primero de Margarita

Colombia
Alvarez Gardeazábal, Gustavo (novelist, b. 1945)
Pepe Botellas
Míos, Los
Ángel, Albalucía (novelist and poet, b. 1939)
Painted Bird Was Sitting on the Green Lemon Tree, The
Andariegas, Las
Caballero Calderón, Eduardo (novelist, 1910-1993)
Cristo de espaldas, El
Buen salvaje, El
Caicedo, Andrés (novelist, 1951-1977)
Que viva la música
Atravesado, El
Carranza, Eduardo (poet, 1913-1985)
Pasos cantados, Los
Canciónes para iniciar una fiesta
Collazos, Oscar (novelist and playwright, b. 1942)
Verano también moja las espaldas, El
Literatura en la revolución y revolución en la literatura
Días de la paciencia, Los
Cruz Kronfly, Fernando (novelist, b. 1943)
Por estos tiempos santos
Abendland
Isaacs, Jorge (novelist, 1837-1895)
Bolívar
María: A South American Romance
Mejía Vallejo, Manuel (novelist, b. 1923)
Tiempo de sequía
Aire de tango

Mutis, Alvaro (essayist, 1923-1975)
Sesenta cuerpos
Amirbar
Rivera, José Eustasio (novelist, 1889-1928)
Vortex, The
Rivera, intelectual
Silva, José Asunción (poet, 1865-1896)
Intimidades
De sobremesa
Valverde, Umberto (short-story writer, b. 1947)
Celia Cruz y Reina Rumba
Bomba camará
Vivas, Eliseo (philosopher, b. 1901)
Schopenhauer as Educator
Moral Life and the Ethical Life, The
Zapata Olivella, Manuel (poet, b. 1920)
Changó, el gran putas
Chambacu: Black Slum

Ecuador
Carrera Andrade, Jorge (poet, 1903-1978)
Wreath of Silence, The
Bulletins of Sea and Land
Cuadra, José de la (journalist, 1903-1941)
Sangurimas, Los
Oven
Mad Monkeys, The
Donoso Pareja, Miguel (poet, b. 1931)
Violencia en Ecuador
Hora de lobo
Exile's First Song, The
Egüez, Iván (poet, b. 1944)
Pájara la memoria
Linares, Las
Gallegos Lara, Joaquin (novelist, b. 1909)
Que se van, Los
Cruces sobre el agua, Las

Gil Gilbert, Enrique (novelist, 1912-1973)
Relato de Emmanuel
Our Daily Bread
Farsa
Hernández y Aguirre, Mario (novelist, b. 1909)
Vida es un cielo cerado, La
Litoral de amor
Abandonando el alba
Mera, Juan León (novelist, 1832-1894)
Porque soy cristiano
Cumandá o un drama entre salvajes
Montalvo, Juan (essayist, 1832-1889)
Cosmopólita, El
Cartas y lecturas
Palacio, Pablo (novelist, 1906-1947)
Vida del ahorcado
Debora
Pareja y Díez Canseco, Alfredo (novelist, 1908-1993)
Casa de los locos, La
Baldomera
Ramírez Estrada, Alsino (novelist, b. 1930)
Perspectiva, La
Ceremonial
Velasco Mackenzie, Jorge (novelist, b. 1949)
Como gato en tempestad
Clown
Vera, Pedro Jorge (novelist, b. 1914)
Pueblo soy yo, El
Luto eterno y otros relatos
Yánez Cossío, Alicia (novelist, b. 1929)
Yo vendo unos ojos negros
Casa del sano placer, La

Paraguay
González Real, Osvaldo (essayist, b. 1938)
Memoria de exilio
Anticipación y reflexión

Plá, Joséfina (poet, 1909-1999)
Rostros en el agua
En la piel de la mujer
Rodríguez Alcalá, Guido (essayist, b. 1946)
Residentas
Ciudad sonámbula
Rodríguez-Alcalá, Hugo (essayist, b. 1917)
Palabras de los días
Danza de la muerte, La
Ruiz Nestosa, Jesús (novelist, b. 1941)
Musarañas, Las
Contador de cuentos, El

Peru
Adán, Martín (poet, 1908-1985)
Travesía de extramares, 1929-46
Piedra absoluta, La
Cardboard House, The
Arguedas, José María (short-story writer, 1911-1969)
Yawar fiesta
Everyone's Blood
Deep Rivers
Congrains, Enrique (novelist, b. 1932)
No una sino muchas muertes
Narrativa cubana
Círculo de novelistas peruanos
Diez Canseco, José (novelist and poet, 1904-1949)
Gaviota
Estampas Mulatas
Duque
Eielson, Jorge (poet, b. 1924)
Reinos
Cuerpo de Giulia-no, El
Canto visible
Jaimes Freyre, Ricardo (short-story writer, 1868-1933)
Tucumán colonial, El
Castalia bárbara

López Albújar, Enrique (short-story writer, 1872-1966)
Palos al viento
Cuentos andinos
Calderonadas
Mariátegui, José Carlos (essayist, 1894-1930)
Seven Interpretive Essays on Peruvian Reality
Selected Essays of José Carlos Maríategui
Heroic and Creative Meaning of Socialism, The
Matto de Turner, Clorinda (novelist, 1852-1909)
Herencia
Aves sin nido
Palma, Clemente (novelist, 1872-1946)
Malignant Tales
Malevolent Tales
Palma, Ricardo (playwright, 1833-1919)
Rodil
Bohemia de mi tiempo, La
Portal, Magda (essayist, 1901-1989)
Vidrios de amor
Constancia del ser
Ribeyro, Julio Ramón (novelist, 1929-1994)
Teatro
Crónica de San Gabriel
Rivera Martínez, Edgardo (essayist, b. 1933)
Hombres, paisajes, ciudades
Azurita
Romualdo, Alejandro (poet, b. 1926)
Rebelión de Túpac Amaru
Cuarto mundo
Salazar Bondy, Sebastián (playwright, 1924-1965)
Rodil
Lima la horrible
Scorza, Manuel (novelist, 1928-1983)
Garabombo, el Invisible
Drums for Rancas
Sologuren, Javier (poet, b. 1921)
Hojas de herbolario
Estancias

Soto, Hernando de (essayist, b. 1941)
Other Path
Mystery of Capital, The
Urteaga Cabrera, Luis (novelist, b. 1940)
Universo sagrado, El
Hijos del orden, Los

Uruguay
Agustini, Delmira (poet, 1886-1914)
Libro blanco, El
Astros del abismo, Los
Amorim, Enrique (novelist, 1900-1960)
Paisano aguilar, El
Carreta, La
Caballo y su sombra, El
Berenguer, Amanda (poet, b. 1921)
Río, El
Contracanto
Chavarría, Daniel (novelist, b. 1933)
Eye of Cybele, The
Adiós muchachos
Conteris, Hiber (novelist, b. 1933)
Ten Percent of Life
Asesinato de Malcolm X, El
Delgado Aparaín, Mario (novelist and scholar, b. 1949)
Terribles ojos verdes
Cuentos del mar
Díaz, José Pedro (poet, b. 1921)
Tratado de la llama
Habitante, El
Espínola, Francisco (novelist, 1901-1973)
Raza ciega
Infierno nazi
Don Juan, el zorro
Estrazulas, Enrique (novelist, b. 1942)
Zitarrosa
Lucifer ha llorado
Confesión de los perros

Herrera y Reissig, Julio (poet, 1875-1910)
Pascuas del tiempo, Las
Opalos
Ciles alucinada
Ibarbourou, Juana de (poet, (1895-1979)
Pasajera, La
Elegía
Levrero, Mario (short-story writer, b. 1940)
Santo varón
Maquina de pensar en Gladys
Aguas salobres
Martínez Moreno, Carlos (novelist 1917-1986)
Tierra en la boca
Infierno, El
Coca
Morosoli, Juan José (children's author, 1899-1957)
Perico
Hombres y mujeres
Hombres
Rodó, José Enrique (essayist, 1871-1917)
Bolívar
Ariel
Rossi, Cristina Peri (novelist, b. 1941)
Solitaire of Love
Ship of Fools, The
Forbidden Passion: Stories, A
Sabat Ercasty, Carlos (poet, 1887-1982)
Verbo de Américas
Oda a Ruben Darío
Somers, Armonía (novelist, 1914-1994)
Tríptico darwiniano
Eye of the Heart
Vicuña, Cecilia (poet, b. 1948)
Unravelling Words and the Weaving of Water
Precarious
Vilarino, Idea (poet, b. 1920)
Suplicante, La
Cielo, cielo

Zorrilla de San Martín, Juan (poet, 1855-1931)
Libro de Ruth, El
Indian Legend of Uruguay, An

Venezuela
Balza, José (novelist, b. 1939)
Marzo anterior
Cuerpos del sueño, Los
Bello, Andrés (scholar and poet, 1781-1865)
Philosophy of the Understanding
Georgic of the Tropics, A
Díaz Rodríguez, Manuel (novelist, 1871-1927)
Sensaciónes de viaje
Idolos rotos
Díaz Sánchez, Ramón (novelist, 1903-1968)
Cumboto
Casandra
Borburata
Garmendía, Julio (short-story writer, 1898-1977)
Tuna de oro, La
Opiniónes para despúes de la muerte
Liscano, Juan (poet, b. 1915)
Edad oscura
Del mar
Carmenes
Massiani, Francisco (novelist, b. 1944)
Primeras hojas de la noche, Las
Piedra de mar
Meneses, Guillermo (novelist, 1911-1978)
Campeones
Cable cifrado
Noguera, Carlos (novelist, b. 1943)
Historias de la calle Lincoln
Eros y Pallas
Otero Silva, Miguel (novelist, 1908-1985)
Fiebre
Agua y cauce

Parra, Teresa de la (novelist, 1890-1936)
  Memorias de Mama Blanca, Las
  Blanca Nieves y companía
Peña, Edilio (essayist, b. 1951)
  Hermanos, Los
  Drágon amarillo, El
Picón-Salas, Mariano (essayist, 1901-1965)
  Tratos de la noche, Los
  On Being Good Neighbors
  Cultural History of Spanish America, A
Pocaterra, José Rafael (novelist, 1888-1955)
  Luis Urbaneja Achelpohl
  Doctor Bebé, El
Quintero, Ednodio (novelist, b. 1947)
  Volveré con mis perros
  Muerte viaja a caballo
Rugeles, Manuel Felipe (poet, 1903-1959)
  Luz de tu presencia
  Canta
Uslar Pietri, Arturo (novelist, 1906-2001)
  Nubes, Las
  Bolívar hoy

Bibliography

Contents

Anthologies

Carlson, Lori Marie, ed. *Cool Salsa: Bilingual Poems on Growing Up Latino in the United States.* New York: Henry Holt, 1994.

_____. *Red Hot Salsa: Bilingual Poems on Being Young and Latino in the United States.* New York: Henry Holt, 2005.

Del Rio, Eduardo R. *The Prentice Hall Anthology of Latino Literature.* Upper Saddle River, N.J.: Prentice Hall, 2001.

Gonzalez, Ray, ed. *Currents from the Dancing River: Contemporary Latino Fiction, Nonfiction, and Poetry.* San Diego, Calif.: Harcourt Brace, 1994.

Kanellos, Nicolás, ed. *Hispanic American Literature: A Brief Introduction and Anthology.* New York: HarperCollins, 1995.

Ortiz Cofer, Judith, ed. *Riding Low Through the Streets of Gold: Latino Literature for Young Adults.* Houston, Tex.: Arte Público Press, 2004.

Salas, Teresa Cajiao, and Margarita Vargas, eds. *Women Writing Women: An Anthology of Spanish-American Theater of the 1980's.* Albany: State University of New York Press, 1997.

Stavans, Ilan, ed. *Wáchale! Poetry and Prose About Growing up Latino in America.* Chicago: Cricket Books, 2001.

Ventura, Gabriela Baeza. *U.S. Latino Literature Today.* New York: Longman, 2004.

General Studies and Reference Works

Augenbraum, Harold, and Margarite Fernández Olmos. *U.S. Latino Literature: A Critical Guide for Students and Teachers*. Westport, Conn.: Greenwood Press, 2000.

Balderston, Daniel, and Mike Gonzalez, eds. *Encyclopedia of Latin American and Caribbean Literature, 1900-2003*. New York: Routledge, 2004.

Bloom, Harold, ed. *Hispanic-American Writers: Modern Critical Views*. Philadelphia: Chelsea House, 1998.

Contemporary Hispanic Biography. 4 vols. Detroit: Thomson Gale, 2002.

Fitz, Earl E. *Rediscovering the New World: Inter-American Literature in a Comparative Context*. Iowa City: University of Iowa Press, 1991.

Flores, Angel. *Spanish American Authors: The Twentieth Century*. New York: H. W. Wilson, 1992.

Foster, David W., and Daniel Altamirada, eds. *Spanish American Literature: A Collection of Essays*. 5 vols. New York: Routledge, 1997.

Foster, David W., and Virginia R. Foster, eds. *Modern Latin American Literature*. New York: Ungar, 1975.

Gonzalez, Juan. *Harvest of Empire: A History of Latinos in America*. New York: Penguin, 2001.

González Echevarría, Roberto, and Enrique Pupo-Walker, eds. *The Cambridge History of Latin American Literature*. 3 vols. New York: Cambridge University Press, 1996.

Herrera-Sobek, Maria, and Virginia Sánchez Korrol, eds. *Recovering the U.S. Hispanic Literary Heritage*. Vol. 3. Houston, Tex.: Arte Público Press, 2000.

Kanellos, Nicolás, ed. *The Hispanic American Almanac: A Reference Work on Hispanics in the United States*. 3d ed. Detroit: Gale, 2002.

_____. *Hispanic Literature of the United States: A Comprehensive Reference*. Westport, Conn.: Greenwood Press, 2003.

Kevane, Bridget A., ed. *Latino Literature in America*. Westport, Conn.: Greenwood Press, 2003.

Lindfors, Bernth, and Ann González, comps. *African, Caribbean, and Latin-American Writers*. 3 vols. Detroit: Gale, 2000.

Luis, William, and Ann González, eds. *Modern Latin-American Fiction Writers*. Detroit: Gale, 1994.

Martínez, Julio A., and Francisco A. Lomelí, eds. *Chicano Literature: A Reference Guide*. Westport, Conn.: Greenwood Press, 1985.

Meyer, Nicholas E., ed. *Biographical Dictionary of Hispanic Americans*. 2d ed. New York: Facts on File, 2002.

Millington, Mark I., and Paul Julian Smith, eds. *New Hispanisms: Literature, Culture, Theory*. Ottawa: Dovehouse Editions, 1994.

Ocasio, Rafael. *Literature of Latin America*. Westport, Conn.: Greenwood Press, 2004.

Sayers Peden, Margaret. *The Latin American Short Story: A Critical History*. Boston: Twayne, 1983.

Smith, Verity, ed. *Concise Encyclopedia of Latin American Literature*. London: Fitzroy Dearborn, 2000.

Sole, Carlos A., ed. *Latin American Writers*. 3 vols. New York: Charles Scribner, 1989.

Stavans, Ilan. *The Oxford Book of Latin American Essays*. New York: Oxford University Press, 1997.

Valdés, Mario J., and Djelal Kadir, eds. *Literary Cultures of Latin America: A Comparative History*. 3 vols. New York: Oxford University Press, 2004.

West-Durán, Alan, ed. *Latino and Latina Writers*. New York: Charles Scribner's Sons, 2004.

Colonialism and Postcolonialism

Abbott, Don Paul. *Rhetoric in the New World: Rhetorical Theory and Practice in Colonial Spanish America*. Columbia: University of South Carolina Press, 1996.

Arias, Santa, and Mariselle Meléndez, eds. *Mapping Colonial Spanish America: Places and Commonplaces of Identity, Culture, and Experience*. Lewisburg, Pa.: Bucknell University Press, 2002.

Armstrong, Jeanne. *Demythologizing the Romance of Conquest*. Westport, Conn.: Greenwood Press, 2000.

Ashcroft, Bill, Gareth Griffiths, and Helen Tiffin. *The Empire Writes Back: Theory and Practice in Post-Colonial Literatures*. London: Routledge, 2002.

Bauer, Ralph. *The Cultural Geography of Colonial American Literatures: Empire, Travel, Modernity.* Cambridge, England: Cambridge University Press, 2003.

Bolaños, Alvaro Félix, and Gustavo Verdesio, eds. *Colonialism Past and Present: Reading and Writing About Colonial Latin America Today.* Albany: State University of New York Press, 2002.

Cevallos-Candau, Francisco Javier, Jeffrey A. Cole, Nina M. Scott, and Nicomedes Suárez-Araúz. *Coded Encounters: Writing, Gender, and Ethnicity in Colonial Latin America.* Amherst: University of Massachusetts Press, 1994.

Greene, Roland. *Unrequited Conquests: Love and Empire in the Colonial Americas.* Chicago: University of Chicago Press, 1999.

Ibsen, Kristine. *Women's Spiritual Autobiography in Colonial Spanish America.* Gainesville: University Press of Florida, 1999.

Johnson, Julie Greer. *Satire in Colonial Spanish America: Turning the New World Upside Down.* Austin: University of Texas Press, 1993.

Kagan, Richard L, ed. *Spain in America: The Origins of Hispanism in the United States.* Urbana: University of Illinois Press, 2002.

Larsen, Neil. *Reading North by South: On Latin American Literature, Culture, and Politics.* Minneapolis: University of Minnesota Press, 1995.

Mignolo, Walter D. *The Darker Side of the Renaissance: Literacy, Territoriality, and Colonization.* 2d ed. Ann Arbor: University of Michigan Press, 2003.

Promis Ojeda, José. *The Identity of Hispanoamerica: An Interpretation of Colonial Literature.* Translated by Alita Kelley and Alec E. Kelley. Tucson: University of Arizona Press, 1991.

Schlau, Stacey. *Spanish American Women's Use of the Word: Colonial Through Contemporary Narratives.* Tucson: University of Arizona Press, 2001.

Thurner, Mark, and Andrés Guerrero, eds. *After Spanish Rule: Postcolonial Predicaments of the Americas.* Durham, N.C.: Duke University Press, 2003.

Toro, Fernando de. *New Intersections: Essays on Culture and Literature in the Post-Modern and Post-Colonial Condition.* Princeton, N.J.: Markus Wiener, 1993.

Fiction

Alonso, Carlos J. *The Spanish American Regional Novel: Modernity and Autochthony.* New York: Cambridge University Press, 1990.

Avelar, Idelber. *The Letter of Violence: Essays on Narrative, Ethics, and Politics.* New York: Palgrave Macmillan, 2004.

Balderston, Daniel, comp. *The Latin American Short Story: An Annotated Guide to Anthologies and Criticism.* New York: Greenwood Press, 1992.

Blayer, Irene Maria F., and Mark Cronlund Anderson, eds. *Latin American Narratives and Cultural Identity: Selected Readings.* New York: Peter Lang, 2004.

Bloom, Harold, ed. *Modern Latin American Fiction.* New York: Chelsea House, 1990.

Brotherston, Gordon. *The Emergence of the Latin American Novel.* Cambridge, England: Cambridge University Press, 1977.

Chandler, Richard E., and Kessel Schwartz. *A New History of Spanish American Fiction.* Rev. ed. Baton Rouge: Louisiana State University Press, 1991.

Craft, Linda J. *Novels of Testimony and Resistance from Central America.* Gainesville: University of Florida Press, 1997.

D'Lugo, Carol Clark. *The Fragmented Novel in Mexico: The Politics of Form.* Austin: University of Texas Press, 1997.

Faris, Wendy B. *Ordinary Enchantments: Magical Realism and the Remystification of Narrative.* Nashville, Tenn.: Vanderbilt University Press, 2004.

González Echevarría, Roberto. *Myth and Archive: A Theory of Latin American Narrative.* Durham, N.C.: Duke University Press, 1998.

Hart, Stephen M. *White Ink: Essays on Twentieth-Century Feminine Fiction in Spain and Latin America.* London: Tamesis, 1993.

Kanellos, Nicolás, ed. *Short Fiction by Hispanic Writers of the United States.* Houston, Tex.: Arte Público Press, 1993.

Larson, Ross. *Fantasy and Imagination in the Mexican Narrative.* Tempe: Arizona State University Center for Latin American Studies, 1977.

Maiorino, Giancarlo. *The Picaresque: Tradition and Displacement.* Minneapolis: University of Minnesota Press, 1996.

Martinez, Elizabeth Coonrod. *Before the Boom: Latin American Revolutionary Novels of the 1920's.* Lanham, Md.: University Press of America, 2001.

Niebylski, Dianna C. *Humoring Resistance: Laughter and the Excessive Body in Latin American Women's Fiction.* Albany: State University of New York Press, 2004.

Nunn, Frederick M. *Collisions with History: Latin American Fiction and Social Science from El Boom to the New World Order.* Athens: Ohio University Center for International Studies, 2001.

O'Connor, Patrick. *Latin American Fiction and the Narratives of the Perverse: Paper Dolls and Spider Women.* New York: Palgrave Macmillan, 2004.

Schroeder, Shannin. *Rediscovering Magical Realism in the Americas.* Westport, Conn.: Praeger, 2004.

Shaw, Donald L. *The Post-Boom in Spanish American Fiction.* Albany: State University of New York Press, 1998.

Swanson, Philip. *Latin American Fiction: A Short Introduction.* Malden, Mass.: Blackwell, 2005.

————. *The New Novel in Latin America: Politics and Popular Culture After the Boom.* Manchester, England: Manchester University Press, 1995.

Williams, Raymond L. *The Postmodern Novel in Latin America: Politics, Culture, and the Crisis of Truth.* New York: St. Martin's Press, 1996.

Identity

Allatson, Paul. *Latino Dreams: Transcultural Traffic and the U.S. National Imaginary.* New York: Rodopi, 2002.

Aparicio, Frances R., and Susana Chávez-Silverman, eds. *Tropicalizations: Transcultural Representations of Latinidad.* Hanover, N.H.: University Press of New England, 1997.

Castillo, Debra A. *Redreaming America: Toward a Bilingual American Culture.* Albany: State University of New York Press, 2005.

Castro-Klarén, Sara, and John Charles Chasteen, eds. *Beyond Imagined Communities: Reading and Writing the Nation in Nineteenth-Century Latin America.* Washington, D.C.: Woodrow Wilson Center Press, 2003.

Cooper, Sara E. *The Ties That Bind: Questioning Family Dynamics and Family Discourse in Hispanic Literature.* Lanham, Md.: University Press of America, 2004.

Durán-Cogan, Mercedes F., and Antonio Gómez-Moriana, eds. *National Identities and Sociopolitical Changes in Latin America.* New York: Routledge, 2001.

Feracho, Lesley. *Linking the Americas: Race, Hybrid Discourses, and the Reformulation of Feminine Identity.* Albany: State University of New York Press, 2005.

Flores, Juan. *From Bomba to Hip-Hop: Puerto Rican Culture and the Latino Identity.* New York: Columbia University Press, 2000.

Fox, Geoffrey. *Hispanic Nation: Culture, Politics, and the Constructing of Identity.* Tucson: University of Arizona Press, 1997.

Gish, Robert Franklin. *Beyond Bounds: Cross-Cultural Essays on Anglo, American Indian, and Chicano Literature.* Albuquerque: University of New Mexico Press, 1996.

Gutmann, Matthew C., ed. *Changing Men and Masculinities in Latin America.* Durham, N.C.: Duke University Press, 2003.

Karem, Jeff. *The Romance of Authenticity: The Cultural Politics of Regional and Ethnic Literatures.* Charlottesville: University of Virginia Press, 2004.

Kushigian, Julia. *Reconstructing Childhood: Strategies of Reading for Culture and Gender in the Spanish American Bildungsroman.* Lewisburg, Pa.: Bucknell University Press, 2003.

Paz-Soldán, Edmundo, and Debra A. Castillo. *Latin American Literature and Mass Media.* New York: Garland, 2001.

Pérez, Janet, and Wendell Aycock, eds. *Climate and Literature: Reflections of Environment.* Lubbock: Texas Tech University Press, 1995.

Ryan-Ranson, Helen, ed. *Imagination, Emblems, and Expressions: Essays on Latin American, Caribbean, and Continental Culture and Identity.* Bowling Green, Ohio: Bowling Green State University Popular Press, 1993.

Sá, Lúcia. *Rain Forest Literatures: Amazonian Texts and Latin American Culture.* Minneapolis: University of Minnesota Press, 2004.

Saldaña-Portillo, Josefina. "Who's the Indian in Aztlán? Rewriting Mestizaje, Indianism, and Chicanismo from the Lacandón." In *The Latin American Subaltern Studies Reader,* edited by Ileana Rodriguez. Durham, N.C.: Duke University Press, 2001.

Sandín, Lyn Di Ioria. *Killing Spanish: Literary Essays on Ambivalent U.S. Latino/a Identity.* New York: Palgrave Macmillan, 2004.

Walter, Roland. *Narrative Identities: (Inter)Cultural In-Betweennss in the Americas.* New York: Peter Lang, 2003.

Poetry

Agosín, Marjorie, ed. *Miriam's Daughters: Jewish Latin American Women Poets.* Translated by Roberta Gordenstein. Santa Fe, N.Mex.: Sherman Asher, 2001

————. *These Are Not Sweet Girls: Latin American Women Poets.* Fredonia, N.Y.: White Pine Press, 1994.

Bush, Andrew. *The Routes of Modernity: Spanish American Poetry from the Early Eighteenth to the Mid-Nineteenth Century.* Lewisburg, Pa.: Bucknell University Press, 2002.

Cussen, Antonio. *Bello and Bolívar: Poetry and Politics in the Spanish American Revolution.* New York: Cambridge University Press, 1992.

DeCaires Narain, Denise. *Contemporary Caribbean Women's Poetry: Making Style.* New York: Routledge, 2002.

Dick, Bruce. *A Poet's Truth: Conversations with Latino/Latina Poets.* Tucson: University of Arizona Press, 2003.

Espinosa, César, ed. *Corrosive Signs: Essays on Experimental Poetry (Visual, Concrete, Alternative).* Translated by Harry Polkinhorn. Washington, D.C.: Maisonneuve Press, 1990.

Fife, Austin E. *Latin American Interlude.* Logan: Utah State University Press, 1966.

Forster, Merlin H. *The Committed Word: Studies in Spanish American Poetry.* University, Miss.: Romance Monographs, 2002.

Gonzalez, Mike, and David Treece. *The Gathering of Voices: The Twentieth-Century Poetry of Latin America.* New York: Verso, 1992.

Gonzalez, Ray, ed. *After Aztlán: Latino Poets of the Nineties.* Boston: David R. Godine, 1993.

————. *Touching the Fire: Fifteen Poets of Today's Latino Renaissance.* New York: Anchor/Doubleday, 1998.

Hart, Stephen M. *Spanish, Catalan, and Spanish-American Poetry from Modernismo to the Spanish Civil War: The Hispanic Connection.* Lewiston, N.Y.: E. Mellen Press, 1990.

Jenkins, Lee M. *The Language of Caribbean Poetry: Boundaries of Expression.* Gainesville: University Press of Florida, 2004.

Kuhnheim, Jill S. *Spanish American Poetry at the End of the Twentieth Century: Textual Disruptions.* Austin: University of Texas Press, 2004.

Lewis, Marvin A. *Afro-Hispanic Poetry, 1940-1980: From Slavery to Negritud in South American Verse.* Columbia: University of Missouri Press, 1983.

Menes, Orlando Ricardo, ed. *Renaming Ecstasy: Latino Writings on the Sacred.* Tempe, Ariz.: Bilingual Press, 2004.

Murray, Frederick W. *The Aesthetics of Contemporary Spanish American Social Protest Poetry.* Lewiston, N.Y.: E. Mellen Press, 1990.

Oliphant, Dave. *On a High Horse: Views Mostly of Latin American and Texan Poetry.* Fort Worth, Tex.: Prickly Pear Press, 1983.

Pérez-Torres, Rafael. *Movements in Chicano Poetry: Against Myths, Against Margins.* New York: Cambridge University Press, 1995.

Rowe, William. *Poets of Contemporary Latin America: History and the Inner Life.* New York: Oxford University Press, 2000.

Ruiz, Reynaldo, ed. *Hispanic Poetry in Los Angeles, 1850-1900.* Lewiston, N.Y.: E. Mellen Press, 2000.

Spooner, David. *The Poem and the Insect: Aspects of Twentieth Century Hispanic Culture.* San Francisco: International Scholars, 1999.

Politics, Modernity, and Migration

Alonso, Carlos J. *The Burden of Modernity: The Rhetoric of Cultural Discourse in Spanish America.* New York: Oxford University Press, 1998.

Altamirano, Teófilo, and Lane Ryo Hirabayashi, eds. *Migrants, Regional Identities and Latin American Cities.* Washington, D.C.: American Anthropological Association, 1997.

Alvarez-Borland, Isabel. *Cuban-American Literature of Exile: From Person to Persona.* Charlottesville: University of Virginia Press, 1998.

Beverly, John, and Marc Zimmerman. *Literature and Politics in the Central American Revolutions.* Austin: University of Texas Press, 1990.

Conlogue, William. *Working the Garden: American Writers and the Industrialization of Agriculture.* Chapel Hill: University of North Carolina Press, 2001.

Dove, Patrick. *The Catastrophe of Modernity: Tragedy and the Nation in Latin American Literature.* Lewisburg, Pa.: Bucknell University Press, 2004.

Franco, Jean. *The Decline and Fall of the Lettered City: Latin America in the Cold War.* Cambridge, Mass.: Harvard University Press, 2002.

Garza-Falcón, Leticia. *Gente Decente: A Borderlands Response to the Rhetoric of Dominance.* Austin: University of Texas Press, 1998.

Geist, Anthony L., and José B. Monleón, eds. *Modernism and Its Margins: Reinscribing Cultural Modernity from Spain and Latin America.* New York: Garland, 1999.

Gonzales-Berry, Erlinda, ed. *Paso por aqui: Critical Essays on the New Mexican Literary Tradition, 1542-1988.* Albuquerque: University of New Mexico Press, 1989.

Hernandez, Guillermo E. *Chicano Satire: A Study in Literary Culture.* Austin: University of Texas Press, 1991.

Kaup, Monika. *Rewriting North American Borders in Chicano and Chicana Narrative.* New York: Peter Lang, 2001.

Larrain, Jorge. *Identity and Modernity in Latin America.* Malden, Mass.: Blackwell, 2000.

McClennen, Sophia A. *The Dialectics of Exile: Nation, Time, Language, and Space in Hispanic Literatures.* West Lafayette, Ind.: Purdue University Press, 2004.

Martinez, Manuel Luis. *Countering the Counterculture: Rereading Postwar American Dissent from Jack Kerouac to Tomás Rivera.* Madison: University of Wisconsin Press, 2003.

Mujcinovic, Fatima. *Postmodern Cross-Culturalism and Politicization in U.S. Latina Literature: From Ana Castillo to Julia Alvarez.* New York: Peter Lang, 2004.

Muller, Gilbert H. *New Strangers in Paradise: The Immigrant Experience and Contemporary American Fiction.* Lexington: University Press of Kentucky, 1999.

Saldívar, Ramón. *Chicano Narrative: The Dialectics of Difference.* Madison: University of Wisconsin Press, 1990.

Sommer, Doris, ed. *The Places of History: Regionalism Revisited in Latin America.* Durham, N.C.: Duke University Press, 1999.

Race

Bost, Suzanne. *Mulattas and Mestizas: Representing Mixed Identities in the Americas, 1850-2000.* Athens: University of Georgia Press, 2003.

Brogan, Kathleen. *Cultural Haunting: Ghosts and Ethnicity in Recent American Literature.* Charlottesville: University of Virginia Press, 1998.

Cox, Timothy J. *Postmodern Tales of Slavery in the Americas: From Alejo Carpentier to Charles Johnson.* New York: Garland, 2001.

Domínguez, Jorge I., ed. *Race and Ethnicity in Latin America.* New York: Garland, 1994.

Edwards, Brent Hayes. *The Practice of Diaspora: Literature, Translation, and the Rise of Black Internationalism.* Cambridge, Mass.: Harvard University Press, 2003.

Ellis, Robert Richmond. *They Dream Not of Angels but of Men: Homoeroticism, Gender, and Race in Latin American Autobiography.* Gainesville: University Press of Florida, 2002.

Feracho, Lesley. *Linking the Americas: Race, Hybrid Discourses, and the Reformulation of Feminine Identity.* Albany: State University of New York Press, 2005.

Hedrick, Tace. *Mestizo Modernism: Race, Nation, and Identity in Latin American Culture, 1900-1940.* New Brunswick, N.J.: Rutgers University Press, 2003.

Hiraldo, Carlos. *Segregated Miscegenation: On the Treatment of Racial Hybridity in the U.S. and Latin American Literary Ttraditions.* New York: Routledge, 2003.

Jackson, Richard. *Black Writers and the Hispanic Canon.* New York: Twayne, 1997.

Jehenson, Myriam Yvonne. *Latin-American Women Writers: Class, Race, and Gender.* Albany: State University of New York Press, 1995.

John, Catherine A. *Clear Word and Third Sight: Folk Groundings and Diasporic Consciousness in African Caribbean Writing.* Durham, N.C.: Duke University Press, 2003.

Kaup, Monika, and Debra J. Rosenthal, eds. *Mixing Race, Mixing Culture: Inter-American Literary Dialogues.* Austin: University of Texas Press, 2002.

Keizer, Arlene R. *Black Subjects: Identity Formation in the Contemporary Narrative of Slavery.* Ithaca, N.Y.: Cornell University Press, 2004.

Luis, William. *Dance Between Two Cultures: Latino Caribbean Literature Written in the United States.* Nashville, Tenn.: Vanderbilt University Press, 2001.

Smith, Paul Julian. *Representing the Other: "Race," Text, and Gender in Spanish and Spanish American Narrative.* New York: Oxford University Press, 1992.

Wade, Peter. *Race and Ethnicity in Latin America.* Chicago: Pluto Press, 1997.

Williams, Claudette M. *Charcoal and Cinnamon: The Politics of Color in Spanish Caribbean Literature.* Gainesville: University Press of Florida, 2000.

Sexuality

Alarcon, Norma, Ana Castillo, and Cherrie Moraga, eds. *The Sexuality of Latinas.* Berkeley, Calif.: Third Woman Press, 1993.

Bacarisse, Pamela, ed. *Carnal Knowledge: Essays on the Flesh, Sex, and Sexuality in Hispanic Letters and Film.* Pittsburgh: Ediciones Tres Rios, 1993.

Balderston, Daniel, and Donna J. Guy, eds. *Sex and Sexuality in Latin America.* New York: New York University Press, 1997.

Bejel, Emilio. *Gay Cuban Nation.* Chicago: University of Chicago Press, 2000.

Bergmann, Emilie L., and Paul Julian Smith, eds. *Entiendes? Queer Readings, Hispanic Writings.* Durham, N.C.: Duke University Press, 1995.

Chávez-Silverman, Susana, and Librada Hernández, eds. *Reading and Writing the Ambiente: Queer Sexualities in Latino, Latin American, and Spanish Culture.* Madison: University of Wisconsin Press, 2000.

Contreras, Daniel. *Unrequited Love and Gay Latino Culture: What Have You Done to My Heart?* New York: Palgrave Macmillan, 2005.

Costa, María Dolores, ed. *Latina Lesbian Writers and Artists.* Binghamton, N.Y.: Harrington Park Press, 2003.

Foster, David W. *El Ambiente Nuestro: Chicano/Latino Homoerotic Writing.* Tempe, Ariz.: Bilingual Press/Editorial Bilingue, 2005.

_____. *Gay and Lesbian Themes in Latin American Writing.* Austin: University of Texas Press, 1991.

_____. *Latin American Writers on Gay and Lesbian Themes: A Bio-Critical Sourcebook.* Westport, Conn.: Greenwood Press, 1994.

_____, ed. *Chicano/Latino Homoerotic Identities.* New York: Garland, 1999.

Foster, David W., and Roberto Reis, eds. *Bodies and Biases: Sexualities in Hispanic Cultures and Literature.* Minneapolis: University of Minnesota Press, 1996.

Smith, Paul Julian. *The Body Hispanic: Gender and Sexuality in Spanish and Spanish American Literature.* New York: Oxford University Press, 1989.

_____. *Laws of Desire: Questions of Homosexuality in Spanish Writing and Film, 1960-1990.* New York: Oxford University Press, 1992.

_____. *Vision Machines: Cinema, Literature, and Sexuality in Spain and Cuba, 1983-93.* New York: Verso, 1996.

Torres, Lourdes, and Inmaculada Pertusa, eds. *Tortilleras: Hispanic and U.S. Latina Lesbian Expression.* Philadelphia: Temple University Press, 2003.

Vilaseca, David. *Hindsight and the Real: Subjectivity in Gay Hispanic Autobiography.* New York: Peter Lang, 2003.

Zimmerman, Bonnie. *The Safe Sea of Women: Lesbian Fiction, 1969-1989.* Boston: Beacon Press, 1990.

Theater

Albuquerque, Severino João Medeiros. *Violent Acts: A Study of Contemporary Latin American Theatre.* Detroit: Wayne State University Press, 1991.

Bottoms, Stephen J. *Playing Underground: A Critical History of the 1960's Off-Off Broadway Movement.* Ann Arbor: University of Michigan Press, 2004.

Broyles-Gonzales, Yolanda. *El Teatro Campesino: Theater in the Chicano Movement.* Austin: University of Texas Press, 1994.

Dauster, Frank, ed. *Perspectives on Contemporary Spanish American Theatre.* Lewisburg, Pa.: Bucknell University Press, 1996.

Flores, Yolanda. *The Drama of Gender: Feminist Theater by Women of the Americas.* New York: Peter Lang, 2000.

France, Anna Kay, and P. J. Corso, eds. *International Women Playwrights: Voices of Identity and Transformation.* Metuchen, N.J.: Scarecrow Press, 1993.

Gladhart, Amalia. *The Leper in Blue: Coercive Performance and the Contemporary Latin American Theater.* Chapel Hill: University of North Carolina Press, 2000.

Juan-Navarro, Santiago, and Theodore Robert Young, eds. *A Twice-Told Tale: Reinventing the Encounter in Iberian/Iberian American Literature and Film.* Newark: University of Delaware Press, 2001.

Larson, Catherine. *Games and Play in the Theater of Spanish American Women.* Lewisburg, Pa.: Bucknell University Press, 2004.

Larson, Catherine, and Margarita Vargas, eds. *Latin American Women Dramatists: Theater, Texts, and Theories.* Bloomington: Indiana University Press, 1998.

Milleret, Margo. *Latin American Women On/In Stages.* Albany: State University of New York Press, 2004.

Ramos-García, Luis A, ed. *The State of Latino Theater in the United States: Hybridity, Transculturation, and Identity.* New York: Routledge, 2002.

Reinelt, Janice, ed. *Crucibles of Crisis: Performing Social Change.* Ann Arbor: University of Michigan Press, 1996.

Román, David. *Acts of Intervention: Performance, Gay Culture, and AIDS.* Bloomington: Indiana University Press, 1998.

Salas, Teresa Cajiao, et al. "Women's Voices in Hispanic Theater." In *International Women Playwrights: Voices of Identity and Transformation,* edited by Anna Kay France and P. J. Corso. Metuchen, N.J.: Scarecrow Press, 1993.

Sandoval-Sanchez, Alberto, and Nancy Saporta Sternbach. *Stages of Life: Transcultural Performance and Identity in U.S. Latina Theater.* Tucson: University of Arizona Press, 2001.

Women's Studies

Adjarian, M. M. *Allegories of Desire: Body, Nation, and Empire in Modern Caribbean Literature by Women.* Westport, Conn.: Praeger, 2004.

Agosín, Marjorie, ed. *A Dream of Light and Shadow: Portraits of Latin American Women Writers.* Albuquerque: University of New Mexico Press, 1995.

Amador Gómez-Quintero, Raysa Elena, and Mireya Pérez Bustillo. *The Female Body: Perspectives of Latin American Artists.* Westport, Conn.: Greenwood Press, 2002.

Anim-Addo, Joan. *Touching the Body: African Caribbean Women's Writing.* London: Mango, 2004.

Anim-Addo, Joan, ed. *Centre of Remembrance: Memory and Caribbean Women's Literature.* London: Mango, 2004.

Aquino, María Pilar, Daisy L. Machado, and Jeanette Rodríguez, eds. *A Reader in Latina Feminist Theology: Religion and Justice.* Austin: University of Texas Press, 2002.

Barbas-Rhoden, Laura. *Writing Women in Central America: Gender and the Fictionalization of History.* Athens: Ohio University Press, 2003.

Brevard, Lisa Pertillar. *Womensaints: The Saintly Portrayal of Select African-American and Latina Cultural Heroines.* New Orleans: University Press of the South, 2002.

Browdy de Hernandez, Jennifer, ed. *Women Writing Resistance: Essays from Latin America and the Caribbean.* Cambridge, Mass.: South End Press, 2003.

Brown, Julie, ed. *American Women Short Story Writers: A Collection of Critical Essays.* New York: Garland, 1995.

Brown-Guillory, Elizabeth, ed. *Women of Color: Mother-Daughter Relationships in Twentieth-Century Literature.* Austin: University of Texas Press, 1996.

Castillo, Debra A., and María Socorro Tabuenca Córdoba. *Border Women: Writing from La Frontera.* Minneapolis: University of Minnesota Press, 2002.

Condé, L. P., and S. M. Hart, eds. *Feminist Readings on Spanish and Latin-American Literature.* Lewiston, N.Y.: E. Mellen Press, 1991.

Davies, Catherine, ed. *Women Writers in Twentieth-Century Spain and Spanish America.* Lewiston, N.Y.: E. Mellen Press, 1993.

Franco, Jean. *Plotting Women: Gender and Representation in Mexico.* New York: Columbia University Press, 1989.

García Pinto, Magdalena, ed. *Women Writers of Latin America: Intimate Histories.* Austin: University of Texas Press, 1991.

Gonzalez, Maria C. *Contemporary Mexican-American Women Novelists: Toward a Feminist Identity.* New York: Peter Lang, 1996.

Green, Carol Hurd, and Mary Grimley Mason. *American Women Writers.* New York: Continuum, 1994.

Horno-Delgado, Asunción, eds, et al. *Breaking Boundaries: Latina Writing and Critical Readings.* Amherst: University of Massachusetts Press, 1989.

Hurley, Teresa M. *Mothers and Daughters in Post-revolutionary Mexican Literature.* Rochester, N.Y.: Tamesis, 2002.

Jones, Anny Brooksbank, and Catherine Davies, eds. *Latin American Women's Writing: Feminist Readings in Theory and Crisis.* New York: Oxford University Press, 1996.

Kafka, Phillipa. *"Saddling la gringa": Gatekeeping in Literature by Contemporary Latina Writers.* Westport, Conn.: Greenwood Press, 2000.

Kaminsky, Amy K. *Reading the Body Politic: Feminist Criticism and Latin American Women Writers.* Minneapolis: University of Minnesota Press, 1993.

Kaup, Monika. *Mad Intertextuality: Madness in Twentieth-Century Women's Writing.* Trier: Wissenschaftlicher Verlag Trier, 1993.

McCracken, Ellen. *New Latina Narrative: The Feminine Space of Postmodern Ethnicity.* Tucson: University of Arizona Press, 1999.

Madsen, Deborah L. *Understanding Contemporary Chicana Literature.* Columbia: University of South Carolina Press, 2000.

Medeiros-Lichem, María Teresa. *Reading the Feminine Voice in Latin American Women's Fiction: From Teresa de la Parra to Elena Poniatowska and Luisa Valenzuela.* New York: Peter Lang, 2002.

Miller, Beth, ed. *Women in Hispanic Literature: Icons and Fallen Idols.* Berkeley: University of California Press, 1983.

— Anna A. Moore

Electronic Resources

Electronic Databases

Electronic databases are integrated electronic sources to which public, college, and university libraries subscribe, installing links on their Web sites, where they are only available to library card holders or specified patrons. Readers can check library Web sites to see if these databases are installed or can ask reference librarians if these databases are available.

General

Academic Search Premier

The world's largest scholarly full-text database, *Academic Search Premier* has indexed and created abstracts for more than 8000 journals, some of which—for example, *Latin American Literary Review*, which is written for the general public—will be of direct interest. The database also includes thousands of peer-reviewed publications.

First Search

Commonly found in academic libraries, this system covers dozens of databases, some of which have links to full-text articles. Students of Latino literature will find helpful information in the *Contemporary Women's Issues, Dissertation Abstracts, MLA Bibliography, Wilson Select,* and *WorldCat* databases.

Gale Virtual Reference Library

The database contains more than 85 reference books, including encyclopedias and almanacs, allowing users to quickly find information about a broad range of subjects.

J-STOR

J-STOR has organized hundreds of journals in both single and multi-disciplinary formats in order to streamline the search process. Their collection includes several journals on Latin American history, as well as the literary journals *Hispania* and *Hispanic Review.*

Oxford Reference Online

A virtual reference library of more than 100 dictionaries and reference books published by Oxford University Press. *Oxford Reference Online* contains information about a broad range of subjects, including art, architecture, military history, science, religion, philosophy, political and social science, and literature. The site also features English language and bilingual dictionaries, as well as collections of quotations and proverbs.

Latin America and Other
Subject-Specific Databases

America: History and Life; Historical Abstracts

This database, produced by ABC-CLIO, provides access to a number of important literary journals and some books. *America: History and Life* focuses on North America and Mexico; information on South America is in *Historical Abstracts*.

Arts and Humanities Citation Index

This database allows users to search across disciplines to find bibliographic and reference material in more than a thousand scholarly journals.

Biography Resource Center

This database, produced by Thomson Gale, includes biographies of more than 320,000 prominent people from throughout the world and from a wide range of disciplines. Searches for Latino authors returned an average of 200 hits.

Chicano Database

The *Chicano Database* is produced by the University of California-Berkeley's Ethnic Studies Department. Its creators have broadened the definition of Chicano to include anyone of Mexican descent living in the United States. As a result, the information available in the database ranges from literature and women's studies to social work. It is particularly useful for information about *El Teatro Campesino*, as well as for Chicano poetry and fiction.

ClasePeriodica

This system enables users to find documents published in 2,600 Latin American journals. Clase is devoted to research in the social sciences and humanities; Periodicas specializes in the sciences and technology. Results include conference proceedings, interviews, essays, articles, and books.

The Columbia Granger's World of Poetry

Columbia University Press compiles thousands of works by hundreds of poets (more than 200 of Pablo Neruda's poems are indexed, for example) in this database, which also includes a comprehensive glossary of poetry-related terms. Biographies and critical essays are available for some writers, and users can search for anthologies by title, category, and editor.

Contemporary Authors

Thomson Gale's database organizes biographical information on approximately 112,000 novelists whose work has been published since 1960.

Contemporary Literary Criticism Select

Published by Thomson Gale, this system catalogs critical essays on approximately 600 major authors. Students can search by author, title, and subject.

Ethnic News Watch

This database functions in both English and Spanish, combing through half a million articles that have appeared in minority and indigenous publications since 1990. Archived material from the mid-1980's is also available. An especially useful resource for hard-to-find newspaper and magazine articles.

Fuente Académica

This Spanish-language database provides full-text links to more than 150 academic journals.

GLBT Life

This database is devoted to discussing issues related to gay, lesbian, bisexual, and transgender issues. The system searches dozens of periodicals specializing in GLBT issues; students will find a number of reviews, interviews, and other articles on such authors as Manuel Puig, Maria Irene Fornes, and Richard Rodriguez.

Hispanic American Periodicals Index (HAPI)

This valuable resource from the University of California-Los Angeles indexes the books, articles, essays, reviews, and many other printed materials that have been produced in and about Latin America over the past twenty-five years. Increasingly, the citations are linked to the full text. More than 400 periodicals are searched regularly for information about Latinos in the United States, the U.S.-Mexican border, Central and South America, and the Caribbean.

History Reference Center

A product of EBSCO Information Services, the History Reference Center is a comprehensive world history database. It contains the contents of more than 650 encyclopedias and other books, the full text of articles published in about 60 history periodicals, and thousands of historical documents, biographies, photographs, and maps.

Latin American Women Writers

Alexander Street Press has assembled a system organizing the memoirs, letters, essays, and works (most are in Spanish only) of Latin American women since the 1600's. Students can combine a number of parameters, including: subject (independence, slavery, love), word, time period, literary movement, birth and death dates, and country of origin.

Latino Literature: Poetry, Drama, and Fiction

Alexander Street Press's highly regarded database focuses on Latino literature in English (although some major works are in Spanish), and places most of its emphasis on writers in the United States after 1850. It includes several hundred novels and plays, and several thousand pages of poetry. Users can narrow their search fields according to a work's major themes, the author's gender, heritage, frequency of word use, and other criteria.

Libros en Venta

This system chronicles all Spanish-language books—both in and out of print—published since 1964. In addition to basic bibliographic information, researchers can also find contact information for publishers and sales distributors.

Literature Resource Center

Literature Resource Center, produced by Thomson Gale, includes biographies, bibliographies, and critical analyses of authors from a wide range of literary disciplines, countries, and eras. The database also features plot summaries, the full text of articles from literary journals, critical essays, and links to Web sites. Users can search by author nationality, theme, literary movement, and genre; for example, a search for Hispanic and Mexican American authors returned 119 results.

MagillOnLiteraturePlus

Salem Press has placed many of its literature reference sources on this database, including *Masterplots, Cyclopedia of World Authors, Cyclopedia of Literary Characters,* and *World Philosophers and Their Works.* The database covers the works of more than 8,500 writers, poets, dramatists, essayists, and philosophers, featuring plot summaries, critical analyses, biographical essays, character profiles, and up-to-date lists of each author's works. Searches can be narrowed according to author's national and cultural identity and literary characters and locales, among other fields; for example, a search for Latino authors returned 292 results.

MLA International Bibliography

Thousands of journals and book citations can be found in the Modern Language Association's electronic bibliography, which is a particularly valuable source of literary theory and critical articles.

Sur Database

This is the online edition of the prominent Latin American literary magazine (1931-1992). It includes images, advertisements, and a searchable index of more than six thousand articles.

World History FullText

A joint product of EBSCO Information Services and ABC-CLIO, this database provides a global view of history with information on a wide range of topics, including anthropology, art, culture, economics, government, heritage, military history, politics, regional issues, and sociology.

World History Online

Facts on File, Inc., has created this reference database of world history, featuring biographies, time lines, maps, charts, and other information.

Wilson Biographies Illustrated

Produced by H. W. Wilson Co., this database offers more than 95,000 biographies and obituaries, and more than 26,000 photographs, of prominent people throughout history.

Web Sites

The sites listed below were visited by the editors of Salem Press in March 2005. Because URLs frequently change or are moved, the accuracy of these sites cannot be guaranteed; however, long-standing sites—such as those of university departments, national organizations, and government agencies—generally maintain links when sites move or upgrade their offerings.

Association for Hispanic Classical Theater, Inc.

http://www.trinity.edu/org/comedia/index.html

This site contains texts for a number of plays, most of which were written during the Golden Age of Spanish Theater (1580-1680). Some of the plays have been translated into English, and a few critical essays are also included.

Brazilian Literature

http://www.unm.edu/~osterloh/BrazLit/BrazLit.htm

This page contains a number of links and information on print-based sources that students of Brazilian, African Brazilian, and Luso Brazilian literatures may find helpful.

The Chicano Literature Index

http://www.accd.edu/sac/english/bailey/mexamlit.htm

A Web site that gives general references, short biographies, lists of major works, and links to other sites about major contemporary Mexican American writers.

Chicano Studies Research Center (CSRC)

http://www.chicano.ucla.edu/

The CSRC is based at the University of California-Los Angeles and is home to significant amounts of important material related to the Chicano movement (online access to the collection is pending). The prestigious journal *Aztlán* is also based at the CSRC, and its contents are listed on the site.

Cultures of the Andes

http://www.andes.org/

Visitors to this site will find original poetry in Quechua, a direct descendant of the language spoken by the Incas that is still common in Bolivia, Peru, and Ecuador. Poems are translated into Spanish and English. Also available are short stories (in Spanish and English) about life in this often-isolated region.

El Andar

http://elandar.com

El Andar bills itself as "a national magazine for Latino discourse," a claim supported by the intelligent and accessible essays and wide array of fiction, poetry, and essays published each month. Highlights of the online edition include readings by prominent Latin American poets of their own work.

Gay and Lesbian Themes in Hispanic Literatures and Cultures

http://www.columbia.edu/cu/lweb/eresources/exhibitions/
sw25/case9.html

Part of the Columbia University exhibition "Stonewall and Beyond: Lesbian and Gay Culture," this page features an essay that locates homosexuality's meaning within Latin American tradition and points out some of the most important differences between North and Latin American perceptions of sexuality. A list of notable literary works is also included.

Handbook of Latin American Studies (HLAS)

http://lcweb2.loc.gov/hlas/

The *HLAS* is an annotated bibliography maintained and updated by the Library of Congress. It includes abstracts for entries, and is useful for locating books, articles, chapters, and papers on almost any topic related to Latin America, covering more than sixty years of scholarly research in the field. An essential starting point for serious research.

Hispanic Culture Review

http://www.gmu.edu/org/hcr/

The online version of this journal, published by students at George Mason University, includes the journal's recent and present contents (poetry, short narrative, essays, and book reviews) and has a number of useful (mostly Spanish-language) links, including George Mason's "The Spanish Page."

Las Culturas.com

http://www.lasculturas.com/lib/libAuthors.htm

An annotated list of links to various webpages about specific authors, sorted alphabetically. Information available varies by author, but several pages contain interviews, images, criticism and official Web sites.

Latin American Network Information Center (LANIC)

http://www1.lanic.utexas.edu/la/region/literature/

LANIC is one of the most comprehensive resources available for information about and direct links to institutions, publications, and projects throughout Latin America. The site has devoted a section to every topic imaginable, and their literature pages—a few of which are in English—are categorized by country, theme, and author. Links to dozens of magazines, journals, and awards as well as region-wide sites are also listed.

Literature of South America

http://gosouthamerica.about.com/od/literature1/

This site, created by About.com, consists largely of book reviews, short stories, biographies of prominent novelists and other information, sorted by country. Only South American countries are featured.

Portals to the World: Resources Selected by Library of Congress Subject Experts

http://www.loc.gov/rr/international/hispanic/countries/
countries.html

The Library of Congress has collected web addresses for sites specializing in specific Latin American languages and dialects, authors, and types of literature, all organized by country. Links are generally to Spanish-language pages. An extremely useful resource for those with some knowledge of the language.

Proyecto Sherezade

http://home.cc.umanitoba.ca/%7Efernand4/

This Spanish-language site has devoted itself to the preservation and presentation of Latin America's strong tradition of fiction. Many of its stories have been chosen as aids for Spanish-language teachers. Each piece is introduced by the webmaster, and a number of author interviews are posted.

Voice of the Shuttle

http://vos.ucsb.edu/

The section titled "Literatures (Other Than English)" contains some useful links to biographies, timelines, and excerpts from works by prominent authors, such as Jorge Luis Borges and Mario Vargas Llosa. However, some of the more general links are outdated.

— *Anna A. Moore*

Chronological List of Authors

Below, authors who are covered in these volumes are arranged chronologically by year of birth.

To 1800
1581   Juan Ruiz de Alarcón
1648   Sor Juana Inés de la Cruz
1776   José Joaquín Fernández de Lizardi

1801-1900
1803   José María Heredia
1834   Ignacio Manuel Altamirano
1834   José Hernández
1839   Joaquim Maria Machado de Assis
1841   W. H. Hudson
1853   José Julián Martí
1866   Euclides da Cunha
1867   Rubén Darío
1871   Enrique González Martínez
1873   Mariano Azuela
1875   Florencio Sánchez
1878   Horacio Quiroga
1883   Hugo Wast
1884   Eduardo Barrios
1884   Rómulo Gallegos
1886   Ricardo Güiraldes
1887   Martín Luis Guzmán
1889   Gabriela Mistral
1889   Alfonso Reyes
1890   José Rubén Romero
1892   César Vallejo
1893   Mário de Andrade
1899   Miguel Ángel Asturias

1899 Jorge Luis Borges
1900 Roberto Arlt

1901-1910

1901 Jesús Colón
1901 José Lins do Rego
1902 Carlos Drummond de Andrade
1902 Nicolás Guillén
1903 Alejandro Casona
1903 Eduardo Mallea
1904 Alejo Carpentier
1904 Pablo Neruda
1904 Agustín Yáñez
1905 Ernesto Galarza
1905 Rodolfo Usigli
1906 Jorge Icaza
1908 João Guimarães Rosa
1909 Demetrio Aguilera Malta
1909 Ciro Alegría
1909 Juan Carlos Onetti
1910 María Luisa Bombal
1910 José Lezama Lima
1910 Rachel de Queiroz

1911-1920

1911 Ernesto Sábato
1912 Jorge Amado
1914 Adolfo Bioy Casares
1914 Julia de Burgos
1914 Julio Cortázar
1914 Nicanor Parra
1914 Octavio Paz
1917 Augusto Roa Bastos
1918 Juan José Arreola
1918 Juan Rulfo
1919 Isidora Aguirre
1919 Jose Yglesias

1921-1930

1921 Raymond Barrio
1924 Claribel Alegría
1924 José Donoso
1924 Osman Lins
1924 José Antonio Villarreal
1925 Ernesto Cardenal
1925 Carlos Castaneda
1925 Clarice Lispector
1928 Carlos Fuentes
1928 Griselda Gambaro
1928 Gabriel García Márquez
1928 Piri Thomas
1929 Guillermo Cabrera Infante
1929 Rolando Hinojosa
1930 Maria Irene Fornes

1931-1940

1932 Manuel Puig
1932 Maruxa Vilalta
1933 Elena Poniatowska
1934 John Rechy
1935 Lionel G. García
1935 Nicholasa Mohr
1935 Tomás Rivera
1936 Ignácio de Loyola Brandão
1936 Luis Rafael Sánchez
1936 Mario Vargas Llosa
1937 Rudolfo Anaya
1937 Severo Sarduy
1938 Rosario Ferré
1938 Mary Helen Ponce
1938 Luisa Valenzuela
1939 Sheila Ortiz Taylor
1940 Eduardo Galeano
1940 Gustavo Sainz
1940 Luis Miguel Valdez
1940 Victor Villaseñor

1941-1950
1941 Nicholas Dante
1942 Isabel Allende
1942 Aristeo Brito
1942 Ariel Dorfman
1943 Reinaldo Arenas
1944 Alejandro Morales
1944 Richard Rodriguez
1944 Thomas Sanchez
1945 Lucha Corpi
1946 Miguel Piñero
1948 Denise Chávez
1949 Victor Hernández Cruz
1950 Julia Alvarez
1950 Laura Esquivel

1951-1960
1951 Oscar Hijuelos
1952 Jimmy Santiago Baca
1952 Judith Ortiz Cofer
1952 Alberto Ríos
1952 Gary Soto
1953 Ana Castillo
1953 Eduardo Machado
1954 Lorna Dee Cervantes
1954 Sandra Cisneros
1954 Helena María Viramontes
1957 Martín Espada
1958 Cristina García

1961-
1961 Abraham Rodriguez, Jr.
1962 Virgil Suárez

INDEXES

Genre Index

Geographical Index

Personages Index

Title Index

Subject Index

Migration, 107, 210, 230, 306,
328, 335, 387, 490, 509, 565,
577, 633, 649, 714, 735
Mile Zero (Sanchez, Thomas),
632-633
Miracle plays, 741
*Miraculous Day of Amalia Gómez,
The* (Rechy), 549
Miranda, Javier. *See* Bioy Casares,
Adolfo
Misiones region (Argentina),
541
Mr. Ives' Christmas (Hijuelos),
392
Mistral, Gabriela, 457-462, 473,
821
Mitío el empleado (Meza), 775
Mito, 678
Mixquiahuala Letters, The
(Castillo), 186
Modern Ladies of Guanabacoa, The
(Machado), 435
Modernism, 155, 245, 784;
Brazilian, 63, 66, 263, 534
Modernismo, 351-352, 453, 573,
687, 773, 817, 862
Mohr, Nicholasa, 463-466, 763,
846
Monkey Hunting (García,
Cristina), 330
Mora, Pat, 810
Morales, Alejandro, 467-471
Morales, Conrad. *See* Dante,
Nicholas
Morales, Rosario, 811
"More Room" (Ortiz Cofer), 491
Moros y cristianos plays, 742
Mothers and Shadows (Traba), 796
"Moths, The" (Viramontes), 843
Moths, and Other Stories, The
(Viramontes), 718
Motivos de son (Guillén), 355-356
Mud (Fornes), 293

*Muerte de Artemio Cruz, La. See
Death of Artemio Cruz, The*
Muerte de Narciso (Lezama Lima),
410
*Mujer del rio Sumpul, La. See
Woman of the River*
Mummified Deer (Valdez), 678
*Mundo alucinante, El. See
Hallucinations*
*Mundo es ancho y ajeno, El. See
Broad and Alien Is the World*
Mundonovismo, 778
Murillo, Rosario, 823
Music in Cuba (Carpentier), 167
Music of the Spheres, The
(Cardenal), 161-162
Música sentimental (Cambacérès),
773
My Son, the Lawyer (Sánchez,
Florencio), 620
My Wicked, Wicked Ways
(Cisneros), 202
Myriam la conspiradora (Wast),
725
Myth in work of Rodolfo Usigli,
669

Nacimientos, Los. See Genesis
*Nada como el piso 16. See Nothing
Like the Sixteenth Floor*
Nada, nadie. See Nothing, Nobody
Nada que ver (Gambaro), 323
Nada que ver con otra historia
(Gambaro), 323
*Não verás país nenhum. See And
Still the Earth*
Nationalism (Latin America),
858
Native Americans. *See*
Geographical Index under
United States
Naturalism, 95, 238, 318, 403,
621, 746, 773